RACHETER

ELEMENTARY POLITICAL ANALYSIS

Donated by
The Public Interest Institute
to The Heartland Institute
2016

ELEMENTARY POLITICAL ANALYSIS

HERBERT JACOB
Northwestern University

ROBERT WEISSBERG
Cornell University

Second Edition

PROPERTY OF
PUBLIC INTEREST
INSTITUTE

McGRAW-HILL BOOK COMPANY

New York   St. Louis   San Francisco   Auckland   Düsseldorf
Johannesburg   Kuala Lumpur   London   Mexico   Montreal   New Delhi
Panama   Paris   São Paulo   Singapore   Sydney   Tokyo   Toronto

Library of Congress Cataloging in Publication Data

Jacob, Herbert, date
    Elementary political analysis.

  1. United States—Politics and government—1945-
2. Political science—Programmed instruction.
I. Weissberg, Robert, joint author. II. Title.
JK274.J17   1975   320.4'73   74-17205
ISBN 0-07-032136-1

ELEMENTARY
POLITICAL
ANALYSIS

Copyright © 1970, 1975 by McGraw-Hill, Inc. All rights reserved. Printed in the United States of America. No part of this publication may be reproduced, stored in a retrieval system, or transmitted, in any form or by any means, electronic, mechanical, photocopying, recording, or otherwise, without the prior written permission of the publisher.

    2 3 4 5 6 7 8 9 0 KPKP 7 9 8 7 6 5

This book was set in Univers by Creative Book Services, division of McGregor & Werner, Inc. The editors were Robert P. Rainier and Barry Benjamin; the designer was Joseph Gillians; the production supervisor was Dennis J. Conroy.
Kingsport Press, Inc., was printer and binder.

CONTENTS

To the Student   vii

To the Instructor   xi

Part One   The Basic Tools of Analysis

1. Reading Tables   3
2. Multivariate Tables and Graphs   25
3. Descriptive Statistics   51
4. Reformulating Problems   77
5. Reformulating Value Statements   91
6. The Interpretation of Textual Data   113

Part Two   Political Analysis

7. Public Opinion   123

   In the United States, the government reflects public opinion.

8. Political Socialization   147

   A democratic and politically active citizenry depends on our system of public education.

9. Political Parties   167

   The Democratic and Republican parties are so similar that citizens are offered no meaningful choices.

10. Presidential Elections   197

    Presidential elections demonstrate that only "middle-of-the-road" politicians can be nominated and elected President.

11. Presidential Power   225

    Despite the intentions of those drafting the Constitution, the President is now unchecked in his power by the other branches of government.

12. Congressional Leadership   253

    Congress is not a representative institution, because not only are congressmen unrepresentative of the public, but congressional leaders, who are even more unrepresentative, dominate law making and thwart their colleagues.

Part Three More Advanced Analysis

13. The Supreme Court   277

Even though the President's power has grown enormously in the twentieth century, the Supreme Court is still a substantially independent branch of government.

14. Minorities in American Politics   291

Discrimination in the political arena against minority groups in the United States has not declined in the last 20 years.

15. Law and Order   305

If government agencies really put their mind to it, they could reduce the amount of crime.

TO THE STUDENT

WHAT THE TEXT IS ABOUT

To understand society, one must learn how to analyze social problems. This requires skills in assessing and manipulating data, in reformulating problems so they are amenable to empirical analysis, and in selecting information that is relevant to the problem at hand. The purpose of this book is to teach these skills so that you can apply the information you acquire in the classroom to the world around you.

The techniques you will learn are those which many social scientists use to apply available data to pressing social problems. This book is not exhaustive, however. There are other techniques, especially some which emphasize more philosophical and value-oriented approaches. The techniques in this book will not necessarily help you in choosing objectives you ought to pursue. But if you are fairly certain about which things you cherish and value highly, the techniques explained in the following pages will help you decide whether your objectives are attainable and how the facts of social life pertain to them.

The goal of the book is to make you adept in finding information relevant to social problems and analyzing it in ways which will help you understand them. The skills taught here are the fundamental techniques of social scientists, but they are not sufficient to make you a professional social scientist. Professional social scientists require many more skills and much more sophisticated techniques in collecting data and analyzing them. The authors assume that most students using this text have not yet decided to become professional social scientists, but wish to learn how to understand the whirlpool of social and political life around them.

The text emphasizes political problems, and is written for use in political science classes. The techniques you will learn, however, are not unique to political science: they are common to all the social sciences. What you learn from this text can be applied to social and economic problems as well as political affairs. In other disciplines the information or data may differ, but the ways in which they are used will be fundamentally similar.

HOW TO USE THE TEXT

Part One is in programmed form: that is, each unit, or frame, requires you to make a judgment, calculation, or decision. Each frame seeks to teach a portion of the required skill. As you read each frame, you should respond by filling in the missing words, choosing among the possible answers, or filling in tables and graphs. While you are reading the frame, keep the right-hand margin covered with the cardboard mask supplied with the book. Keep the margin covered until you have written, in the appropriate space within the frame, the response you think correct. Always write your answers within the question or frame itself. Then remove the cardboard mask to see whether your response is in fact correct. If it is correct, go on to the next frame. If your answer is wrong, reread the frame and try to understand why the answer in the margin is correct and yours is wrong. Then proceed.

You may work through the first six chapters at your own pace. You will be your own judge about how well you are doing and how quickly you should proceed. It is essential, however, that you finish Chapters 1 to 6 before proceeding with Part Two. The first six chapters teach the basic skills which are required to analyze the problems presented in later chapters. You may later wish to refer back to Part One when you are in doubt about some technique which was discussed there. It can serve you as a reference source for your later work.

Part Two is organized differently. Each chapter presents a political problem that you are to analyze. The chapters are divided into sections, with each section devoted to one portion of the analysis process. While the chapters in Part Two are not programmed, correct answers are provided for all questions at the end of the chapter. You may find it convenient to tear the answer sheet out and lay it to the side of your book for easy reference. You should read each section, complete each task, answer the questions which are posed, and compare your answers with the correct ones. Finally, at the end of each chapter, you are asked to write a memorandum analyzing the chapter's problem. You are to base your memorandum on the analysis you have performed in the earlier pages of the chapter. The pages for writing these memoranda are provided in the book, together with blanks for your name and section number. These memoranda may be torn out of the book and handed in to your instructor.

Part Two is organized so that the earlier chapters provide you with more help than the later ones. It is therefore essential that you work one of Chapters 7 through 9 before attempting any of the other chapters. After you have completed at least one of Chapters 7 through 9, you may complete whatever other chapters your instructor assigns in Part Two.

The chapters in Part Two are self-contained. They provide sufficient data to complete the analysis. However, you may wish to analyze the problem with different data, taking a somewhat different approach than that of the authors. Each chapter contains a bibliography, which guides you to sources of data that you can use for the chapter. If you use your own data, be sure to indicate that in your memorandum. We hope you will take the opportunity to do this often, since the book has been designed to provide maximum flexibility to exercise initiative and independent thinking.

Part Three provides less guidance and requires more independent analysis. You may find these chapters especially challenging, but you should not attempt them until you have successfully completed several assignments in Part Two.

The entire book is designed to enable you to work at your own pace. Always check your answers with the correct ones. We have organized the text to teach a correct way of analyzing problems and to alert you to errors as soon as you make them. By checking your answers immediately, you can avoid becoming habituated to fallacious thinking. However, you may sometimes feel that your answer is just as good as the one given in the text. When this occurs, consult your instructor. There sometimes are several correct ways of thinking about the problems discussed in this book. Your instructor can help you decide whether your answer is in fact as good as the one given in the text.

Herbert Jacob
Robert Weissberg

TO THE INSTRUCTOR

Introductory political science courses should teach students how to think about politics, in addition to acquainting them with the range of political values and the facts of political structure and behavior. Students need to learn how to use facts in a disciplined way. Facts are the materials of the political scientist's trade; his tools are analytic techniques which enable him to organize facts into propositional statements and permit him to analyze political situations.

Many texts acquaint students with the structural facts of political life or with political philosophy, but few focus on the analytic processes without which facts remain meaningless. This book seeks to provide the necessary analytical skills. It introduces students to some of the techniques political scientists use to think through political problems. Its objective is to produce citizens who can make more intelligent use of the facts they have at their disposal.

Many of the skills which political and other social scientists use are within easy reach of the beginning student. They involve prudent logic and thorough examination of relatively simple data. One does not need to be a statistician to think clearly about political life. But thinking clearly is a skill that must be taught: it cannot be taken for granted. College students often come to campus with their heads filled by slogans; they are impatient to reform the world. This book attempts to teach them some of the techniques required for clear thinking and to help them to make a detached analysis of their political environment.

We do not recommend teaching complex statistics in an introductory course. More harm than good is done by exposing students to powerful statistical techniques without teaching them the inherent limitations of statistical measures. Nor do we believe in burdening students with the busywork of research—collecting data, coding it, punching it, etc. Most students have no desire to become researchers, and such skills will be quickly forgotten.

We emphasize "consumer" skills. Although our students may not become researchers, they will probably have to read articles which use statistical measures. They are constantly exposed even in the simplest texts to data in tabular or graphic form. Therefore we first teach the skills of reading tables and graphs, recognizing (but not calculating) simple statistical measures, and learning what kinds of inferences may be drawn from each.

We then turn to the problem of using data to analyze propositions which students are likely to encounter in their reading or in their private discussions. Perhaps the most important skill (usually taken for granted by professional political scientists) is recognizing when a proposition is stated in terms that permit empirical analysis. Therefore we emphasize the skills of distinguishing factual from value statements and reformulating each into a statement permitting empirical analysis.

A NOTE ON THE SECOND EDITION

Responses from both teachers and students to the first edition have been encouraging. The combination of programmed learning of analytical skills and structured, data-based exercises has successfully equipped students to analyze complex political questions. Hence, in undertaking a second edition we have followed the format established in the original edition. Our major goals have been to refine the sections on analytical skills and provide students with richer, less clerically cumbersome opportunities to use their newly acquired abilities. Besides the clarification of certain ambiguities within the first five chapters of the first edition, this second edition differs from the first in five ways.

First, we have added a completely new chapter (Chapter 6) on the interpretation of nonquantitative data. Much of our information about politics comes from newspaper accounts, documents, speeches, and other "textual" data, and understanding the uses and limitations of these types of data is as important as knowing how to read a table. In view of our orientation toward "consumer" skills this new chapter emphasizes the detection of biases and distortions in nonquantitative materials as opposed to the development of research techniques such as content analysis.

Second, many chapters examining political problems now contain significant portions of nonquantitative materials. Included are such things as party platforms, political speeches, expert opinions, journalistic commentary, and court decisions. Not only does the inclusion of such material make for a richer, more complete analysis of each chapter's problem, but it should also make the student aware of the relevance of readily available information for examining important political questions.

Third, in addition to changes in subject matter in some of the chapters, we have also varied chapters by their length. Some chapters present large quantities of data and allow for highly complex analyses; others are much briefer and more straightforward. Such variations in length and complexity reflect both the nature of the particular question being examined and our desire to provide students with a range of analytical experience.

Fourth, we have sought to eliminate as much of the "busywork" of analysis as possible while still maintaining the essential structure. *Elementary Political Analysis* is still based on the belief that the student will learn how to analyze complex problems by proceeding through explicit steps, but wherever possible we have abolished time-consuming checklists and intermediate steps. This should allow more time for the actual analysis of data without any dilution of guiding structure.

Finally, the analytic exercises in the later chapters encourage students to compose a number of alternative reformulations. Better students may tackle more complex reformulations; instructors are less likely to have a whole class writing memoranda on the same reformulation.

SPECIAL FEATURES

This book has been carefully planned and pretested to permit its use in a wide range of situations. It is designed to minimize busywork for both students and instructors; it focuses their interactions on fundamental questions of analysis rather than on detailed problems of calculation. Its special features are as follows:

Reinforcement of Correct Responses through Programmed Instruction
Correct responses are given and wrong answers are analyzed. The student is urged to check his own answer with that in the book as soon as he has finished a paragraph or section so that errors will not become imbedded in his mind. Unlike most other books on the subject, this text does not require the student to proceed through long exercises, only to find at the end that he made a mistake somewhere along the way. In this text, if he makes an error, he discovers it immediately and can correct it before proceeding to the next section.

Focus on Meaningful Tasks for Both Students and Instructors
The students are taught skills which they will use in their reading of other materials for the course. They are asked to analyze propositions that are relevant to their course. The end product of each of the analysis chapters is a memorandum in which the students draw conclusions based on their understanding of relevant facts and their inferences from them.

Instructors are relieved of the burden of meaningless paperwork. They do not need to check dozens of calculations or routine steps in the analysis. The programmed text does this for them.

The only papers which students need to turn in for grading are the memoranda that constitute the final product of each analysis chapter. These memoranda may be considered miniature papers or important elements of a term paper.

Adaptability to Large Courses

Because the text minimizes the amount of grading and checking which instructors need to do, it is readily adaptable to large courses. Furthermore, it provides useful foci for discussion sections where it may be necessary for the professor to use teaching assistants who are less experienced than he in planning and leading discussion groups.

Emphasis on Analytic Skills

The text is a supplement to other materials. But unlike most supplements, it does not simply present additional reading on a particular topic. It adds an entirely new dimension to the introductory course by enabling the instructor to teach methods of thinking about political problems in addition to facts about political life.

Adaptability to a Variety of Course Contents

The book is written for use in most elementary American Government or Introduction to Political Science courses. We believe it can be used as a supplement to most introductory texts. Within the limits described below, it permits complete flexibility for the instructor.

Adaptability to a Variety of Course Formats

The book may be used as homework reading assignments for students, as the material for a political science laboratory, or as the basis for discussion groups. It can be used in both small and large classes.

THE DESIGN OF THE BOOK

The first three chapters of *Elementary Political Analysis* are devoted to the learning of basic technical skills. These include reading tables and graphs, understanding measures of central tendency and dispersion, and interpreting measures of association. The emphasis is on recognition and comprehension, though in some cases simple arithmetical calculations are required. These skills are not political analysis, but without them the student cannot make effective use of empirical research in his own analysis of substantive issues.

Chapters 4 and 5 deal with the essential but seldom taught skill of changing ambiguous statements into propositions that can be analyzed. Chapter 4 explains how to reorganize general or vague problems into more specific and testable propositions. Chapter 5 describes the different kinds of value statements and how each can be transformed into a factual proposition. The students learn that, while personal values are not irrelevant to politics, value statements must be converted into factual equivalents if they are to be empirically analyzed.

These skills are essential to political analysis; unless substantive political questions can be made manageable and testable, the narrower technical skills are of little value. Chapter 6 focuses on the interpretation of nonquantitative data. Particular emphasis is put on potential sources of bias in the mass media, since so much of our daily political information comes from newspapers and television. In each chapter exercises are provided to give the students an opportunity to practice these skills.

The first six chapters are in programmed form. Each frame teaches one portion of the required skill. Students must supply missing words, choose between alternatives, or fill in tables or graphs. The correct answers are provided to allow the student to correct himself instantly to gain the immediate satisfaction of answering correctly. Answers are also given to the problems at the end of each chapter so that errors are immediately corrected and learning is reinforced.

The next nine chapters provide the student with a chance to practice his analytic skills. Each chapter examines one statement about American politics. These statements deal with such topics as public opinion, political parties, presidential power, congressional leadership, the Supreme Court, and other subjects relevant to an introductory course in political science. Each chapter guides the student in his analysis, yet allows alternative conclusions to be reached from the available data.

The first step in each of these chapters is reformulating the original problem so that it can be analyzed with data. This modification must meet certain criteria learned in Chapters 4 and 5 and repeated in every lesson. In early chapters, Chapters 7 to 9, the student decides which of a number of reformulations are correct or incorrect. Then he compares his answers with the correct ones found on the page immediately following his answers. Thus the student sees why some approaches to the problem are unworkable or unproductive. Time is not wasted pursuing fruitless lines of inquiry, and by example the student learns how to approach complex problems. In Chapters 10 to 15, discussions on the reformulation are presented, but students are responsible for devising their own reformulations.

The second step is to decide on the data necessary to analyze the reformulated statement. This decision is made before examining actual data. In Chapters 7 to 9 students choose among different sets of data and explain why particular data are necessary or unnecessary for analysis. Again, the text provides answers, so correct decisions are reinforced and errors corrected. In later lessons the student describes the necessary data and then compares his listing with specified criteria.

Having decided what data he needs, the student examines actual data. These data are taken from the published research of political scientists and from government documents and are sufficient to provide analyses for a variety of reformulations of the problem. Bibliographies are included in each chapter for students who wish to use additional or more current information. These bibliographies list specific sources of usable data.

After examining the data, the student is presented specific questions and answers on the data in Chapters 7 through 12. The questions guide students in interpreting the data but do not constitute the analysis of the original problem. Their purpose is to avoid mistaken inferences due to a misreading of the information. Correct answers for each question follow the student's own answer; thereby errors are promptly corrected. In Part Three, *More Advanced Analysis,* this format is replaced by a brief discussion of some aspects of the data in Chapters 13 and 14 while in Chapter 15 the student is left entirely on his own to analyze the data.

With the completion of these steps, the student writes a brief memorandum on the proposition, using the reformulated version as the basis for his analysis. These conclusions can be torn free from the book and handed in for grading by the instructor.

GUIDELINES FOR USING ELEMENTARY POLITICAL ANALYSIS

In Part One, Chapters 1 to 6, the materials are cumulative. The student first learns to read two-variable tables, then three-variable tables, graphs, and simple statistical measures. Chapter 4 (Reformulating Problems) and Chapter 5 (Reformulating Value Statements) are of particular importance for later chapters. The authors strongly recommend that none of these lessons be omitted, since each teaches a skill necessary for the successful completion of the problem chapters. Because these chapters are all self-grading, their assignment places no burden on the instructor, other than answering questions about particular difficulties.

The second part of *Elementary Political Analysis* contains two types of chapters: (1) highly structured chapters in which students choose among alternatives (Chapters 7 to 9) and (2) less structured ones, where students reformulate the problem and specify the necessary data, and are allowed greater range in writing memoranda (Chapters 10 to 12). Depending on the design of a course, any of these chapters may be omitted. However, it is suggested that students be assigned at least one of the highly structured chapters before attempting a less structured lesson.

Part Three should be assigned only after several of the other chapters have been successfully completed. The chapters in this section require more independent work but, for that reason, may be more challenging to those students who have completed earlier assignments without difficulty.

While this general sequence should be adhered to in most cases, the book intentionally contains more material than most instructors can use in one semester or quarter. We have done this in order to provide flexibility and variety. Chapters can be assigned in the sequence best suited for a particular course. The skills we are addressing can usually be taught through the assignment of five of the last nine chapters. We do not recommend that every chapter be assigned in one term except in unusual circumstances.

Herbert Jacob
Robert Weissberg

Part One
THE BASIC TOOLS OF ANALYSIS

Among the benefits of taking a political science course is that it can teach you new ways of thinking about politics and give you more information about government. The first chapters of this book seek to teach you some of the ways in which you may understand political problems more thoroughly and more realistically.

Two skills are especially important. The first involves understanding information in the special form in which it is often found. Data about politics often are published in numerical form, in tables and graphs; often they are reduced to statistical indices like means, medians, and correlation coefficients. One needs to develop the skill of understanding these special forms of data presentation in order to use the information in analyzing political problems.

The second skill involves learning a systematic way of thinking through problems. That requires learning how to sort out various elements of a problem—normative and empirical elements. It requires mastering the technique of disentangling complex problems into their component parts and analyzing each part separately. It necessitates choosing information which is relevant to a problem. And finally, it requires the ability to reassemble the parts of one's analysis in a statement which is an analysis of the entire original problem.

The five chapters which follow are designed to teach these skills. They are an essential prologue to the later chapters, which provide opportunities to use them.

Chapter 1
READING TABLES

Most quantitative information in newspapers, magazines, and books is presented in tabular form. We use tables because they allow us to convey a great deal of information in little space. If one knows how to read tables correctly, this condensation of information makes it easy to comprehend a lot of data at a glance. On the other hand, it is easy to be misled by tables. To take advantage of the information presented in tabular form, we need to learn how to read them correctly.

This chapter concentrates on some of the fundamental skills of interpreting information in tables. It will teach you to identify:

1. The content of a table
2. The form of the numbers
3. The source of the information
4. The relationship between phenomena represented in the table
5. The flow of causality in a table

Each of these characteristics of tables will help you to make correct inferences from them. Thus you will want to interpret raw numbers differently than percentages, you will want to treat with proper caution data that come from biased sources, and you will want to know when you can make causal inferences (e.g., being Italian causes one to vote for Democrats) in contrast to associational inferences (e.g., most Italians also vote Democratic). In this chapter you will work with simple two-variable tables. In the next chapter you will learn to read complex three- and four-variable tables, as well as graphs.

The first part of this chapter is written in programmed form. Cover the right-hand margin with a suitable card mask. As you read, you will find that many of the paragraphs have missing words or ask questions. Fill in the missing words or answer the questions as you read. Immediately after doing so, check to see whether you were right by looking at the answer printed in the right-hand margin. If you answered correctly, proceed to the next paragraph. If your answer was wrong, reread the preceding paragraph so that you understand why it was wrong.

The second part of this chapter provides you with an opportunity to use your skills with tables taken from reading in the social sciences. You will discover how much your ability to read tables has improved.

IDENTIFIERS IN TABLES

Every table contains many identifiers—labels which tell the reader what the table is about. You will find such identifiers in the (1) title, (2) column and row labels, (3) body of the table, and (4) footnotes. It is important to read these identifying labels carefully, because they tell you what you may and may not infer from the table.

1. Refer, for example, to Table 1.1. The title and footnote of this table carefully define its content. They indicate that the table shows the relationship between conservatism and liberalism (as measured by attitudes toward change) and education. You may draw conclusions from the table about the relationship between people's education and their attitudes toward change. Can you also draw conclusions about intelligence and attitudes toward change? [Yes. No]. You cannot because the table contains no information about intelligence.

    No

2. Numbers in a table may have several forms. They may be absolute numbers, index numbers, or percentages. Note that the numbers in Table 1.1 are [absolute numbers, percentages]. Furthermore, they are based

    percentages

TABLE 1.1 RELATIONSHIPS BETWEEN EDUCATION AND CONSERVATISM-LIBERALISM IN A RANDOM MINNESOTA SAMPLE

	Education		
Conservatism-Liberalism	Grade School	High School	College
Liberal	6%	16%	30%
Moderately liberal	16	33	36
Moderately conservative	35	32	24
Conservative	43	19	10
Total	100%	100%	100%
	(277)	(512)	(293)

SOURCE: Adapted from Herbert McClosky. "Conservatism and Personality," American Political Science Review, vol. 52, p. 35, 1958. Conservatism is defined as resistance to change, liberalism as favoring change.

on the column totals. This means that you can compare the proportion of liberals in each educational group regardless of the fact that there are many more persons who have a high school education than those who went to college. You can also compare the proportion who are moderately liberal, those who are moderately conservative, and those who are conservative. So you may note that 43 percent of grade-school-educated respondents were conservative but only _____ percent of college-educated respondents were conservative. Can you assert that 6 percent of the liberals had a grade school education? [Yes, No] No, because 6 is the proportion of grade-school-educated persons who are liberal. If we substitute the number of people in each cell of the table for the percentages, this becomes clear. See Table 1.2. There are _____ grade-school-educated liberals. They constitute 6 percent of all people with a grade school education but 17/190, or 9 percent, of all liberals. Returning to Table 1.1, can you assert that 19 percent of the conservatives had a high school education? [Yes, No] Nineteen percent represents the proportion (95/512) of high-school-educated people who were conservative. The proportion of conservatives who had a high school education is _____ .

10

No

17

No

95/245, or 39%

3. Tables 1.1 and 1.2 indicate that the Minnesota sample asked these questions of 1,082 people. The fact that it is a random sample allows us to have considerable confidence in the results. Were we told that the 1,082 were people attending a Baptist church in one city, we would have much less confidence in

TABLE 1.2 RELATIONSHIP BETWEEN EDUCATION AND CONSERVATISM-LIBERALISM IN A RANDOM MINNESOTA SAMPLE

Conservatism-Liberalism	Education			
	Grade School	High School	College	Total
Liberal	17	84	89	190
Moderately liberal	44	168	104	316
Moderately conservative	96	165	70	331
Conservative	120	95	30	245
Total	277	512	293	1,082

SOURCE: As in Table 1.1.

generalizing from those data to the entire population, because Baptists attending a single church would clearly be a very special group and could not be representative of the whole state.

4. Finally, the tables show the source of the information. It comes from [*Time Magazine, American Political Science Review*]. If we want to learn more about this study, we know where to look.

American Political Science Review

5. Examine Table 1.3 now. Does it allow us to compare the proportion of narcotics violators sentenced to prison with the proportion of robbers sent to prison? [Yes, No]

Yes

6. Do the percentages in Table 1.3 permit us to assert what percentage of all suspended sentences were given to people charged with assault? [Yes, No] We would need row percentages to draw such conclusions.

No

7. Does Table 1.3 permit us to generalize about the administration of justice in the United States? [Yes, No] The table refers only to New York City.

No

TABLE 1.3 SENTENCES GIVEN DEFENDANTS BY TYPE OF CHARGE IN NEW YORK CITY, 1960

		Charge				
Sentence	Assault	Carrying Dangerous Weapons	Larceny	Narcotics	Robbery	Other
Suspended	42%	30%	42%	41%	22%	43%
Prison	58	70	58	59	78	57
Total	100%	100%	100%	100%	100%	100%
	(26)	(10)	(40)	(17)	(18)	(14)

SOURCE: Adapted from Ares, Rankin, and Sturz. "Administration of Bail in New York." *New York University Law School Review*, vol. 38, p. 85, 1963.

If you got all these answers right with respect to Table 1.3, proceed to the next section. If you made a mistake, reread the first four frames of this section before proceeding.

HOW TO INTERPRET A TABLE— THE CHARACTERISTICS OF VARIABLES

1. Authors use tables to show how several phenomena vary (or change) together. Wealth and vot-

ing, for instance, tend to vary in such a way that the wealthier a person is, the more likely it is that he will vote. A table presenting this information would present two phenomena, wealth and voting, both of which vary. Look at the skeletal table on the next page.
    Tendency to vote varies from high to _____.Wealth [varies, does not vary], ranging from rich to poor. Phenomena which have a range of values are called variables. Phenomena which have only a single value and do not vary are called constants. *All phenomena in tables are variables.*

                                                           low; varies

TABLE _____ RELATIONSHIP BETWEEN THE WEALTH OF RESPONDENTS AND VOTING TURNOUT

	Wealth		
Voting Turnout	**Rich**	**Middle Income**	**Poor**
High			
Medium			
Low			

2. Some variables are used to explain others. For instance, an author might use the wealth of people to explain whether they voted Republican or Democratic. The variables used to explain something else are called *independent* variables. If you wish to explain voting behavior by wealth, wealth is an _____ variable. If you wish to explain the incidence of war by the incidence of nationalism, nationalism is the _____ variable.

            independent

            independent

3. There is also a name for the phenomenon which is being explained; it is called the dependent variable. In frame 2, nationalism is used to explain the incidence of war. Nationalism is the independent variable, war is the _____ variable. Alternatively, if we try to explain Supreme Court decisions by the partisan affiliation of the justices, Supreme Court decisions are the _____ variable and the partisan affiliation of the justices is the _____ variable.

            dependent

            dependent
            independent

4. Whether a variable is used as a dependent (the explained phenomenon) or as an independent variable (the explaining phenomenon) depends entirely on the author's analytic strategy. You may identify variables by asking the following questions:

8 The Basic Tools of Analysis

a. *What is the author trying to explain?* This will be the _____ variable in the table, so labeled because its values depend on the values of other variables.

dependent

b. *How does the author account for changes in the dependent variable?* He implies that some other variable causes the dependent variable to assume different values. The "causal" variables are called _____ variables. The implication in a table is that the independent variables cause changes in the dependent variables, and not the other way around.

independent

c. *In what direction do percentages run?* When the percentages run down the columns (indicated by the 100 percent at the bottom of each column), the independent variable will be found along the top of the table and the dependent variable along the side. This is the most common form. When the percentages read across the rows with the 100 percent figure to the right of the table, the dependent variable is at the top and the independent variable at the left side of the table. The correct procedure is:

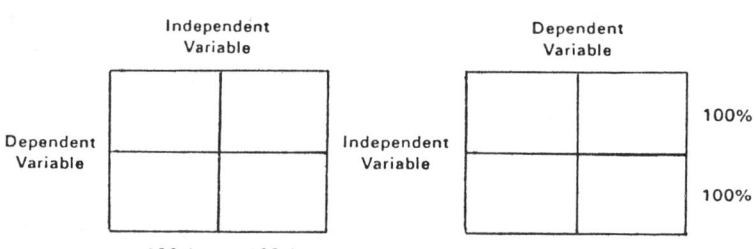

d. *Are some variables logically or chronologically prior to others?* Independent variables are generally logically or chronologically prior to dependent variables.

5. Let us take some examples to illustrate frame 4. Look again at Table 1.1. Here the relationship is between education and conservatism-liberalism. The percentages run down the education columns, implying that education is the [dependent, independent] variable. This also implies that education occurs [before, after] an attitude of conservatism or liberalism. A different research may be more in-

independent

before

terested in the effects of liberalism and conservatism on education and thus percentage Table 1.1 on the rows rather than the columns. However as presently constructed, the causal connection runs from _____ to conservatism-liberalism. Education is the _____ variable, and conservatism-liberalism is the _____ variable.

education

independent
dependent

6. Now examine Table 1.3 again. The percentages are calculated [down the columns, across the rows], indicating that "charge" is the independent variable which is being used to explain "sentence," the _____ variable. Note that this causal connection is reasonable, since the charge against a defendant may affect his sentence, but his sentence cannot possibly help determine the crime with which he is charged.

down the
columns

dependent

TABLE 1.3 SENTENCES GIVEN DEFENDANTS BY TYPE OF CHARGE IN NEW YORK CITY, 1960

		Charge				
Sentence	Assault	Carrying Dangerous Weapons	Larceny	Narcotics	Robbery	Other
Suspended	42%	30%	42%	41%	22%	43%
Prison	58	70	58	59	78	57
Total	100%	100%	100%	100%	100%	100%
	(26)	(10)	(40)	(17)	(18)	(14)

SOURCE: Adapted from Ares, Rankin, and Sturz. "Administration of Bail in New York." *New York University Law School Review,* vol. 38, p. 85, 1963.

7. Suppose you were the author and wished to explain the occurrence of high or low racial prejudice in terms of people's race (white or black). Place the variables properly in Table 1.4 below for which the numbers have already been supplied.

TABLE 1.4 RACIAL PREJUDICE BY RACE OF RESPONDENT

60%	30%
40%	70
100%	100%

SOURCE: Simulated.

In columns:
White, black
  (in either order)
In rows:
Racial prejudice
  (high, low in
  either order)

Check your answer with the rules outlined earlier.

a. What are you trying to explain? This identifies the dependent variable.

b. With what variable are you trying to account for change in the dependent variable? This will be the independent variable.

c. How do the percentages run to 100 percent? They should run down (or across) the *independent* variable to total 100 percent.

Not all tables are quite so simple. Sometimes the author is not implying causality. He simply wants to point out a relationship between two phenomena. They exist together, without one necessarily causing the other. For example, the level of education is not a *cause* of criminality although the incidence of crime may be associated with levels of education. Likewise, we may be interested in the distribution of Republican votes in various sections of a metropolitan area without asserting that living in a suburb causes people to vote Republican; indeed, the causal explanation is much more likely to be that wealthier people are both Republican and likely to live in suburbs. So wealth is the causal factor, but living in suburbs is related to voting Republican.

When we are looking simply at the association between two variables without implying causality, we use two independent variables, and the table is said to be symmetrical, that is, the percentages can run either way, and either variable can be placed in the column or row.

We can identify such symmetrical tables by asking:

a. Is a causal relationship implied in a symmetrical table? No

b. Does it make as good sense to have the percentages run across the rows to 100 percent as down the columns to 100 percent? If yes, the table is symmetrical.

Reading Tables 11

8. Examine Table 1.5. It shows the vote for mayor in two cities according to party. The numbers in the table are [absolute numbers, percentages]. We do not want to imply causality. Therefore the table is _____ .

    absolute
      numbers
      symmetrical

TABLE 1.5   VOTES FOR MAYOR BY PARTY IN TWO CITIES

	Greenville	Redwood City	Total
Republican	450	1,550	2,000
Democratic	550	450	1,000
Total	1,000	2,000	3,000

SOURCE: Simulated.

9. Because we do not want to imply causality, but simply to examine the relationship between city and vote, we may show the relationship with either column or row percentages. Which you use depends on your purpose. Suppose you want to show the proportion of Democrats and Republicans in each city. Fill in the percentages for such a table, using Table 1.6 below.

10. Now suppose the two cities are the only two in a state and you wish to determine from which city most of the Republican (or Democratic) votes came in state-wide elections. You would now run the percentages (down the columns, across the rows) because you wish to find out the proportion of the total Republican (or Democratic) vote coming from each city. Fill in the percentages for Tables 1.6 and 1.7, using Table 1.5 as your base data.

    across the rows

TABLE 1.6 PROPORTION OF REPUBLICAN AND DEMOCRATIC VOTERS IN EACH OF TWO CITIES

	Greenville	Redwood City
Republicans		
Democrats		
Total	100%	100%

SOURCE: Simulated.

Greenville:
45%
55%
Redwood City:
77.5%
22.5%

12 The Basic Tools of Analysis

TABLE 1.7 DISTRIBUTION OF PARTY VOTERS IN TWO CITIES

	Greenville	Redwood City	Total
Republican			100%
Democratic			100%

SOURCE: Simulated.

Republican
22.5%; 77.5%
Democratic
55.0%; 45.0%

11. Before concluding that a relationship exists between two variables, we also want to make certain that the differences in the numbers are large enough to be significant. Significance has two meanings. The first is a statistical one. By statistical significance we mean that the difference in the numbers is so large that it is unlikely to be the result of chance or error. When a table footnote asserts that its results are statistically significant, it means that neither _____ nor _____ is likely to explain the results, and the relationship is probably a true one. When the data come from a national sample with more than 1,500 respondents, we can as a rule of thumb use a range of 5 percent as our gauge of significance. If differences between groups are less than 5 percent, the result is probably not statistically _____ . The results are statistically significant when the difference is [greater, smaller] than 5 percent. When a sample is smaller, the size of the difference between two groups has to be larger before we can consider the relationship statistically significant.

chance
error

significant
greater

Examine Table 1.8. It shows the difference between boys and girls in the third grade on scores of

TABLE 1.8 RELATIONSHIP OF SEX TO SENSE OF POLITICAL EFFICACY* AMONG THIRD GRADERS

Sex	Low Efficacy	Medium Efficacy	High Efficacy	Total Percent	$N^\dagger$	N Not Scored
Boys	55%	28	17	100%	669	164
Girls	57%	29	14	100%	576	269

*Political efficacy is the belief that one can influence government and that public officials are responsive to public demands.

† Used as a base for percentages.

SOURCE: By permission from David Easton and Jack Dennis, "The Child's Acquisition of Regime Norms: Political Efficacy," *American Political Science Review,* vol. 61, March, 1967.

political efficacy. The difference between the two is [more, less] than 5 percent. We would conclude that there [is, is no] relationship between sex and sense of political efficacy at the third-grade level.

less
is no

The second meaning of significance is a *substantive* one. A relationship may not be caused by chance or error, but it may nevertheless have little meaning for our analysis. For instance, crime rates seem to grow with expenditures on policing. The extra police are not causing the added crime but simply unearthing more of the crime that already existed. Substantive significance means that the relationship makes sense in terms of the proposition we are testing or the theory we hold. To be substantively significant, a relationship must fit into the _____ or _____ we are testing.

theory
proposition

Summary

To review the most essential elements of the reading of tables: First, we must examine the title and footnotes carefully to determine the content of the table and the sources of its data. We also need to ascertain the form of the numbers in the table.

Second, we need to determine whether the table is symmetrical. If it is symmetrical, it contains two independent variables and the author does not claim that one causes the other. Many tables, however, are not symmetrical, and the author claims that one variable is logically or chronologically prior to the other and probably causes it. In such a table, the variable which represents the phenomenon being explained is the dependent variable. The variables used to explain that phenomenon are the independent variables. Once you can identify the dependent and independent variables correctly, you know what the author is explaining and how he is trying to do it.

Finally, we need to determine whether the differences in numbers are significant. The differences between groups must be large enough so we can discount chance or error as being the cause of the difference. We call that statistical significance. In addition, the data must have substantive significance; they must make sense in terms of the theory or proposition we are testing.

PROBLEMS

These are the fundamental rules for interpreting tables. To interpret them correctly requires practice. On the following pages you will find problems which will help you test yourself on the objectives of this lesson, to identify the variables in a table and the flow of causality in it.

14 The Basic Tools of Analysis

Each of the problems consists of three sections. The first is the problem section; it consists of a table with several statements about it. Following the problem section is your answer section. Label each statement correct or incorrect and *explain your answer briefly* in a sentence or two. If, for example, a statement does not follow from the data in the table, all that has to be said is that it does not follow and why it does not follow. Likewise, if the statement is a misinterpretation of a percentage, a sentence on why it is a misrepresentation will suffice. More than one correct answer is possible. The third section follows your answers and gives the correct answers. If all your answers were correct, proceed to the next section of the exercise. If some of your answers were wrong, reread the preceding frames until you understand the correct answers.

Problem 1

CHANGING SOUTHERN ESTIMATES OF RACE RELATIONS, 1957–1963

"Do you think the day will ever come in the South when Whites and Negroes will be going to the same schools, eating in the same restaurants, and generally sharing the same public accommodations?"

Date	Percent Expecting Eventual Integration	Percent Not Expecting Eventual Integration	Uncertain
August, 1957	45%	33%	22%
October, 1958	53	31	16
January, 1961	76	19	5
July, 1963	83	13	4

SOURCE: American Institute of Public Opinion (Gallup Poll), July, 1963.

A. In 1963 over 80 percent of Southerners supported total integrattion.

B. In only six years (1957—1963) much of Southern life became integrated.

C. A small minority of Southerners are blocking civil rights progress.

D. By 1963, eventual racial integration was expected by most Southerners.

Your Answers to Problem 1
A.

B.

C.

D.

Now check your answers with the correct ones on p. 23.

Problem 2
ATTITUDE TOWARD THE UNITED STATES AS "NOT WORTH FIGHTING FOR" AMONG RESIDENTS OF THE BLACK GHETTOS OF DETROIT AFTER THE 1967 RIOTS

"Is the country worth fighting for in a major world war?"

	Behavior		
	Rioters*	Noninvolved*	Counter-rioters*
Worth fighting for	55.3%	75.0%	86.9%
Not worth fighting for	39.4	15.5	3.3
Don't know	5.3	9.5	9.8
Total	100.0%	100.0%	100.0%

*Respondents were drawn by random-sampling techniques two weeks after the riot ended. "Rioters" were those who said they participated; "noninvolved" were those who claimed they did not participate; "counter-rioters" were those who claimed they tried to halt the riot.

SOURCE: Report of the National Advisory Commission on Civil Disorders (New York: Bantam Books, Inc., 1968), p. 178.

A. The data show that believing that one's country is worth fighting for is related to behavior in riots among Negroes.

B. Most of the rioters do not believe their country is worth fighting for.

C. The data show that in the black ghetto in Detroit, a majority believe that America is worth fighting for.

D. Over half (55.3 percent) of those believing America is worth fighting for took part in the riots.

Your Answers to Problem 2
A.

B.

C.

D.

Now check your answers with the correct ones on p. 23.

Problem 3

VOTING PREFERENCES OF MIDDLE-CLASS AND WORKING-CLASS PEOPLE IN 1964*

Voting Preference	Middle-class Voters ($N = 470$)	Working class Voters ($N = 570$)
Democratic	56%	77%
Republican	43	21
Other, don't know	1	2
Total	100%	100%

*The 1964 presidential-election survey conducted by the University of Michigan's Survey Research Center. The respondents are a random sample of the national population. Class identification is based on self-identification.

SOURCE: Marian D. Irish and James W. Prothro, *The Politics of American Democracy,* 3d ed. (Englewood Cliffs, N.J., Prentice-Hall, Inc., 1959, 1962, and 1965), p. 177. By permission of the publisher.

A. Over three-quarters of working-class voters are members of the Democratic party.

B. This table shows that there are more working- than middle-class voters in America.

C. The Republicans did better among middle-class voters than among the working class.

D. The farther down the economic ladder one goes in American society, the greater the proportion of Democratic voters.

Your Answers to Problem 3
A.

B.

C.

D.

Now check your answers with the correct ones on p. 24.

Problem 4
EDUCATIONAL DIFFERENCES IN CONSERVATISM-LIBERALISM AS MEASURED BY ATTITUDE TOWARD CHANGE

Relationship between Education and Conservatism-Liberalism in a Minnesota Random Sample

Conservatism-Liberalism	Grade School	High School	Some College
Liberal	6.2%	16.3%	30.5%
Moderately liberal	15.9	32.7	35.7
Moderately conservative	34.6	32.3	23.8
Conservative	43.3	18.7	10.0
Total (*N* = 1,082)	100.0%	100.0%	100.0%

SOURCE: Adapted from Herbert McClosky, "Conservatism and Personality," *American Political Science Review,* vol. 52, p. 35, 1958. Conservatism-liberalism is defined as attitude toward change.

A. This table disproves the idea that college-educated people favor the Republican party.

B. On the whole, conservatives tend to be poorly educated.

C. Less well-educated people are more likely to accept the ways of the past and resent innovation than those who have attended college.

D. Only 10 percent of the extreme conservatives have had some college education compared with 30.5 percent of the liberals.

Your Answers to Problem 4
A.

B.

C.

D.

Now check your answers with the correct ones on p. 24.

CORRECT ANSWERS

Correct Answers to Problem 1

A. Answer A is incorrect because the question asked is not whether a person supports integration, but whether he thinks integration will *eventually* come to the South. The expectation of some future occurrence, e.g., death, does not necessarily mean that one favors it.

B. Incorrect. The table shows changes in expectations of Southerners; it tells nothing about the actual integration of schools, restaurants, and public accommodations.

C. Incorrect. It may be true that a small minority of Southerners are blocking civil rights progress, but this table says nothing about this subject. Believing that integration will never come to the South is not the same thing as opposing civil rights.

D. Correct. In 1963 over half (83 percent) of the Southerners in this sample believed that some day schools, restaurants, and public accommodations would be integrated. This does not mean, of course, that they favored such integration.

Correct Answers to Problem 2

A. Correct. The data show that believing one's country is worth fighting for is related to participation in riots. Looking across the first row, the percentages increase as one goes from the rioters to those not involved to those who opposed the rioting. Reading across the second row ("not worth fighting for"), we see that the proportions decrease: fewer counter-rioters believe this than rioters.

B. Incorrect. Though behavior in riots and belief that one's country is worth fighting for are related, this does not mean that most rioters do not feel that America is worth fighting for. On the contrary, 55.3 percent of the rioters think America is worth fighting for.

C. Correct. In no column in Table 2.4 is there a majority believing that America is not worth fighting for. Therefore we can say that more than half of the total sample believe this. However, because the number of people in each category is unknown, we cannot tell exactly how many hold each opinion. All we can say is that more than 55.3 percent of the total sample agree that America is worth fighting for

D. Incorrect. The figure 55.3 percent represents rioters who think America is worth fighting for, not those with this opinion who rioted. Answer D reads the percentage as if it were calculated across the row, but the location of the 100 percent sign indicates that the percentages are calculated down the columns.

Correct Answers to Problem 3

A. Incorrect. Voter *preference* is described here, not party *membership*. Because preference is not the same as membership, answer A is incorrect. Many football fans prefer the Green Bay Packers, but most of them are not members of the team. Nowhere in the table is "membership" mentioned.

B. Correct. This answer indicates a careful reading of the table by looking at the N's at the head of each column. It does assume that the sample is random and gives accurate population estimates. The Survey Research Center at the University of Michigan is one of the most scientific polling organizations in America, and their samples can generally be relied upon to be random.

C. Correct. In 1964 the Republican party was preferred by 43 percent of the middle-class voters compared with only 21 percent of the working-class voters.

D. Incorrect. Only two broad classes are presented here, and this is not an "economic ladder." Here, as in many other instances, you cannot project tendencies without additional information. It is possible that as you move down the ladder you encounter more people who are politically indifferent. Before answer D can be verified, many more data are needed.

Correct Answers to Problem 4

A. Incorrect. Conservatism and liberalism *as defined in the source* do not mean Democraticness or Republicanism. Attitude toward change *may* be related to partisan identification, but party affiliation is not described in this table.

B. Incorrect. The percentages run down the columns; so we can only say that poorly educated people tend to be conservative. We do not know how many of the conservatives had a grade school or a high school or a college education. To know that, we need percentages that run across the rows. This kind of percentage could be calculated if the number of people in each class of education were known (but these figures are not given).

C. Correct. 43.3 percent of those with grade school education were "conservative" compared with 10.0 percent of those with some college. Likewise, only 6.2 percent of those with grade school education were "liberal" compared with 30.5 percent of those with some college.

D. Incorrect. In this table, the percentages run down the columns. Answer D is a column percent incorrectly read as a row percent. The 10 percent figure is based on the number of people who attended college, not the number of people who are "conservative." Hence the 10 percent figure should be read: 10 percent of those with "some college" are conservative.

Chapter 2
MULTIVARIATE TABLES AND GRAPHS

More complicated tables than those examined in Chapter 1 are often used for the purpose of analyzing information. Rather than use a single independent variable to explain a phenomenon, several independent variables which simultaneously affect a dependent variable may be studied. Alternatively, tables may not be used at all, but data are presented in graphic form. This chapter will teach interpretation of multivariate tables and graphs by identifying:

1. The independent and dependent variables of multivariate tables
2. The flow of causality in multivariate tables
3. Independent and dependent variables in graphs
4. The metric of graphs and its significance

MULTIVARIATE TABLES

Often, more than one variable is needed to explain a social phenomenon. For instance, if we want to understand racial tensions in the United States, we need to take into account at least the relative size of the black community in an area and whether the communities are in the North or the South. Thus we must examine two independent variables in order to explain one dependent variable.

Presenting such data in a table, the social scientist will hold one of the independent variables constant to show the effect of the other one on racial tension. For instance, he may examine the relationship between racial tension and the proportion of Negroes in a community in the South, and then in the North. When he does this, he holds the independent variable "regionalism" constant and thereby controls for its effect on racial tensions.

1. Refer to Table 2.1. According to its title, it shows the relationship between [1, 2, 3, 4] variables. The variables are (1) race-relations symbols, (2) attitudes toward them, and (3) the race of the respondents.   3

TABLE 2.1 ATTITUDES TOWARD RACE-RELATIONS SYMBOLS BY RACE OF RESPONDENTS

Race-relations Symbol	White				Negro			
	Helpful	Neutral	Harmful	N	Helpful	Neutral	Harmful	N
Open housing	53%	26%	22%	482	95%	3%	1%	236
Integration	46	31	33	468	87	7	6	238
School busing to facilitate integration	23	18	59	484	67	16	17	222

SOURCE: Reprinted from "Social Strain and Urban Violence," by Everett F. Cataldo, Richard M. Johnson, and Lyman A. Kellstadt, in *Riots and Rebellion, Civil Violence in the Urban Community,* Louis H. Masotti and Don R. Bowen (editors). (Beverly Hills, Calif., Sage Publications, Inc., 1968), p. 293. By permission of the publisher.

2. The authors of this table have "nested" their variables. Thus the race-relations symbols and attitudes toward them are presented first for whites and then for Negroes. Whenever you see such nesting, you know that one of the variables is being held constant. The variable which is held constant is the one that contains all the others. In Table 2.1, race contains both attitudes and the three symbols. Therefore [race, attitudes] is the variable being held constant. By controlling for race, the authors can show that both whites and Negroes are most likely to endorse "open housing" and least likely to endorse "school busing to facilitate integration." However, a much higher proportion of Negroes than whites endorses all three symbols.

race

3. Next, examine Table 2.2. It shows the relationship between [2, 3] variables. The variable in which the two others are nested is income, since place of resi-

3

TABLE 2.2 VOTING TURNOUT BY INCOME AND PLACE OF RESIDENCE

	High Income		Low Income	
	Voted	Did Not Vote	Voted	Did Not Vote
Urban	85%	15%	60%	40%
Rural	55	45	40	60

SOURCE: Simulated.

dence and voting turnout are shown separately for high-income and low-income respondents. Thus the authors control for [income, voting turnout]. Within each category of income, place of residence makes a difference in the percentage voting.

income

4. Three-variable tables are often shown in a condensed form. Refer to Table 2.3, which has been condensed from Table 2.2. Note that the subcolumn representing those not voting has been omitted.

TABLE 2.3 VOTING TURNOUT BY INCOME AND PLACE OF RESIDENCE

	High Income	Low Income
Urban	85%	60%
Rural	55	40

SOURCE: Simulated.

The rules for interpreting such tables are similar to those for two-variable tables.

a. Count the number of variables referred to in the title.

b. Note where each variable is referenced in the table. One will be referenced in the rows; one will be referenced in the columns. If the table is condensed, one will not be in either column or row headings. This last, or remaining, variable is represented by the numbers in each cell (or square) of the table.

c. If causality is implied by the table, the dependent variable will be the one represented by the numbers in the cells of the table.

5. Let us apply these rules to Table 2.3. There are a total of _____ variables listed in the title. The variable _____ is placed in the rows; _____ is placed in the columns. The remaining variable is _____ and must be represented by the numbers in each cell of the table.

three
place of residence
income
voting turnout

6. Table 2.3 seeks to explain voting turnout by two independent variables, income and place of residence. The dependent variable is _____ . Thus we conclude from the table that voting turnout is highest in high-income, urban areas and lowest in _____ , _____ areas.

voting turnout

low-income; rural
(either order)

Now look at Table 2.4.

28 The Basic Tools of Analysis

TABLE 2.4 PERCENTAGE OF NEGROES REGISTERED TO VOTE IN 1958 IN SOUTHERN COUNTIES, BY LYNCHING RATE AND RACIAL VIOLENCE

Lynching Rate 1900–1931	Amount of Racial Violence, 1955–1960	
	None	Some
Low	15% (576)	29% (80)
High	27% (216)	7% (16)
Total	18% (792)	26% (96)

NOTE: A "low" lynching rate is less than 10 lynchings per 100,000 population in 1930. Racial violence is defined as acts against institutions and individuals involved in the civil rights movement. The numbers in parentheses are the total number of counties on which the percentages are based.

SOURCE: Adapted from Donald Matthews and James Prothro, *Negroes and the New Southern Politics* (New York: Harcourt, Brace & World, Inc., 1966), p. 167, reproduced with permission.

7. The three variables identified by the title are _____ , _____ , and _____ .

       voter registration rate, the lynching rate, racial violence

   The lynching rate is placed in the [rows, columns]; the amount of racial violence in 1955–1960 is in the _____.

       rows

       columns

   The third variable is the voter registration rate, and is represented by the numbers in each cell. The authors of this table mean to imply causality; i.e., they are asserting that Negro registration is affected by past and present racial violence. Therefore "Negro voter registration rate" is the [dependent, independent] variable and is represented by the numbers in each cell of the table.

       dependent

8. Interpreting Table 2.4, we see that the two almost identically high registration rates (27 percent and 29 percent) occur where there was violence either in the past or present but not at both times. The lowest Negro voting registration occurs when there was a [high, low] past rate and [none, some] present violence. Thus we have a complicated relationship. Many Negroes register to vote where there has been violence in the present or past; few register where violence occurred at both times.

       high; some

9. As a test of your ability to interpret such complex tables, examine Table 2.5. It seeks to explain

TABLE 2.5 ILLITERACY BY AGE, RACE, AND SEX, 1952

| | Percent Illiterate | | | | | |
| | White | | | Non-white | | |
Age	Male	Female	Both	Male	Female	Both
14–24	1.2	0.5	0.8	7.2	1.4	3.9
25–34	0.8	0.6	0.7	9.7	3.8	6.4
35–44	1.2	0.5	0.8	7.5	5.9	6.6
45–54	2.2	1.4	1.8	12.8	10.4	11.5
55–64	3.6	3.4	3.5	19.4	16.9	18.1
65 +	5.6	4.4	5.0	35.8	31.2	33.3

SOURCE: Bureau of the Census. Based on a sample of about 25,000. Persons unable to read and write in any language were classified as illiterate, except that literacy was assumed for all who had completed 6 or more years of school. Only the civilian, noninstitutional population 14 years of age and over is included.

_____ by three independent variables: _____, _____, and _____. The table title [explains, does not explain] what is meant by illiteracy. To find the explanation one must search [the body of the table, the footnote].

illiteracy
age, race, sex
does not explain

footnote

10. The independent variables are placed in the [rows and columns, in the cells] of Table 2.5. The dependent variable, which is _____, is placed in the cells.

rows and columns
illiteracy

11. We may interpret Table 2.5 in a number of different ways. Let us first look at the portion representing the relationship between illiteracy and age among men and women who are "whites." In general, as we move down to the older age groups, illiteracy [increases, decreases]. Thus, among all whites, _____ percent of those 65 or older are illiterate while among the 14-to-24-year-olds, only _____ percent are illiterate.

increases
5

0.8

12. Next, in Table 2.5, we can compare men and women among the whites. In every age group proportionately [more, fewer] men are illiterate than women. Thus, among whites, we may conclude that both age and sex are related to illiteracy. Those with the highest illiteracy are _____ and _____.

more

older
male (either order)

13. Next we look at some relationships among non-whites in Table 2.5. Is there a relationship be-

tween age and illiteracy? [Yes, No] Is there a relation- Yes
ship between sex and illiteracy? [Yes, No] For non- Yes
whites, most illiterates are found among the
_____ _____ . older men

14. Finally, we can look at the relationship between race and illiteracy in Table 2.5. Are whites or nonwhites more often illiterate? Comparing white and nonwhite males in every age group, we find a [larger, smaller] percentage of nonwhites are illiterate than whites. Among females, we find a [larger, smaller] percentage of nonwhites illiterate than whites.   larger

larger

15. Thus, from the foregoing analysis, we may conclude that race is also related to illiteracy. In fact, if we hold sex and age constant by comparing only men or only women of a specific age group, we still find a very large difference in the illiteracy rate between whites and non-whites. For instance, among 65-year-old men, _____ percent of the whites are illiterate, while   5.6
_____ percent of the nonwhites are illiterate.   35.8
Therefore we may say that race is related to illiteracy even when we hold constant (or control for) the effects of sex and age.

16. Does Table 2.5 show that most of the illiterates in America are nonwhite males? [Yes, No] Though   No
illiteracy is much higher among nonwhites, remember that there are about 10 times as many whites as nonwhites in the United States. Notice that in almost all age categories in the total column, nonwhite rates are not 10 times higher. This means that the actual number of white illiterates is probably [smaller, larger]   larger
than the number of nonwhite illiterates.

17. Notice also that there are conclusions that you *cannot* make from Table 2.5. You [can, cannot]   cannot
conclude that men are less intelligent than women or that whites are more intelligent than nonwhites. You cannot infer intelligence from the table because the dependent variable is _____ , not intelligence.   illiteracy
You also cannot infer that whites are more often literate than nonwhites *because* they get better schooling, are wealthier, or come from more stable homes. You cannot make these inferences because the table's independent variables are _____ , _____ ,   age, sex,
and _____ and tell nothing about education,   race
wealth, or family stability.

Summary

Three- and four-variable tables contain a great deal of information. You can interpret them correctly if you follow the rules outlined earlier.

1.   Count the number of variables referred to in the title.

2.   Note how the table is constructed.

a.   If several variables are nested in another one, the variable in which they are nested is the *control* variable.
b.   If the table is condensed so that one variable is referenced in the rows, another is referenced in the columns, and one is missing, the missing variable is the dependent variable and is represented by the numbers in the cells of the table.

3.   If causality is implied by the table, the dependent variable will be the one represented by the numbers in the cells of the table.

PROBLEMS

On the following pages are some problems which provide further practice in interpreting such tables. Each of the problems consists of three sections. The first is the problem section; it consists of a table with several statements about it. Following the problem section is your answer section. Label each statement correct or incorrect and *explain your answer briefly* in a sentence or two. If, for example, a statement does not follow from the data in the table, all that has to be said is that it does not follow and why it does not follow. Likewise, if the statement is a misinterpretation of a percentage, a sentence on why it is a misinterpretation will suffice. More than one correct answer is possible. The third section is the answer section, giving the correct answers. If all your answers were correct, proceed to the next section of the exercise. If some of your answers were wrong, reread the previous frames until you understand the correct answers.

Problem 1

RELATIONSHIP OF SEX TO SENSE OF POLITICAL EFFICACY* AMONG SCHOOL CHILDREN IN GRADES 3 TO 8

Grade	Sex	Low Efficacy	Medium Efficacy	High Efficacy	Total Percent[†]	N[‡]	N Not Scored
3	Boys	55%	28%	17%	100	669	164
	Girls	57	29	14	100	576	269
4	Boys	52	27	20	99	764	131
	Girls	57	27	16	100	663	191
5	Boys	35	28	37	100	825	86
	Girls	34	31	35	100	798	94
6	Boys	31	24	45	100	819	64
	Girls	28	30	43	101	784	82
7	Boys	23	28	49	100	805	48
	Girls	23	30	47	100	820	50
8	Boys	18	30	52	100	762	37
	Girls	16	29	55	100	854	42

*Political efficacy is the belief that one can influence government and that public officials are responsive to public demands.
†Percentages fail to add to 100 percent in some cases due to rounding error.
‡Used as base for percentages.
SOURCE: By permission from David Easton and Jack Dennis. "The Child's Acquisition of Regime Norms: Political Efficacy," *American Political Science Review,* vol. 61, March, 1967.

A. The data show that sense of political efficacy is related to grade in school.

B. According to this table, schools are generally successful in teaching children how to influence government.

C. Sense of political efficacy is related to sex.

D. A careful reading of the table shows that while girls develop a high sense of efficacy early, by the eighth grade the boys have caught up and passed the girls.

Your Answers to Problem 1
A.

B.

C.

D.

Now check your answers with the correct ones on p. 40.

Problem 2

PERCENTAGE WHO APPROVE PRESIDENT JOHNSON'S VIETNAM POLICY BY PARTY AFFILIATION AND VOTE IN 1964

"In general, do you approve or disapprove of the way the Johnson administration is handling the situation in Vietnam?"

	Political Affiliation	
Vote in 1964	Republican	Democratic
Johnson	67%* ($N = 80$)	71% ($N = 608$)
Goldwater	45 ($N = 225$)	39 ($N = 56$)

*The percentages are the proportions approving of Johnson's policy.

SOURCE: By permission from Sidney Verba, Richard A. Brody, Edwin B. Parker, Norman H. Nie, Nelson W. Polsby, Paul Ekman, and Gordon S. Black, "Public Opinion and the War in Vietnam," *American Political Science Review,* vol. 61, p. 319, June, 1967.

A. The data show a relationship between the 1964 presidential vote and approval of President Johnson's Vietnam policy.

B. 67 percent of the Republicans in this sample voted for Johnson in 1964.

C. The data show that that the war in Vietnam is generally perceived as the policy of President Johnson, not the policy of Congress or of any other government group.

D. This table indicates a relationship between political affiliation and voting in the 1964 presidential election.

Your Answers to Problem 2

A.

B.

C.

D.

Now check your answers with the correct ones on p. 40.

Problem 3

PERCENT OF SOUTHERN NEGROES POLITICALLY ACTIVE BY STRENGTH OF PARTY IDENTIFICATION AND POLITICAL INTEREST

	Extent of Political Interest		
	Much	Some	Not Much
Strong partisans	85% (93)	77% (44)	63% (57)
Weak partisans	67% (45)	66 (47)	42 (90)
Leaners and independents	81 (26)	64 (25)	37 (52)
Apoliticals	25 (12)	24 (21)	15 (104)

NOTE: Numbers in parentheses are the totals on which the accompanying percentage is based.

SOURCE: From Donald R. Matthews and James W. Prothro, *Negroes and the New Southern Politics* (New York: Harcourt, Brace & World, Inc., 1966), p. 283, reproduced with permission.

A. The data show that among Southern Negroes strength of partisan identification is related to political activity.

B. The data show that extent of political interest is related to political activity.

C. Southern Negroes who are "apolitical" are the least active group, regardless of their interest in politics.

D. According to this sample, a majority of Southern Negroes have at least some interest in politics (i.e., they either have "much" or "some" political interest).

Your Answers to Problem 3

A.

B.

C.

D.

Now check your answers with the correct ones on p. 41.

Problem 4

POLITICAL PARTICIPATION AND SEX IN NORWAY AND THE UNITED STATES

Political Behavior	Norway			United States		
	Total	Men	Women	Total	Men	Women
Did not vote	21%	15%	26%	27%	20%	33%
Voted (but did nothing else)	57	55	60	59	64	55
Voted and took part in other political activities	22	30	14	14	16	12
Total	100%	100%	100%	100%	100%	100%
Number of respondents	1,406	688	718	1,722	791	981

SOURCE: Stein Rokkan and Angus Campbell, "Citizen Participation in Political Life: Norway and the United States of America," *International Social Science Journal,* vol. 12, 1960.

A. The data show no relationship between nation and political activity.

B. More people in Norway are politically active beyond voting than in the United States.

C. Sex is related to political participation.

D. By holding sex constant, i.e., comparing only males or females, we see that differences between the United States and Norway do not disappear. This means that national differences in political participation are not due to one nation having a greater proportion of males or females.

Your Answers to Problem 4
A.

B.

C.

D.

Now check your answers with the correct ones on p. 41.

CORRECT ANSWERS

Correct Answers to Problem 1

A. Correct. Sense of political efficacy is related to grade. Reading down the columns (going from third to eighth grade), we see that the proportion having a low sense of efficacy decreases, while the percentage with high efficacy increases. While over half of the third-graders are low on efficacy, less than a fifth of the eighth-graders score low on efficacy.

B. Incorrect. Though sense of efficacy increases with grade, the data say nothing about the causes of this relationship. It may be true that schools teach children how to influence government, but the fact that efficacy increases with grade does not mean that schools are directly responsible for the increase. Children may acquire feelings of efficacy outside of school, among friends or in the family.

C. Incorrect. Within each grade there is very little difference between the distributions of male and female efficacy scores. In the third grade, for example, 55 percent of the boys and 57 percent of the girls are low on efficacy. What differences exist between the percentages for boys and girls are very small and show no meaningful pattern.

D. Incorrect. There is no relation between sex and political efficacy in these data. Reading down the low-efficacy column, we see that the differences between boys and girls are very small and show no pattern. The same is true for the middle- and high-efficacy column.

Correct Answers to Problem 2

A. Correct. A much larger proportion of those who voted for Johnson in 1964 approve of his Vietnam policy than those who voted for Goldwater. Reading across the first row (those who voted for Johnson), we see that 67 and 71 percent approve of Johnson's Vietnam policy. Reading across the second row, we see that only 45 and 39 percent of the Goldwater voters approve.

B. Incorrect. The figure of 67 percent indicates that 67 percent of the Republicans who voted for Johnson in 1964 approve of his Vietnam policy, not that 67 percent of the Republicans voted for Johnson.

C. Incorrect. This may be true, but this table says nothing about the subject. There is no mention of the question of whose policy the Vietnam war is.

D. Correct. A careful examination of the data shows that most Republicans voted for Goldwater in 1964 and most Democrats voted for Johnson. Of 305 Republicans in the sample, 225 (73.8 percent) voted for Goldwater, while about 92 percent of the Democrats voted for Johnson (608 of 664).

Multivariate Tables and Graphs 41

Correct Answers to Problem 3

A. Correct. In general, the stronger the feeling of partisan identification, the greater the percentage of political activists. Reading down each of the three columns of political interest, we see that the proportions that are politically active decrease. In other words, those with weaker partisan feelings are less likely to be politically active. The only exception to this pattern are "leaners and independents" with "much" interest, who are more active than weak partisans. However, in all the other cases, the relationship between partisan identification and activity holds up.

B. Correct. The data show that as extent of political interest declines (from "much" to "not much"), there are proportionately fewer people who are politically active. Reading across each row of political interest ("strong partisan," etc.) we see that the percentages decrease. In each row, the proportion with "some" political interest is less than that for "much" political interest.

C. Correct. Southern Negroes who are apolitical are the least active, regardless of their interest in politics. The percentages in the last row are the lowest in the entire table.

D. Correct. By adding the total number of cases in each column, we see that there are 176 with much political interest, 137 with some, and 303 with not much interest. 176 plus 137 totals 313, a majority of the total number in the sample. Thus we can say that a majority have at least some ("much" plus "some") political interest. To be more exact, 313/616, or 50.8 percent, have at least some interest in politics. Note, however, that due to sampling error, this estimate may be incorrect, and slightly more or less than a majority have some interest in politics.

Correct Answers to Problem 4

A. Incorrect. Comparing the total column of Norway with that of the United States, we see that there are proportionately more nonvoters in the United States than in Norway. Also, a larger proportion of Norwegians (22 percent) took part in political activities beyond voting than Americans (14 percent).

B. Incorrect. *Proportionately* more Norwegians than Americans are active beyond voting in this sample, but in *absolute* terms (i.e., total number in each country), there are many more Americans than Norwegians taking part in activities beyond voting. Though the *samples* in the country are, roughly, the same size remember that the total population in the United States is very much larger.

C. Correct. In each country, men are politically more active than women; there are proportionately fewer male nonvoters and proportionately more males who politically participate beyond voting.

42 The Basic Tools of Analysis

D. Correct. When we hold sex constant by comparing American and Norwegian men and American and Norwegian women, we see that there are still differences between Norway and the United States (e.g., 15 percent of the Norwegian males are nonvoters compared with 20 percent of the U.S. males). This comparison allows us to say that Norway differs from the United States even when we control for the effects of sex. In other words, differences between the nations are not due to the United States' having proportionately more women who are less politically active. When we examine two variables "controlling" for a third (in this case, nation and political participation controlling for sex), we want to know if the relationship between the two variables is really due to a third factor (e.g., sex). Because the original relationship does not disappear when we control for sex, we can say the relationship between nation and political participation is not due to the third variable (sex).

Graphs

Graphs are much like tables, but they are usually simpler. They try to give a picture of the relationship between variables. Most graphs show only two variables.

1. Like tables, you must examine the titles of graphs carefully, because they will tell you what is depicted in the graph. You will remember that table titles identify and define the variables. Graph titles do the same; they usually _____ and _____ the variables.   identify; define

It makes little difference on a graph where the dependent or independent variables are placed. Thus one cannot identify the dependent and independent variables from their position on the graph. One needs to understand the author's use of the variables. As with tables, independent variables must be chronologically or logically prior to the dependent variables if they are to be useful in explaining the occurrence of the dependent variable.

2. For instance, look at the graphs in Fig. 2.1. It makes no difference where the variables are placed. If the population were placed on the horizontal axis, the figures would look the same as if you turned the page around sideways so that "population in millions" is at the bottom. The curve does not change.

There are two variables in the graphs, _____ and _____ . Time is the _____ variable since, over time, population may change. Hence population is the _____

time (or years)
population
independent
dependent

variable. Note that time cannot be the dependent variable because a change in population cannot cause a change in time. Thus, by inspection of the table and examination of the chronological or logical relationship between variables, you can identify the independent and dependent variables.

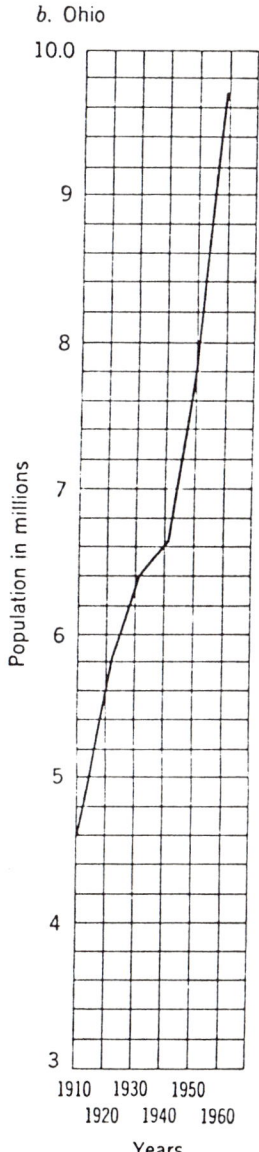
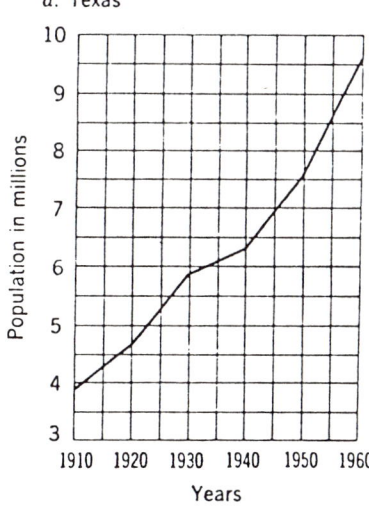

FIGURE 2.1 Population growth in Texas and Ohio, 1919–1960. (Source: U.S. Bureau of the Census)

44 The Basic Tools of Analysis

There is only one special difficulty with graphs. It is very important to note the space used to depict units of dependent and independent variables. These distances should be clearly marked on the two edges (called axes) of the graph. These unit distances are important because they can change the shape of the line and mislead the reader.

3. Examine, for instance, graphs a and b in Fig. 2.1. Their titles indicate that they show the relationship between _____ and _____ in Texas and Ohio. Graph b appears to show a steeper rise in population between 1910 and 1960. In fact, both graphs show the same thing. Look at 1910. The population for that year on graph a is _____ ; on graph b it is _____ . In 1960, the population on graph a is _____ ; on graph b it is _____ . The difference is that on graph a, each large square represents ½ million people; on graph b, each large square represents only _____ . Consequently, the curve on graph b looks steeper, although the relationship between population growth and time is very nearly the same on both graphs.

population; time (in years)

3.9 million
4.6 million
9.6 million
9.7 million

1/5 million

4. To convince yourself that the population growth in Ohio was very much the same as in Texas, mark off the points for the population of Ohio on graph a. You can read them off graph b; thus we have already said that the 1910 population was 4.6 million. The 1920 population is _____ ; that for 1930 is _____ ; that for 1940 is _____ ; that for 1950 is _____ . Also find and mark off the 1960 population. Then connect the points by straight lines. Now the lines for the two states are almost identical.

5.6
6.4; 6.6
7.8

PROBLEMS

For practice in interpreting graphs, turn to the following section and work each of the problems in the same fashion as for the multivariate tables.

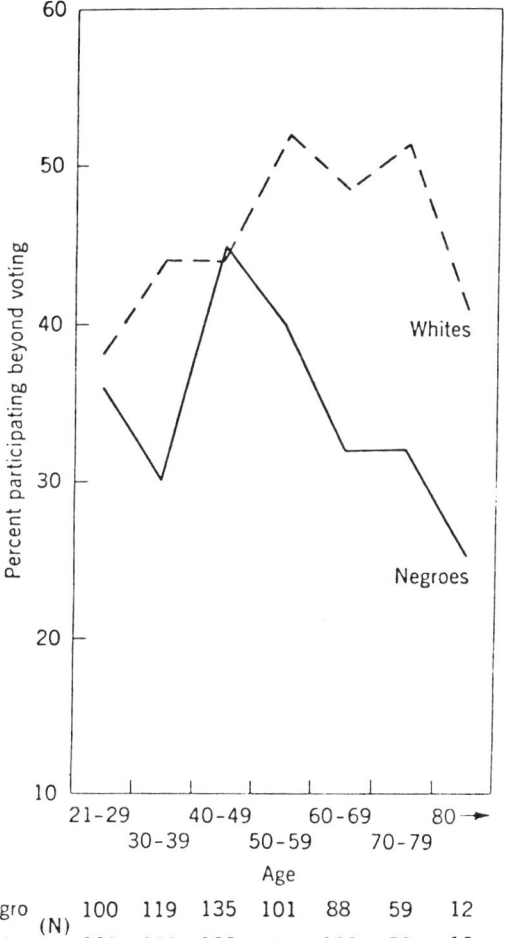

Political participation in the South, by race and age. (Source: Donald R. Matthews and James W. Prothro, Negroes and the New Southern Politics; *New York: Harcourt, Brace & World, Inc., 1966, p. 71, reproduced by permission.)*

Problem 5

A. Both Negro and white political participation has decreased in the last 80 years.

B. The difference between white and Negro participation rates is generally constant for those over 60 years old.

C. Since white and Negro political participation rates are about the same for 21-to-29-year-olds, it must be later experiences that cause lower political participation among older Negroes.

D. Whites generally have a higher voting rate than Negroes.

Your Answers to Problem 5
A.

B.

C.

D.

Now check your answers with the correct ones on p. 49.

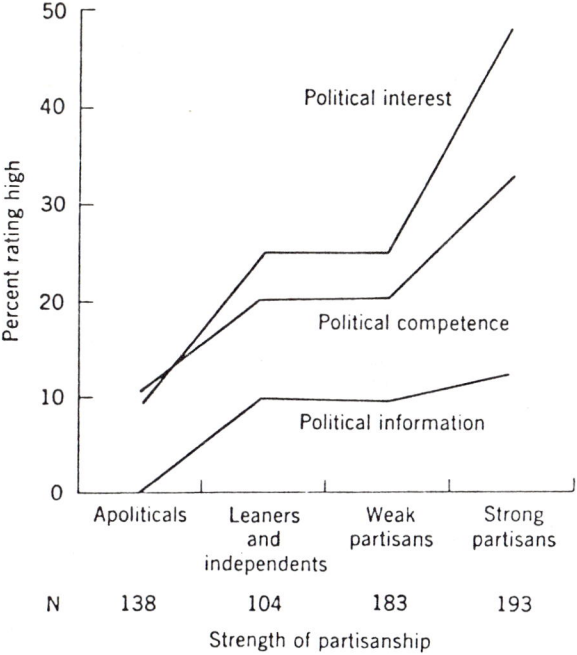

Strength of partisanship and high ratings on political interest, information, and sense of competence among Southern Negroes. (Source: Donald R. Matthews and James W. Prothro, Negroes and the New Southern Politics, New York: Harcourt, Brace & World, Inc., 1966, p. 282, reproduced by permission.)

Problem 6

A. Fewer Southern Negroes rate high on political information than on political competence or political interest.

B. Political interest is more significant than political information.

C. Strength of partisanship is related to political information, feeling of competence, and political interest.

D. Weak partisans are higher than leaners and independents on all three measures.

Your Answers to Problem 6

A.

48 The Basic Tools of Analysis

B.

C.

D.

Now check your answers with the correct ones on p. 49.

Correct Answers

Correct Answers to Problem 5

A. Incorrect. The horizontal axis (the lower line) indicates age groups, not years. Thus we read on the graph that 21-to-29-year-olds have one participation rate, 31-to-39-year-olds have another rate, etc.

B. Correct. It is important to qualify your inference from the graph in this fashion because the differences between Negroes and whites are not maintained among the younger age groups. Past 60, a 16 to 19 percent difference constantly separates the two groups.

C. Incorrect. It may be true that Negroes have certain experiences later in life which reduce political participation, but this cannot be proved with these data. An alternative explanation of this pattern is that younger Negroes are better-educated, and education is related to political participation. Whatever the reasons, there are not enough data here to reach a conclusion on the causes of participation.

D. Incorrect. The graph defines political participation as behavior "beyond voting." The graph gives no information about voting among whites and Negroes.

Correct Answers to Problem 6

A. Correct. The line representing political information is lower for every category of partisanship than the lines representing political competence and political interest.

B. Incorrect. More Southern Negroes exhibit political interest than exhibit political competence or information. But whether it is more significant or important depends on other facts, such as whether interest is more strongly related to voting, violence, mobility, etc.

C. Correct. Each of the three lines rise from apoliticals (who rate lowest on all three measures) to the strong partisans (who rate highest on all three measures). As strength of partisanship increases, so do the other factors.

D. Incorrect. About the same proportion of weak partisans and leaners and independents rate high on the three measures, as shown by the almost flat lines connecting the two categories.

Chapter 3
DESCRIPTIVE STATISTICS

Many tables in books on the social sciences use numbers which represent neither raw numbers nor percentages. Instead, authors frequently use summary measures (also called descriptive statistics) to describe complicated phenomena in a very condensed form. You may already be familiar with some of these measures, such as an average. But you need to be able to recognize what kind of an average is being used and how to interpret it. In addition, there are measures which show how closely phenomena cluster around their average value and how closely several variables are related to one another.

In this chapter you will learn:

1. To distinguish between the mean and median

2. To interpret the mean and median

3. To identify situations in which one or the other is the more informative and accurate measure

4. To learn the meaning of dispersion and standard deviation

5. To identify and know how to interpret commonly used measures of association

This chapter is not a lesson in how to calculate statistics. We are interested in teaching how to *read* statistics and understanding how authors employ them in their analyses. Therefore the calculations in this chapter are quite simple and are used only as concrete illustrations of various measures. After mastering the material in this chapter, you should rarely again be in the position of finding the numbers in a table meaningless, and you will not easily be confused by statistics.

WHAT ARE STATISTICS?

Few words convey such terror to innocent readers as statistics, and completely without cause. Statistics are nothing more than numerical facts.

52 The Basic Tools of Analysis

statistics we will learn are descriptive and summary devices. This means that they describe some of the characteristics of the phenomena we are interested in, and summarize them in a succinct fashion. Thus they enable us to state complicated relationships in simple ways.

AVERAGES

Suppose we are interested in studying the amounts of money spent by the states in each region. Table 3.1 presents those data.

1. When you examine the table, you note that the data are presented in [absolute numbers, percentages] for each state. The states are arranged according to regional boundaries. You will find an explanation for the choice of boundaries in the [footnote, appendix].

    absolute numbers

    footnote

Table 3.1 presents a bewildering array of numbers. There are so many that it is difficult to say anything meaningful about regional variations in state expenditures. We need some simpler way to compare regions. Let us see how we can arrive at a revised table that will make it easier to formulate meaningful statements about the comparative state expenditures of the eight regions of the United States.

Our first task is to produce one number for each region so that we can compare that region with the others. What we need is an average of some sort to replace the per capita expenditure figures for each state with one number for an entire region.

To calculate the most common kind of average, called the *mean,* we simply add all the numbers together and divide by the number of cases we have added. In simple mathematical terms:

$$\bar{x} = \frac{\Sigma x}{N}$$

which is read "mean equals the sum of the observations divided by the number of cases," where

    $\bar{x}$ = mean x = observations
    Σ = sum of N = number of cases

2. To calculate the mean for each region in Table 3.1, we simply total the expenditures in the region and divide by the number of states in the region. For in-

TABLE 3.1   STATE GOVERNMENT EXPENDITURES PER CAPITA BY STATES AND REGIONS, 1967

New England

Maine	$251.56	
New Hampshire	218.65	Mean =
Vermont	404.55	
Massachusetts	256.95	Median =
Rhode Island	320.48	
Connecticut	178.74	

Mid-Atlantic

New York	$321.11	
New Jersey	168.73	Mean =
Pennsylvania	200.00	
Maryland	252.42	Median =
Delaware	458.00	

Southeast

Virginia	$234.76	
West Virginia	301.46	
North Carolina	245.44	
South Carolina	227.82	
Georgia	244.09	
Florida	217.78	Mean = 258.22
Kentucky	286.77	Median = 244.76
Tennessee	237.00	
Alabama	260.49	
Mississippi	237.99	
Arkansas	247.62	
Louisiana	357.46	

Great Lakes

Ohio	$187.50	
Indiana	234.04	Mean = 250.52
Illinois	210.26	
Michigan	294.88	Median = 234.04
Wisconsin	325.92	

Plains

Minnesota	$291.45	
Iowa	268.68	
Missouri	209.79	Mean = 267.59
North Dakota	363.44	
South Dakota	283.68	Median = 268.68
Nebraska	215.78	
Kansas	240.35	

54 The Basic Tools of Analysis

TABLE 3.1 (Continued)

Mountains

Montana	$305.30	
Wyoming	498.98	Mean = 351.30
Colorado	308.11	
Idaho	287.64	Median =
Utah	356.47	

Southwest

Oklahoma	$325.74	Mean = 322.17
Texas	206.44	
New Mexico	418.95	Median = 331.65
Arizona	337.57	

Far West

Washington	$377.14	Mean =
Oregon	333.47	
Nevada	378.10	Median =
California	353.26	

Far Far West

Alaska	$968.33	Mean = 744.79
Hawaii	521.25	Median = 744.79

SOURCES: Expenditure data from U.S. Bureau of the Census, *State Government Finances in 1967* (Washington: Government Printing Office, 1968). Regions adapted from Harvey S. Perloff et al., *Regions, Resources, and Economic Growth* (Baltimore: The Johns Hopkins Press, 1960).

stance, for New England we add together the expenditures for the six states and divide by 6:

$$\begin{array}{r} \$251.56 \\ 218.65 \\ 404.55 \\ 256.95 \\ 320.48 \\ \underline{178.74} \\ 6\,\overline{\smash{)}1{,}630.93} \\ \$271.82 \end{array}$$

3. Now calculate the mean state expenditure for Mid-Atlantic, Great Lakes, and Far West regions. For

the Mid-Atlantic, the mean is _____; for the   286.06
Great Lakes, the mean is _____; and for the   250.52
Far West, the mean is _____. Place the correct 360.49
answers in the blanks on Table 3.1.

4. Another kind of average is called the median. It is the middle number in a range of figures ranked from the highest to the lowest. For the Mid-Atlantic region, we would arrange the states from the highest (Delaware, 458.00) to the lowest (New Jersey, 168.73). The middle state in this array is Maryland, with expenditures of 252.42. Thus the median expenditures for Mid-Atlantic states is 252.42. To calculate the median for the Mountain region, arrange the states from highest to lowest like this:

Wyoming	$498.98
Utah	356.47
Colorado	308.11
Montana	305.30
Idaho	240.35

The middle state is _____, and the region's   Colorado
median expenditure is _____.   308.11

5. When there is an even number of observations in a list—as in the New England region where there are six states—the median is the average of the two middle cases. In the case of the New England region, the two middle cases are the third and fourth states when you list them from highest to lowest.

Vermont	$404.55
Rhode Island	320.48
Massachusetts	256.95
Maine	251.56
New Hampshire	218.65
Connecticut	178.74

The third and fourth states in this array are   Massachusetts
_____ and _____. The average of their   Maine
expenditures is the median and is _____.   254.25

Now calculate the median for the Far West region.
The middle states are the second and _____.   third
The average of their expenditures is the median, which
is _____.   365.20

6. The mean and the median represent quite differ-

ent kinds of summaries of the range of figures. Comparing the mean and median, you see that they are almost always different in Table 3.1.

a. The mean is the arithmetic center of a set of numbers. If there are a few very high or a few very low numbers in the group, the value of the mean is much influenced by these "deviant" cases. In Table 3.1, this is true for the New England region, where Vermont's expenditure of 404.55 is much higher than any other state's. It would also be true if we placed the two Far Far West states (Alaska and Hawaii) with the other four Far West states. That would make the mean for the six states _____ , much higher than the original mean. Therefore the mean is most accurate as a summary statistic when most of the values in a group of numbers cluster around the arithmetic center. The mean is best when there are *few* extremely high or extremely low values.

488.59

b. The median is the middle value of a range of numbers. Half the values lie below the median, and half lie above it. If you know the median, you can immediately say that half the values are greater than the median value and half are less. For instance, in Table 3.1, you can say that half the states in New England spend more than _____ and half spend _____ . The median is less sensitive to extreme values. For instance, when we add Alaska and Hawaii to the Far Western region, the median remains the middle value, which is now the average of the third and fourth highest spenders, or _____ . This is not very different from the original median for the four Western states of 365.20.

254.25, less

377.62

7. It would be useful to have a measure of dispersion, or spread, of the numbers in a group so that we would be able to make our judgments about the accuracy of a mean value without having to scan the whole table to make our decision. Such a statistic is called the *standard deviation*.* The standard deviation measures the degree to which values of a group or distribution are clustered close to the mean or are dispersed broadly over the whole range of possible values. When

---

*Calculation of the standard deviation is more complicated than of the mean or median. For a relatively simple explanation, see Hubert M. Blalock. *Social Statistics* (New York: McGraw-Hill Book Company, 1960), pp. 67–73.

the standard deviation is large compared with the value of the mean, it indicates that the values are dispersed, and the mean is not a very reliable summary of the distribution. When the standard deviation is small compared with the mean, it indicates that most of the values are clustered around the mean, and the mean is a reliable summary of the distribution. So when we see the mean value, we also look for the standard deviation. If the standard deviation is large compared with the mean, the mean is relatively [reliable, unreliable] as a summary measure of the distribution. If the standard deviation is small compared with the mean, we know that the mean is a [reliable, unreliable] summary of the values in the original distribution.

unreliable

reliable

8. Examine, for example, the two following distributions: Calculate the mean for each and place it in the blank provided in the table opposite its label. For distribution A, the mean is _____; for distribution B, the mean is _____. Notice that the two means are almost identical, but distribution A is much more widely dispersed than distribution B, where six of the numbers are almost at the mean. The standard deviation shows that the mean of distribution A is a [more reliable, less reliable] summary measure than the mean of distribution B.

5.5
5.4

less reliable

9. The median is not affected by the extreme values as the mean is. It is simply the middle figure. Half of all

	A	B
	1	3
	2	4
	3	5
	4	5
	5	5
	6	5
	7	6
	8	6
	9	7
	10	8
Sum	55	54
Mean		
Standard deviation	2.83	1.72

58 The Basic Tools of Analysis

cases lie above it; half lie below it. Thus, when we say that the median family income of Connecticut is $4,677, we mean that half of all families in Connecticut earn less than $4,677 and half earn _____ than $4,677. But we do not know how many families are earning close to the median amount because we have no statistic comparable with the standard deviation for the median.

more

10. The comparison of the mean to the standard deviation has another function too. It enables us to compare variability in two sets of data. When we divide the standard deviation by the mean and multiply by 100, we obtain the coefficient of variation. The formula

$$V = 100 \; \frac{\text{standard deviation}}{\text{mean}}$$

produces the _____, which allows us to _____ the variability of two sets of data. For instance, in the example above, the coefficient of variability for A is $2.83 \div 5.5 \times 100$ which equals 51.4. The coefficient of variability for B is $1.72 \div 5.4 \times 100$ equals _____ . This shows that the data in set B is clustered much [more, less] closely around the mean than for set A. Let us look at another example, Table 3.2. It shows the criminal homicide rate for selected states and the number of persons those states sent to prison for a homicide offense. To find the median, we rearrange the numbers so that they run from the smallest to the largest and pick the [average, middle] number. In this case the middle number for criminal homicides is _____ . The median for the number of homicide prisoners is _____ . We calculate the mean by adding all the numbers in each column and dividing by the number of states. For the homicide rate, the mean is _____ ; for the number of homicide prisoners the mean is _____ . Enter your results in Table 3.3.

coefficient of variation
compare

31.8
more

middle

5.7
15

5.89

56.6

11. Table 3.3 shows the medians, means, and standard deviations for the data in Table 3.2. This allows us to compare the median and mean. The median shows us the [middle, highest, lowest, most frequent] state for homicide rate and persons sent to prison on homicide charges. Thus half the states above

middle

TABLE 3.2 MURDER RATES AND NUMBER OF PERSONS SENT TO PRISON FOR MURDER IN SELECTED WESTERN STATES, 1970

	Murder Rate*	Rank	No. of Persons sent to Prison for Murder	Rank
Arizona †	9.5	11	44	10
California	6.9	8	424	11
Colorado	6.2	7	39	9
Hawaii	3.6	4	8	1.5
Idaho	4.6	5	12	4
Montana	3.2	1	15	6
Nevada	8.8	9	13	5
New Mexico	9.4	10	22	7
Utah	3.4	2	8	1.5
Washington	3.5	3	29	8
Wyoming	5.7	6	9	3

* Murder Rate is criminal homicides per 100,000 population.

† Some Western states are omitted because complete data for them is unavailable.

SOURCES: Murder rate: U.S. Department of Justice, FBI *Uniform Crime Report for 1970*; Number of persons sent to prison for murder: U.S. Department of Justice, Federal Bureau of Prisons, *National Prisons Statistics: State Prisoners, Admissions and Releases 1970*.

_____ had more homicides and half had less in 1970. The mean tells us the arithmetic average for homicides and prisoners. Note that the coefficient of variation for homicides is much smaller compared to the coefficient of variation for the number of prisoners. That permits us to conclude that the mean is a better summary of the data for the homicide rate than for the number of homicide prisoners. The coefficient of variation also allows us to conclude that these states show more variation in sentencing persons to prison for homicide than the homicide rate itself would suggest.

5.7

TABLE 3.3 MEAN, MEDIAN, STANDARD DEVIATION, AND COEFFICIENT OF VARIATION OF MURDER RATE AND NUMBER OF PERSONS SENT TO PRISON FOR MURDER IN SELECTED WESTERN STATES, 1970

	Median	Mean	Standard Deviation	Coefficient of Variation
Murder rate	5.7		2.47	41.9
Persons sent to prison for murder			122.48	216.3

All four measures provide us important information about the two sets of data. The best measures are the mean *plus* the coefficient of variation because the two together tell us that these are a group of figures with many extreme values and that leads us to exercise greater caution in drawing conclusions from any kind of average.

Summary

Two kinds of averages are often used. They lead to quite different interpretations and are reliable in different situations.

1. The *mean* is the arithmetic center of a group of numbers. It is most reliable when most of the numbers cluster around the middle, that is, when there are few very large or very small numbers. To make certain that the mean is a reliable summary, you need to look at the *standard deviation* of the set of numbers. If it is small relative to the mean, the mean is a reliable summary of the numbers. If it is large relative to the mean, the mean is unreliable.

2. When you have determined that the *mean* is reliable, you interpret it as the *average value,* the one value that best represents the whole set of numbers.

3. The *median* is the middle number of a group of numbers. Half the cases are smaller, and half are larger. The median is not affected very much by large or small numbers. Therefore, if you decide that the mean is unreliable, the median is probably the best summary.

4. The *median* allows you to specify that half the values are smaller and half larger. It does not give you any clue as to how much larger or how much smaller the other values are.

PROBLEMS

On the following pages are two pieces of data which make use of summary measures. Each of the problems consists of three sections. The first is the problem page; it consists of a table and several interpretations about it. The second section is your answer page. Label each statement correct or incorrect (if necessary, refer back to the first part of this lesson), and *explain your answer briefly* in a sentence or two. If, for example, a statement or interpretation does not follow from the data in the table, all that has to be said is that it does not follow and why it does not follow. Likewise, if the statement is a misinterpretation, a sentence on why it is a misinterpretation will suffice. More than one correct answer is possible. The third section is an answer section giving the correct answers. If all your answers were correct, proceed to the next section of the exercise. If some of your answers were wrong, reread the previous frames until you understand the correct answers.

Problem 1

MEDIAN YEARS OF ACTIVE PARTY WORK IN WISCONSIN

Party Officers	No. of Party Workers	Median Years of Party Work
Republican:		
County chairmen	62	16.5
County secretaries	58	10
Milwaukee unit officers	22	10
Democrat:		
County chairmen	62	7
County secretaries	63	6
Milwaukee unit officers	26	7

SOURCE: By permission from Leon D. Epstein, *Politics in Wisconsin* (Madison: The University of Wisconsin Press, copyright, 1958), p. 87.

A. On the average, Democratic party workers had served fewer years in active party work than their Republican counterparts.

B. For Milwaukee unit officers of both parties, the median number of years of party work should be interpreted cautiously since there are fewer cases here than in the other categories, so that a few individuals with either very long or very short service can distort the average.

C. The data show that most Republican county chairmen had served 16.5 years, compared with only 7 years for the Democratic county chairmen.

D. These data show that the Republican party in Wisconsin is run by old people.

Your Answers to Problem 1

A.

62 The Basic Tools of Analysis

B.

C.

D.

Now check your answers with the correct ones on p. 65.

Problem 2

MEAN CONTINUOUS SERVICE IN SENATE OF COMMITTEE MEMBERS (DEMOCRATS). JANUARY 3, 1955

Committee	Mean Service in Years	Committee	Mean Service in Years
Appropriations	13.9	Banking and Currency	7.1
Foreign Relations	10.7	Public Works	4.3
Rules and Administration	10.5	Interior	4.2
Finance	10.3	Post Office and Civil Service	4.0
Armed Services	8.5	District of Columbia	3.7
Agriculture	8.0	Government Operations	3.6
Labor	8.0	Interstate and Foreign Commerce	3.1
Judiciary	7.5		

SOURCE: Donald R. Matthews, *U.S. Senators and Their World* (New York: Vintage Books, Inc., Alfred A. Knopf, Inc., 1960), p. 156.

A. The data show that it is virtually impossible for Democrats to get on the Appropriations Committee unless they have almost 14 years of continuous Senate service.

B. The Interstate and Foreign Commerce Committee is not very attractive for Democrats as evidenced by the fact that no Democrat has stayed on the Committee more than 3.1 years.

C. As Democrats serve longer in the Senate, they become more interested in serving on the Appropriations and Foreign Relations Committees.

D. Among Democrats, positions on such committees as Appropriations and Foreign Relations are generally held by those with the most continuous Senate service.

Your Answers to Problem 2
A.

64 The Basic Tools of Analysis

B.

C.

D.

Now check your answers with the correct ones on p. 65.

Correct Answers

Correct Answers to Problem 1

A. Correct. For each of the three officeholders, the median number of years of active party work by Republicans was larger than the figures for Democrats.

B. Incorrect. The median, unlike the mean, is insensitive to extreme values. Even if a Milwaukee unit officer had served 50 years, the median would still be 7.

C. Incorrect. The median is that point which divides the list of figures into two equal parts, not the most common number. For example, the median for 5, 5, 7, and 8 is 6, yet 6 does not appear in the series. The median may be the most common number, but it does not have to be and very rarely is.

D. Incorrect. This answer misreads the title. The figures are years of party work, not age. People who have served a long time may be old, but one cannot tell this from these data.

Correct Answers to Problem 2

A. Incorrect. The figure 13.9 is a mean and is composed of a number of different values that could be well above or well below the mean. For example, if there were two members of the Appropriations Committee, one of whom had served for 27 years and the other for 1 year, the mean for these two cases would be 14 years of service.

B. Incorrect. The number 3.1 refers to the number of years spent in the Senate, not the years spent on the committee. Even if the figure referred to years on the committee, the statement would still be wrong—a mean includes a range of values, some higher, some lower than the mean value.

C. Incorrect. This statement may or may not be true, but because these data do not mention a senator's changing interest, one cannot know one way or another. Additional data would be needed.

D. Correct. Members of the Appropriations and Foreign Relations Committees have on the average (mean) served a greater number of years in the Senate than members of other committees (although there is only a small difference in *average* length of service between Foreign Relations, Rules and Administration, and Finance).

MEASURES OF ASSOCIATION: r, r^2, R, AND R^2

Both the mean and the median deal with a single quantity, e.g., "average" income in a city, "average" number of school years completed in a particular

66 The Basic Tools of Analysis

city, etc. It frequently happens that in dealing with a particular unit (such as a group of people, a city, a state, etc.) you have a number of different measures (say, figures on personal income and education). Not only do you have this information, but you are interested in determining or showing how one phenomenon is related to another, e.g., how education is related to income. For example, we might want to know whether state-local receipts are related to federal revenues. We can, of course, look at the long columns in Table 3.2 to attempt our comparisons. While this technique would show whether a relationship existed, the large number of figures makes such an exercise difficult and awkward. Here, as in the easier examples, we need measures which will summarize complex relationship as simply as possible.

The statistics which indicate whether two (or more) phenomena are related are called measures of association. One of the most common is the *correlation coefficient.* It tells us in one precise number the degree to which variables are correlated, that is, related to one another.

1. The correlation coefficient is a statistical tool which indicates the degree of association between two or more phenomena. By association we mean the extent to which phenomena vary together. To say, for example, that education and income are correlated means that some levels in education are associated with certain levels in _____ .   income

2. Statisticians use a special symbol for the correlation coefficient, r; r indicates the _____   correlation
coefficient. The r is a handy index. It has a very limited range of values; it can be any number between -1 and $+1$. The correlation coefficient (r) is a standardized score, which means we can directly compare the value of one coefficient with the value of another coefficient. Thus, if we have three sets of relationships which yield r's of .25, .53, and .92, we can say that the relationship with an r of .53 is stronger than that with .25, and the strongest relationship of all among these three is indicated by the r of _____ .   .92

3. The closer the r is to $+1$ or -1, the stronger the relationship. Thus an r of .65 indicates a [stronger,   stronger
weaker] relationship than an r of .47. An r of $-.87$
indicates a [stronger, weaker] relationship than an r of   stronger
$-.23$, because $-.87$ is closer to -1 than $-.23$. An r of
$-.92$ indicates a [stronger, weaker] relationship than   stronger
an r of .90 because $-.92$ is closer to -1 than .90 is
to $+1$. The strength of a relationship is thus indicated
by the value of r. The closer r is to _____ or $+1$

_____, the stronger the relationship. The closer r is to _____, the weaker the relationship.

4. The sign of the correlation coefficient r can be either positive or negative. If the sign is *positive* (for example, r = .7), it means that the two variables are changing in the same direction. So, if one increases, the other increases, and if one decreases, the other also decreases. If we find that the relation between education and income is represented by r = .6, this means that as education rises, income also _____, and as education falls, income also _____ .

5. A *negative* sign (for example, r = −.7) means an inverse relationship; i.e., as one variable increases, the other *decreases*. A negative correlation between percent Democratic vote and income would mean that as income rises, percent Democratic vote _____.

6. In Table 3.4, you see the correlation coefficients between the rankings of the states (from highest to lowest turnout) in 1952, 1956, and 1960. These coefficients tell you that there was a closer relationship between the [1952–1956 vote, 1952–1960 vote] than between the 1956–1960 vote. The direction of all the relationships is [positive, negative] That means that the states which ranked high in one year ranked [high, low] in the other year.

−1 (either order)
zero

rises
falls

falls

1952–1956

positive
high

While a correlation coefficient tells you that one variable increases or decreases as a second variable changes, it does not tell you *how much* one variable increases or decreases for every change in another variable. With correlations you cannot state that each

TABLE 3.4 CORRELATIONS BETWEEN 1952, 1956 AND 1960 VOTING-TURNOUT RANKINGS

	Correlation Coefficient
1952 and 1956 turnout	.94
1956 and 1960 turnout	.92
1952 and 1960 turnout	.90

SOURCE: Based on data from U.S. Bureau of the Census

68 The Basic Tools of Analysis

year of education increases income by $1,000; this may be true, but you could not deduce this from the correlation coefficient. Correlations indicate whether phenomena vary together, and how strong this relationship is, not how large an increase in one variable brings a unit increase (or decrease) in a second variable.

    The correlation coefficient yields still a third bit of information. When we square its value, the number tells us how much of the variation (technically, variance) in one variable is accounted for or explained by the second variable. For instance, if the relationship between income and education yields an r of .80, $r^2 = .64$, which indicates that education explains 64 percent of the variance in income. Thus, in Table 3.4, we can say that 1956 voter-turnout rankings account for [85 percent, 92 percent] of the variation in 1960 turnout rankings.

    85%

7. Turning to another example, in Table 3.5, you see that the correlation r between the percentage of Negroes registered to vote and "percent of population Negro in 1950" is _____ . The sign of this correlation indicates that as the percentage of Negroes in a county increases, the proportion of Negroes of voting age actually registered to vote _____ .

    −.46

    decreases

8. By squaring −.46 (i.e., multiplying −.46 by −.46), you are able to conclude that [46 percent, 21 percent] of the variation in percent Negroes registered to vote is accounted for by _____ . Similarly,

    21%

    "percent of population Negro in 1950"

TABLE 3.5 CORRELATIONS BETWEEN SOCIAL AND ECONOMIC CHARACTERISTICS OF COUNTIES AND PERCENT OF VOTING-AGE NEGROES REGISTERED TO VOTE IN 11 SOUTHERN STATES

Median number of school years completed by Negroes	.22
Median income of Negroes	.19
Median income of whites	.08
Median number of school years completed by whites	−.26
Percent of population Negro in 1950	−.46

SOURCE: Donald R. Matthews and James W. Prothro, "Social and Economic Factors and Negro Voter Registration in the South," *American Political Science Review*, March, 1963.

the median number of school years completed by Negroes explains [5 percent, 22 percent] of the variation in Negro voting registration.

5%

When using either r or r^2, the figures cannot be added together to increase the amount of explained variation. If, for example, the r^2 between intelligence and income were .50, and the r^2 between education and income were also .50, you could not say that these two factors explained 100 percent of the variation in income.

9. However, an entirely different measure, the multiple correlation coefficient R, may be used to indicate the total relationship between several independent variables and one dependent variable. For example, we may want to determine whether there is a relationship between the independent variables education and intelligence and the dependent variable income. In such a case, we would use R, which is the _____ correlation coefficient.

multiple

10. Unlike r, R varies only between 0 and 1. R cannot have a negative value. This means that R cannot tell us the direction of the relationship. It cannot tell us whether income and intelligence combined are positively or inversely related to income. So if that relationship is .87, we can say that education and intelligence are [closely, remotely] related to income; we [can, cannot] say that as education and intelligence rise, income rises.

closely
cannot

11. As with r, the values of R are comparable with one another. If we have a series of values for R, for example, .97, .62, and .10, we can say that the relationship indicated by .97 is [closer, more remote] than the one indicated by .62, and the relationship indicated by the R of .10 is [closer, more remote] than that indicated by the R of .62.

closer

more remote

12. An advantage of using R as compared with r is that you can usually explain something better by using a number of variables than by using one. One of the disadvantages of R is that as you add more variables, the interpretation of the association becomes more complex. For example, an $r = .6$ between wealth and voting Republican is simple to understand; an $R = .9$ between 25 variables and voting Republican accounts for more variation, but would be more difficult to inter-

pret. Consequently, when simplicity of interpretation is desired, [r, R] is a better measure; when a more complete explanation is sought. [r, R] is more useful.
    r
    R

13. As R was analogous to r, so R^2 is analogous to r^2. Like r^2, R^2 varies between 0 and 1 and is computed by squaring the value of R. Thus, if R = .80, R^2 = [.80, 64] Its interpretation is the same as for r^2; it indicates the percentage of the variance in the dependent variable accounted for by the independent variables. Thus an R^2 of .64 indicates that [80 percent, 64 percent] of the variance of the dependent variable is accounted for by the independent variables used in the analysis. For instance, if we have an R^2 of .7 between four indicators of economic development and the amount of money spent on education in American states, we can conclude that these four indicators of economic development account for [49 percent, 70 percent] of the variance in education expenditures in American states.

    64

    64%

    70%

PROBLEMS IN INTERPRETING CORRELATIONS

1. You have seen that when we say that two (or more) factors are highly correlated, we mean that they are closely associated with one another. The fact that two things vary together is commonly taken to mean that one variable explains or causes the other. While this extension of the meaning of correlation is not necessarily incorrect, you still cannot *automatically* assume that correlation (covariation) means explanation or causation. Thus an r^2 = .8 between X and Y does not *necessarily* mean that X causes or explains 80 percent of Y. Rather, it means that X often occurs together with Y. You need other information (such as time sequence, or theoretical relationships) to give a causal interpretation to the relationships. Thus we may conclude that a high value of R or r [can, cannot] be said to indicate causality.

    cannot

2. Moreover, in interpreting correlations, a high numerical value by itself does not indicate whether a relationship is meaningful. An r^2 = .9 between income and wealth indicates a high relationship, but it is a *tautological* one; i.e., income is virtually identical with wealth. Correlating two variables that mean practically the same thing, e.g., attitudes toward big-car man-

ufacturers and attitudes toward General Motors, will produce high values for r, but these correlations [are, are not] meaningful.   are not

3. In addition to numerical value, what can make a correlation meaningful is the *theoretical* connection between the variables. To try to explain a person's voting behavior by the size of his shoes is of no theoretical importance (even if the correlation were high). On the other hand, the use of social class to explain voting behavior is of theoretical importance; so correlation between these variables will be meaningful (whether high or low). To know that the correlation between X and Y was significant, you should ask whether the theoretical connection between the variables is [important, unimportant].   important

4. Using both criteria of significance (high numerical value and an important theoretical connection between the variables), there are many possible combinations. As Table 3.6 illustrates, correlations may be high but tautological (e.g., income and wealth) or moderately high but only of questionable theoretical significance or they may be high and of great theoretical importance. There are no hard-and-fast rules for correct interpretation; judgments must be made on a case-by-case basis. The two important things to observe are the _____ of the correlation coefficient and the _____ between the variables.   value (or size)
  theoretical
  connection

TABLE 3.6 INTERPRETATION OF CORRELATION COEFFICIENTS

Theoretical Relationship	Numerical Value of r^2 or R^2		
	Low (0)	Medium	High (1)
None or tautological	Not meaningful	Not meaningful	Not meaningful
Important theoretical link	Doubtful	Meaningful	Very meaningful

PROBLEMS

On the following pages are two tables which make use of measures of association. Each of the problems consists of three sections. The first is the problem section; it consists of a table and several interpretations of it. The second consists of your answers. Label each statement correct or incorrect and *explain your answer briefly* in a sentence or two (it may be helpful in the cases of incorrect answers to refer back to the various rules in the second part of this lesson). If, for example, a statement does not follow from the data in the table, all that has to be said is that it does not follow and why it does not follow. Likewise, if the statement is a misinterpretation, a sentence on why it is a misinterpretation will suffice. More than one correct answer is possible. The third section is an answer section, giving the correct answers. If all your answers were correct, proceed to the next chapter. If some of your answers were wrong, reread the preceding frames until you understand the correct answers.

CORRELATION OF ATTIDUES OF CONGRESSMEN AND ATTITUDES OF THE PEOPLE THEY REPRESENT—THREE SELECTED ISSUE AREAS

Issue Area	Correlation of Constituency Attitude with Representative's Own Attitude, r
Social welfare	.26
Foreign involvement	.32
Civil rights	.50

SOURCE: Angus Campbell, Philip E. Converse, Warren E. Miller, and Donald E. Stokes; *Elections and the Political Order* (New York: Copyright by John Wiley & Sons, Inc., 1966), p. 363.

A. These data show only a small positive relation between a representative's attitude and the attitudes of the people in his district on social welfare issues.

B. The three correlation coefficients r indicate only a moderate relation between the three issue areas.

C. The predominance of low correlations shows that most representatives do not vote in accordance with the wishes of their constituents.

D. Of all three issues, representatives are most in agreement with the people they represent on the issue of civil rights.

Your Answers to Problem 3
A.

B.

C.

D.

Now check your answers with the correct ones on p. 76.

Problem 4

CORRELATIONS BETWEEN PER CAPITA WELFARE EXPENDITURES AND URBAN POPULATION AND EDUCATION IN SOUTHERN AND NON-SOUTHERN STATES

Independent Variable	Southern States, r	Non-Southern States, r
Percent population in urban areas	.12	.12
Median school years completed	−.32	−.06
	$R^2 = .50$	$R^2 = .02$

SOURCE: Robert Weissberg, "Public Welfare Expenditures and the Fifty States," unpublished paper.

A. In the South, percent of population in urban areas and median school years account for 50 percent of the variation in per capita public welfare expenditures.

B. In Southern states there is a positive relationship between education and per capita welfare expenditures.

C. In the non-Southern states, it makes little difference how urban the state is or how well-educated its people are in relation to the amount of money spent on public welfare.

D. Outside of the South, percent of people in urban areas and education are unrelated to each other.

Your Answers to Problem 4
A.

B.

C.

D.

Now check your answers with the correct ones on p. 76.

Correct Answers

Correct Answers to Problem 3

A. Correct. The correlation r between a representative's attitude and the attitudes of the people in his district on social welfare issues is .26. The numerical value of this correlation indicates only a small relationship.

B. Incorrect. The correlation coefficients show the relationship between attitudes of representatives and their constituents on each of three issues, not the relationship between the three issues.

C. Incorrect. It is impossible to tell from these data if this statement is true or false since there are no data on how congressmen vote.

D. Correct. The correlation of .50 between the constituency's attitude on civil rights and the congressman's attitudes is the highest value of the three in the column. The value of .50 indicates a moderate relationship.

Correct Answers to Problem 4

A. Correct. Fifty percent (R^2 = .50) of the public welfare expenditures in the Southern states are explained by the two independent variables (population in urban areas and median school years completed).

B. Incorrect. The correlation r between median school years completed and public welfare expenditures per capita is *minus* .32. As education increases, expenditures per capita for welfare *decrease* in the South.

C. Correct. The relationship between each independent variable and the dependent variable is very small (.12 and −.06), so there is no relationship among these factors.

D. Incorrect. In this table percent in urban areas and median school years completed are not correlated. They are correlated with the dependent variable, public welfare expenditures, not with each other.

Chapter 4
REFORMULATING PROBLEMS

Analyzing problems involves more than reading a table or graph. One of the crucial steps in analyzing complex problems is reducing them to more manageable proportions. Most problems are difficult to analyze correctly when phrased in broad general terms. Suppose, for example, someone asked if you would pass this course. Left in these terms, the problem is difficult to examine. If you began your analysis by asking what is required to pass the course, you have made the problem a little more manageable. If you further specify that the requirements are doing the assigned reading, taking careful class notes, and passing examinations with a grade of C or better, you have reformulated the original question into one much easier to analyze correctly. Your answers to the narrower questions of fulfilling course requirements provide you with a good response to the original question. Changing general problems into more specific and narrower statements makes it easier to collect information for complete and systematic answers.

This process of modifying general problems to make them more manageable is known as *reformulation*. Except for very simple problems, almost every problem must be reformulated before it can be correctly analyzed.

This chapter will teach you how to reformulate problems so that you can solve them with information that is readily available to you. In order to do that you will learn:

1. How to distinguish between fact and value statements

2. How to alter questions so that they can be answered with quantitative or qualitative information

3. How to break down broad questions into a number of narrowly defined ones, none of which presumes a single-factor solution by its very formulation

4. How to break down broad questions into a number of more narrowly defined ones, which nevertheless retain the meaning of the original question.

Breaking down large problems into small and more manageable ones is a skill essential to political analysis. Many errors can occur in this process; no

78   The Basic Tools of Analysis

set of rules, no matter how detailed, can provide a formula for instant success. Much will have to be learned by experience, but careful reading of this chapter and working its problems will greatly help the process. Since much of your success in the future will depend on how well you learn this skill, careful attention should be paid to the rules of reformulating problems and to the illustrations that will accompany these rules.

Reformulations Must Be Statements of Fact, not Value Statements.

1. When you reduce a large problem to smaller questions, these questions must be answerable with actual data. Only statements of fact, not value statements, can be answered with data; so any reformulation must be a _____ statement.   factual

2. A value statement, i.e., a statement which reflects your personal preference as to what is good or bad, is not, of course, irrelevant to politics. Any decision regarding a personal preference, e.g., whether an increase in the government's role in the economy is desirable, must be made on the basis of _____, as well as facts.   values

3. The statement that rich people vote more than poor people is a _____ statement. If you said   factual
that not everyone ought to have the right to vote, this would be a statement of _____ .   value

4. If you began, for example, with the problem of whether the senator from your state will win reelection and you reduce this question to the lesser one of whether he has been a good senator, your reformulation would be a _____ statement.   value

5. On the other hand, if you asked: "What factors influence the election of a senator and what is the state of each of these factors at the present time?" your reformulation would be a _____ statement.   factual

6. A value question cannot be answered solely by facts. To decide whether President Nixon has been a good President, we need a statement of your own [facts, values] as well as generally known facts. Your values may differ from your neighbor's.   values

7. A factual question can be answered by facts alone. To determine what factors lead to the election of a man as President, we need only learn _____ .   facts
These facts can be established so that everyone agrees they are true.

Reformulations Must Be Specific.

1. In the preceding section you learned that problems had to be reformulated as factual statements in order to be analyzed with empirical data. The process of providing data for testing statements is not as simple as it may seem. We have to know what data are needed, and we have to find them. Consequently, in addition to being factual, testable statements must also specify the data which will be needed to establish their truth. Thus the second criterion for reformulating statements is that the statement [identifies, denies] the facts which will be used to test its validity.   identifies

2. When we speak of the need for data which are clearly defined, we mean that key terms must have a concrete rather than a vague or general meaning. A reformulation which required data on whether people who voted were more rational thinkers than those who did not would be incorrect, for the key term "rational" is too [vague, specific] to be of much use.   vague

3. Let us take another example, the proposition: *Poor people fight America's wars, while the sons of the rich stay at home.* Is this a fact or value statement? _____   Fact

It is a fact statement because it does not state a preference. Note that it might be incorrect, but statements can assert facts and be incorrect. Our decision on whether a statement is fact or value does not depend on its validity, but on whether it asserts a fact or asserts a value preference.

4. Can we test the validity of the statement without reformulating it? [Yes, No.]   No

5. No, we cannot, because we have to define what we mean by rich and poor. Let us try the following reformulation: *More sons of poor people are in the armed forces than sons of rich people.* This is a [fact, value] statement. Does it sufficiently concretize the original statement? [Yes, No]   fact

   No

Not entirely. It does make the original statement more specific—"More sons of poor . . . than sons of rich . . ."—but it does not define rich or poor. Let us try again: *More sons of people earning less than $4,500 per year are soldiers than sons of people earning more than $4,500 per year.* Is this statement fact or value? _____   Fact

6. Does it sufficiently define the key terms? [Yes, No]

Yes

Yes. Now we have defined poor as earning $4,500 a year or less and rich as earning more than $4,500. We can perform the operation of checking the income of every soldier's father and then classifying him as the son of a rich man or of a poor man.

Note that you might disagree with the use of the $4,500 criterion. The authors would. We might well choose a different definition, such as $6,000-a-year income, or whether the soldier comes from a family on welfare. Each would be an operational and specific definition of rich and poor.

7. Let us take as another example the statement: *Streets of American cities are less safe now than 50 years ago.* Is this a fact or value statement? _____

Fact

8. Can we analyze the statement as it stands? [Yes, No]

No

No, we need to define "safe streets." Let us try the following reformulation: *More crimes are committed now than 50 years ago in American cities.* Does this concretize the original statement? [Yes, No]

No

No, "crimes committed" is more specific than "unsafe streets," but not specific enough. How do we define crimes: all those committed, all those reported, just crimes of violence, or also such crimes as burglary (which is never committed on the streets), embezzlement, and narcotics addiction? In addition, we need to define what we mean by cities. So let us try again. We now reformulate the statement as follows: *More crimes of violence against persons per 100,000 population are now reported by the police in American cities with over 1 million population than were reported in equally large cities 50 years ago.*

9. This reformulation is a [fact, value] statement. It [does, does not] reformulate the problem in concrete terms. Note that we now can count the number of crimes reported to the police, and we know which cities to use in testing the proposition. Thus we have a reformulated statement that permits fruitful analysis.

fact
does

10. Because your reformulation must be specific, you may have to substitute less relevant but more measurable data for more relevant but vague data. To

continue with the example used above, data on the number of crimes reported to the police are not equivalent to the number of crimes actually committed, but reported crimes have the advantage of being more [measurable, factual].

measurable

11. When you discuss political questions, you will inevitably use terms that are vague and undefinable. In talking about why a particular bill did not pass Congress, you may speculate that the time was not "ripe" for such a bill or that it was "unfair" legislation. However useful terms like "ripe" and "unfair" may be in informal discussions, they are of little use in political analysis. In reformulating the problem you should always ask yourself the question, "If I were looking for information with which to analyze this problem, what data would directly clarify it for me?" If you cannot decide exactly what data to collect, you have not made your restatement specific enough.

For instance, to analyze why Congress did not pass a particular civil rights bill, you might formulate the statement: "Congress did not pass a civil rights bill in 1969 because public feeling was against it." Such a statement is [specific, vague]. It is vague because "public feeling" has not been defined. Another reformulation might be: "Most Americans disapproved of additional civil rights legislation when asked by public opinion polls in 1969, and therefore Congress did not pass such a bill." Such a statement is [specific, vague].

vague

specific

The statement "Civil rights legislation tends to foster immorality" is [specific, vague] and a statement of [fact, values]. It is vague because we need to define "foster" and "immorality." Does "foster" indicate mere associations between civil rights legislation and "immorality," or must there be an established cause-and-effect relationship? "Immorality" must be defined in terms of specific activities which can be observed. The statement is a factual statement since it does not express any preferences.

vague
fact

12. Another problem in making a statement specific is the practical problem of whether information is actually available. The statement, "Urban millionaires vote more often than rural millionaires" is specific, but there is little chance that this information exists. As

82 The Basic Tools of Analysis

was the case with measurability, you may have to settle for something less relevant, but something which is available; e.g., "Do people living in urban areas with incomes over $10,000 vote more than those with the same income living in rural areas?" Thus, when you reformulate the original problem, you must always ask yourself whether the information you are seeking is _____ .   available

13. Since you are obviously not aware of all the data that exist in the world, you will not always know what data are actually available or unavailable. Nevertheless, there are some kinds of information that are rarely, if ever, available. In the problem above, you saw that data on the activities of very small groups of people (e.g., rural millionaires) are difficult to obtain. Likewise, information on what certain people "really thought" when they did something or who did what when a group met secretly is usually unobtainable. They only guideline in searching for data that can be offered is that the information being sought should concern actions (or records) that can be seen, e.g., voting in Congress, or something that could be asked about, e.g., whether a person voted in an election. In all likelihood, data about how Southern congressmen *really* felt about Negroes or what *really* went on in the 1968 Republican presidential convention [can, cannot] be   cannot
obtained because it is advantageous to the informants to remain secretive.

Reformulations Must Not Automatically Narrow the Problem to a Single Factor.

1. When analyzing political problems, it is easy to assume what is most important without much evidence. The whole purpose of these lessons is to teach you to give answers to problems *after* examining data, not before examining them. If, for example, you were given the problem "Will President Nixon be reelected in 1972?" and you began by reformulating the problem to read "Has Nixon enacted most of his program?" You have already assumed that what determines whether a President will be reelected is _____ .   whether he has enacted his program
2. A better reformulation of the same problem would begin by asking, "What factors influence people's vote for the presidency and, at the present time, what is the

Reformulating Problems 83

state of each of these factors?" This reformulation does not assume that there is a _____ factor which determines whether a President is reelected.

single

3. To use another illustration, suppose you were given the problem of determining whether the federal government acts on the basis of public opinion. A reformulation that reads "Does the President ask Congress to pass legislation for which there have been street demonstrations?" assumes that the only way public opinion affects government policy is through _____.

demonstrations

4. On the other hand, a reformulation which reads "Has the government enacted laws which the majority of the population approves, and defeated bills which only a minority supports?" makes no assumptions that one factor in the problem is the most important one. It avoids using a [single-, multi.] factor solution.

single-

Reformulations Must Be Relevant.

1. In an earlier section of this chapter you saw that making a reformulation specific sometimes entailed a slight change in focus. While a slight change in meaning is occasionally necessary so that data can be obtained, a restatement that makes too great a change will be irrelevant to the original problem. Among other things, a correct reformulation is [relevant, irrelevant] to the original problem.

relevant

2. One of the things to keep in mind when reformulating the original problem is whether the restatement, if supplied with the appropriate data, would also provide an answer to the original problem. If a reformulation is irrelevant or too narrow, your answer to the original problem will be either _____ or _____, and thus incorrect.

irrelevant
too narrow

3. If, for example, you wanted to examine the importance of the Negro vote to President Nixon's victory in November, 1972, a restatement of the problem which asked "What factors affect Negro voting turnout?" would be [relevant, irrelevant], while a reformulation of "Was the winning candidate's margin of victory larger or smaller than the net number of Negro votes he received?" would be [relevant, irrelevant] to the original problem.

irrelevant

relevant

Summary

Before turning to practice problems, a summary of all the important rules in the reformulation process will be helpful.

1. *Reformulations must be factual statements,* not value statements. You should be able to apply data to the reformulation without making decisions based on personal values.

2. *Reformulations must be specific.* This means that terms must be *clearly defined and measurable,* and the necessary data should be *available.* A reformulation which is vague or which requires unobtainable information is of no help in solving a problem.

3. *Reformulations must not assume in advance that there is only one important factor. A correct reformulation must take into account all the factors which have a direct bearing on the problem.*

4. *Reformulations must be relevant* to the original problem. While you may have to modify terms so that they are operational, too great a modification will make your reformulation irrelevant to the original problem. Always ask whether the answer to the reformulation would also be an answer—even if only a partial one—to the original problem.

Now restate the prerequisites for correctly reformulating problems in your own terms. Reformulated problems must be:

1.

2.

3.

4.

Check your answers with the rules summarized on the preceding page to make sure you have written their equivalents.

PROBLEMS

On the following pages are problems of the type you will deal with in future chapters. Following each one of these problems are four reformulations, one or more of which is correct. Your job is to indicate the correct ones *and* explain why the others are incorrect. In this explanation, it is suggested that you make use of the rules you have just learned.

Each of the problems consists of two sections. The first is the problem section; it consists of the problem and the alternative reformulations. The second is your answer section. Indicate which reformulations are correct and why the others are incorrect. Then compare your answers with the correct ones following page 90. Since the ability to reformulate problems correctly is crucial to all social analysis, accuracy and understanding are more important than speed.

Problem 1

"With recent Republican victories in many Southern states, the South has finally become a two-party region like the North."

A. Southern political thinking has changed in recent years, and this thinking is compatible with two-party politics. On most important issues, Southerners differ very little from other Americans.

B. The political features characteristic of two-party states are presently found in a majority of Southern states. These features are: in the last election each party received at least 40 percent of the vote for governor and controls at least 30 percent of the seats in the state legislatures.

C. Southern Republican successes are victories by real Republicans, not by renegade Democrats who do not support the Republican philosophy. Thus the South now has a choice of governmental philosophies.

D. With such things as a rising standard of living and growing racial integration, Southern social and economic structure no longer differs from the rest of the nation. These changes provide the basis for a viable two-party system.

Your Answers to Problem 1

The correct reformulation(s): _____ .

In the space below, indicate why each one of the other answers is incorrect.

A.

B.

C.

D.

Now check your answers with the correct ones on p. 91.

Problem 2

"Congress represents the American people."

A. Most of the laws passed by Congress are in the best interest of the public.

B. Congress represents the American people, as evidenced by the fact that all its members are elected by the people and can be defeated if they dissatisfy the public.

C. Congress is representative of the American people insofar as its members are similar to the public in terms of education, previous occupation, and income, religion, race, and sex.

D. Congress represents the American public, as evidenced by the fact that a majority of people approve of the bills Congress passed and disapprove of the laws not passed.

Your Answers to Problem 2

The correct reformulation(s): _____ .

In the space below. indicate why each one of the other answers is incorrect.

A.

B.

C.

D.

Now check your answers with the correct ones on p. 92.

Problem 3
"In the United States, getting elected to important political office is a matter of money—candidates without lots of money don't have a chance."

A. Candidates for the presidency and Congress who can afford the best advertising agencies and the best campaigns are more successful than those who cannot.

B. In the most recent election, the presidential candidate and congressmen who spent more money than their opponents (according to official records) usually won.

C. Candidates for Congress who spend the most money to get elected are more in debt to wealthy individuals and thus are more economically conservative, as indicated by their votes on important economic issues.

90 The Basic Tools of Analysis

D. Most Americans think money is the most important factor in getting elected to important political office.

Your Answers to Problem 3

The correct reformulation(s): _____ .

In the space below indicate why each one of the other answers is incorrect.

A.

B.

C.

D.

Now check your answers with the correct ones on p. 92.

Correct Answers

Correct Answers to Problem 1

A. Incorrect. This reformulation is incorrect for two reasons. First, the term "political thinking" is not precise enough. What would you look for when collecting data on "political thinking"? A more precise concept is attitude about the value of two-party politics or desire for a two-party system. Second, the reformulation assumes that attitudes (or "political thinking") are the only factor in two-party competition. Suppose you found, for example, that 80 percent of Southerners were in favor of a two-party system. Would this prove that the South had finally become a two-party area?

B. Correct. This reformulation clearly and concretely defines two-party competition in terms of voting for the governor and state legislature. The statement is factual; all terms are specific; it narrows the original problem but does not assume that only one factor makes for party competition, and an answer to it would also answer the original problem. You may disagree with the dividing lines (a majority of states, 40 percent of the vote for governor, and 30 percent of the legislative seats), but without some specific criteria, the problem is unanswerable. Election results are public records.

C. Incorrect. The concept of "Republican philosophy" must be further defined. What would you look for when getting data on the "Republican philosophy"? In addition, suppose you found that elected Republicans did believe in some philosophy (which you had concretely defined); does this tell you whether the South is a two-party region? An answer to this reformulation would not be an adequate answer to the original problem.

D. Incorrect. The reformulation is irrelevant. Southern economic and social structure may be relevant to a discussion of why the South has a particular party system, but it has nothing to do with the question of whether a two-party system actually exists. Furthermore, the concepts of economic and social structure must be defined more precisely if they are to be useful.

Correct Answers to Problem 2

A. Incorrect. The concept of "best interest" is a value judgment. Any decision on whether a law was in the "best interest" of the public would depend on your personal values. Reformulations must be statements of fact.

B. Incorrect. This formulation does use a common definition of representation. However, it assumes that elections are lost when the people are dissatisfied with their congressmen. Many people may be dissatisfied and yet return their congressman to office because no better candidate is available. Further, senators are elected for six years; so a long time may elapse between public dissatisfaction and defeat at the polls.

C. Correct. This reformulation defines representative in terms of similarity of personal characteristics. These personal characteristics are clearly and concretely spelled out; education, occupation, and so on. These data are available for the public from the census and for congressmen in official biographies. The reformulation does not limit itself to only one factor, e.g., education, and an answer to it would answer the original problem (if you defined representation this way).

D. Correct. This reformulation defines representation in terms of agreement on issues; if Congress acts in agreement with public opinion, it "represents" the public. This definition of representation is very different from the one in alternative C, but it is also a reasonable definition of representation. Data for this reformulation are available from various public opinion polls.

Correct Answers to Problem 3

A. Incorrect. Terms in this reformulation are value statements. How do you judge which is the "best " advertising agency (largest number of clients, reputation?) or what is the "best" campaign? Even if you made these terms factual, this reformulation would not be an adequate answer to the original problem; the reformulation would deal with advertising and campaign strategy as related to election, not money's association with election. Money may be related to advertising and campaigns, but you cannot assume that one equals the other.

B. Correct. This reformulation changes the original statement to the more manageable assertion that those who spent more money than their opponents were elected. Important political offices are specifically defined—the presidency and Congress. By examining only the most recent election and official records (which are available), you limit the scope of the conclusions you can draw, but unless you put some limitations on what to examine, your analysis will be unmanageable. An analysis of this statement would be relevant to the original proposition. If you found, for example, that winning candidates usually spent more, you could say there was a relationship between money and getting elected, although the relationship might be spurious and that possibility would have to be examined with further analysis.

C. Incorrect. This reformulation is irrelevant to the original problem. The problem deals with money as a cause of election, not the consequences of money in politics.

D. This reformulation is technically correct, but it does not deal with the most important issue in the statement—the importance of money in getting elected to important office. Knowing that most Americans think money is the most important factor does not tell you whether it really is the key factor. Reformulating the original statement this way would have led to an analysis that told you very little about the relationship between finances and elections.

Chapter 5
REFORMULATING VALUE STATEMENTS

In the preceding chapter we noted that there is an important difference between statements of fact and statements which reflect personal values. Many statements about politics are value statements and as such cannot be empirically tested. Thus it is essential to distinguish between fact and value statements and to reformulate value statements into their factual counterparts before attempting to subject them to empirical analysis.

In the following pages you will learn:

1. To distinguish value statements from factual statements
2. To reformulate value statements into factual equivalents

These skills are of crucial importance; you cannot engage in political analysis without mastering them. After completing this chapter, you should have no difficulty in performing these analytic tasks.

DEFINITION OF FACTUAL STATEMENTS

1. A factual statement can be either proved or disproved with data. Statements such as "Sixty percent of the electorate votes," "The President always appoints Democrats," "Millionaires pay no income tax" can be proved or _____ with the appropriate data.   disproved

2. Not all statements that you think are true or false are factual statements. You may feel that the statement "The Democratic party is the greatest party in the world" is true or false. But your decision on the truth of such a statement is not based on data; it is based on your personal preferences. Such statements assert the value of something, and their verification depends on your own value preferences rather than on facts alone. Consider, for instance, the statement

96 The Basic Tools of Analysis

"Rich people are better than poor people." This is a [fact, value] statement because _____ .

DEFINITION OF VALUE STATEMENTS

1. A value statement reflects an individual's personal preference, e.g., what is "good" or "bad," and is either accepted or rejected on the basis of these values. For example, the statement "Every American should vote" can be accepted or rejected only on the basis of whether you think voting is good or _____ .

2. Value statements frequently require that key terms be defined according to your own values. A statement like "Nixon is a better President than Johnson" requires a personal definition of the key term _____ if this assertion is to be accepted or denied.

3. Likewise, the assertion "People are free in the United States" is a [value, fact] statement because the meaning of "free" depends on your personal values as well as on facts. For instance, many people feel all Americans are equally free, while some people who live in ghettos feel they are less free than those who live in the suburbs.

DIFFERENT KINDS OF VALUE STATEMENTS

1. Up to this point statements have been distinguished only insofar as they were value or factual. Actually, there are a number of different kinds of value statements, and familiarity with each type will help you to identify all assertions that reflect personal values. The simplest type is the *evaluative statement,* e.g., "Americans are good people." What makes statements like "Americans are good" value statements is that the meaning of words like good, bad, beautiful, or ugly depends on your personal [facts, values], not objective data.

2. A second kind of value statement is the *comparative statement.* This kind of statement indi-

value
its verification depends on value preferences

bad

"better"

value

values

Reformulating Value Statements 97

cates a *personal preference* for one thing over another. "Capitalism is better than communism" would be an example of a comparative value statement, for there are no objective _____ which could prove or disprove this statement (in its present form). Whether this statement was accepted or rejected would depend on your [facts, values] regarding either capitalism or communism.

facts

values

3. Comparative value statements are not always as simple as the above illustration. What may appear to be something based on fact frequently reflects preferences more than data. In the statement "It is better to lock up a few innocent people accidentally than to let dangerous sex maniacs roam the streets," locking up innocent people is _____ to having sex maniacs roam the streets.

preferred

4. A third kind of value statement is a *prescriptive statement,* e.g., "Americans *ought* to vote." What characterizes such a statement is the expression of an imperative, i.e., you *ought* to do this, you *should* do that, etc. The statement "You should play close attention to these lessons" is a [fact, value] statement. However, "People who do not pay close attention to these lessons always fail this course" is a statement of _____ .

value

fact

5. Three kinds of value statements are *evaluative, comparative,* and *prescriptive.*

a. For example, the statement "The Chinese Communists are evil" is an _____ statement.

evaluative

b. The statement "All true-blooded Americans should be eager to fight in their country's defense" is a _____ value statement.

prescriptive

c. The statement "Western civilization is superior to the native cultures of Asia and Africa" is a _____ value statement.

comparative

d. Each of these is a value statement because it [can, cannot] be proved true or false with facts.

cannot

Thus you need to beware of value statements when something is being described, compared, or prescribed. However, not all comparative statements are value statements; many of them are factual statements. Prescriptions and evaluations are always value statements.

TRANSFORMING VALUE STATEMENTS INTO FACTUAL STATEMENTS

We can transform value statements into close factual equivalents by altering them in one of several ways. The first is to change the frame of reference. An evaluative statement, for instance, asserts that "Americans are free," which really means, "I think Americans are free." The factual equivalent changes the reference from "I think . . ." to "Most people think. . . ." So a factual equivalent to "Americans are free" is "Most people think Americans are free." This statement can now be tested empirically by asking a sample of people whether they think Americans are free. The altered statement can be demonstrated to be true or false, whereas the original evaluative statement is an assertion of values and cannot be subjected to empirical analysis.

1. Let us try some further transformations by changing the reference. Take the statement "America was right to send troops to fight for South Vietnam." This is a [factual, value] statement.   value

2. If we transform the statement to read, "Sending troops to fight for South Vietnam was illegal," the statement is [factual, evaluative]. It is still evaluative, because legal and illegal, like "right and wrong," is a value judgment about which reasonable men may differ.   evaluative

3. Let us try again. If we reformulate the statement: "Most world leaders in 1967 thought America was wrong in sending troops to fight for South Vietnam," we have a [factual, evaluative] statement. This is a factual statement because we can empirically demonstrate whether or not most world leaders thought America was right or wrong in sending troops to fight for South Vietnam.   factual

4. Let us try another example: "Urban renewal is bad." This statement is [factual, evaluative]. The reformulation "Most Americans disapprove of urban renewal" is a [factual, evaluative] statement because we can measure the number of Americans who favor or oppose urban renewal and then demonstrate the truth or falsity of the statement.   evaluative

    factual

A second way to transform value statements is to define the value terms in specific, factual terms.

Reformulating Value Statements 99

5. For example, the author of the statement "Urban renewal is bad" may have meant that he thought it was bad because it led to much dislocation for Negroes. We might substitute "Negro removal" for the evaluative term "bad," so that the reformulated statement reads "Urban renewal is Negro removal." This statement is [factual, evaluative]. It is factual because we can find data about "Negro removal" and test the truth or falsity of the statement.

factual

6. Let us take another example: "Public housing is more immoral than private housing." This is a [factual, value] statement. We may reformulate it by changing the value term "immoral." For instance, we might interpret "immoral" as "associated with higher crime rates."

value

7. Then the statement would read: "Public housing has _____ than private housing." This is a [factual, value] statement because we can test its truth or falsity.

a higher crime rate
factual

8. Note, we can also transform this statement by changing the reference, as we did earlier. "Most Americans think public housing is immoral" is a [factual, value] statement.

factual

A third way to transform value statements into factual equivalents is particularly appropriate to prescriptive statements. Take, for example, the prescription "The courts should not coddle criminals." Implicit in this prescription is an "if . . . then . . ." logic: if the courts did not coddle criminals, we would have less crime. When we make the "if . . . then . . ." logic explicit, we transform the prescription into a factual statement that can be demonstrated to be true or false.

9. Examine the following statement: "Welfare recipients should be made to work." This is a [factual, value] statement. The statement is [evaluative, comparative, prescriptive].

value
prescriptive

10. Consider the following transformation: "If welfare recipients worked, they would no longer need public assistance." This is a [factual, value] statement. Note that we can demonstrate its truth or

factual

falsity by collecting the appropriate information and analyzing it.

11. Consider the statement "Cars should be prohibited from the center of metropolitan areas." This statement is [factual, evaluative, comparative, prescriptive].   prescriptive

12. The reformulation "Most city planners think that cars should be prohibited from the center of metropolitan areas" is [factual, evaluative, comparative, prescriptive]. The reformulation "If cars were banned from the central cities of metropolitan areas, air pollution would be greatly reduced" is [factual, evaluative, comparative, prescriptive].   factual

factual

Note that in our last example we have reformulated a value statement in two quite different ways. "Most city planners think that cars should be prohibited from the center of metropolitan areas" is certainly not saying the same thing as "If cars were banned from central cities of metropolitan areas, air pollution would be greatly reduced." Both are proper reformulations. You should notice that we *do* change the meaning of value statements when we reformulate them into factual equivalents. As the preceding chapter emphasized, you must retain as much of the relevance of the original statement as possible in your reformulation if you wish to have your empirical analysis applicable to the original statement.

PROBLEMS

In the following exercise, there are 15 statements. Some of the statements are value statements, others factual. In this exercise, it makes no difference whether a statement is true or false, what is important is whether it can be demonstrated as true or false (a factual statement) or whether it expresses a value (a value statement).

If it is a factual statement, simply write "fact" in the space beneath the statement. If, on the other hand, you feel that it is a value statement, write "value," and then translate it into a factual statement that can be analyzed. You will recall from Chapter 4 that a statement that can be analyzed must be stated in concrete and precise terms.

In reformulating your value statements, be sure you attempt to use all three ways of rewriting them wherever appropriate. Restate them so that:

1. You change the reference from the value preference of a single person to what most people think.

2. You change the reference from a value preference to its equivalent factual term, e.g., "Education is good" to "Education permits people to earn higher incomes."

3. You change prescriptive value statements to if-then statements.

Problem 1
"Politics is a dirty business."

Your Answer

Now check your answer with the correct one on p. 108.

Problem 2
"The average politician, compared with the businessman or professional comes from a lower-income family."

Your Answer

Now check your answer with the correct one on p. 108.

Problem 3
"Americans have an obligation to help the Negro."

Your Answer

Now check your answer with the correct one on p. 109.

Problem 4
"On the whole, Negroes in America are financially better off today than they were 10 years ago."

Your Answer

Now check your answer with the correct one on p. 109.

Problem 5
"Even though there are defects, American courts are the fairest in the world."

Your Answer

Now check your answer with the correct one on p. 109.

Problem 6
"A majority of people in the United States don't even know who their congressman is."

Your Answer

Now check your answer with the correct one on p. 109.

104 The Basic Tools of Analysis

Problem 7
"The average citizen in a democracy must be well-informed."

Your Answer

Now check your answer with the correct one on p. 109.

Problem 8
"Every time a Democrat is elected President, either the income tax rate goes up or war breaks out or both."

Your Answer

Now check your answer with the correct one on p. 110.

Problem 9
"The American factory worker has a higher disposable income than workers in other countries."

Your Answer

Now check your answer with the correct one on p. 110.

Problem 10
"Jews tend to support the Democratic party, while most white Protestants support the Republican party."

Your Answer

Now check your answer with the correct one on p. 110.

106　The Basic Tools of Analysis

Problem 11
　"Foreign nations would do well to copy the American Constitution in order to become prosperous."

Your Answer

Now check your answer with the correct one on p. 110.

Problem 12
　"Labor unions have far too much power over the economy."

Your Answer

Now check your answer with the correct one on p. 111.

Problem 13
"Southern congressmen generally serve longer terms than their colleagues from the North and West."

Your Answer

Now check your answer with the correct one on p. 111.

Problem 14
"Americans of the twentieth century are much more immoral than they were in 1776."

Your Answer

Now check your answer with the correct one on p. 111.

Problem 15

"The Supreme Court is not representative of the American public."

Your Answer

Now check your answer with the correct one on p. 111.

Correct Answers

Correct Answer to Problem 1

Value. The problem with this descriptive statement lies in the word "dirty." "Dirty" can mean almost anything from criminal activity to a willingness to compromise, and whatever one decides on depends on personal values. If the statement were "Most Americans feel that politics is dirty" or "All politicians have taken bribes" or "Politicians are more likely to have a criminal record than the rest of the population," it would have been a factual statement. In order to prove or disprove the last statement, for example, you would need data on how many people in public office had been convicted of some crime, as well as the rate for the rest of the population. Besides any technical problem in acquiring this information, you would have to realize that not everyone who commits a crime is caught, and the crimes politicians are likely to commit may be more (or less) difficult to police. Hence the crime rate may not be a completely accurate reflection of the actual amount of crime.

Correct Answer to Problem 2

Fact. To prove or disprove this assertion, you would compare the average income of a politician's family (his mother and father) with that of the businessman's and professional's family. The obvious problem, of course, besides the technical one, is that not everyone may be honest about financial matters. Some may magnify the poverty in their background to emphasize their present success, while others may minimize it because of their recent ascent to a high-status position.

Correct Answer to Problem 3

Value. This is, clearly, a prescriptive statement. But by modifying it to "Most Americans have given active support to Negro rights" or "Only college-educated people feel an obligation to help the Negro" or "Most Americans feel they have some obligation to help the Negro," it would be changed into a statement that could be proved or disproved. Here, as in almost all questions of this type that are asked of the general public, you have to assume that most people are telling the truth.

Correct Answer to Problem 4

Fact. You would compare the average Negro income of 10 years ago with the present figure. Also, you might want to compare these figures with the equivalent ones for whites. It just may be that while Negro incomes have risen, white incomes have risen faster, and that, compared with the white population, Negroes are poorer today than 10 years ago. This consideration, however, is a secondary one and does not make the original statement a value statement.

Correct Answer to Problem 5

Value. This assertion is a comparative value statement, for it compares American courts with the rest of the world with regard to a concept—"fairest"—that necessarily depends on personal interpretation (to a person very much against suspected criminals being set free, certain decisions seem "fair," while to a person who greatly fears innocent people being locked up, the same decision may be grossly "unfair"). To make this into a fact statement you would have to select a measurable standard, e.g., difficulty in obtaining justice as measured by financial cost to persons involved or length of time it takes to obtain a judgment. Another way would be to say, "Americans, compared with other nationalities, have a very high regard for their court system." In order to answer this last statement, you would need public opinion polls on American attitudes toward their courts, as well as the equivalent information for other countries.

Correct Answer to Problem 6

Fact. This can be proved or disproved by the use of public opinion polls. Here, in comparison with the problem encountered in statement 3 above, there is little problem of people answering dishonestly.

Correct Answer to Problem 7

Value. This assertion is a subtle prescriptive statement (owing to the word "must"). Had it read "Citizens are better informed in democracies than in dictatorships" or "Most people in democracies are not well-informed," it would have been a factual statement. In both of these examples, you would need data on the level of citizen information (in both democracies and dictatorships in the first case, only in democracies in the second). One of the practical problems with both statements is that it may be difficult to compare the knowledge of citizens in different countries: e.g., does an American's knowledge of his representative in the House equal an Englishman's knowledge of his representative in Parliament?

Correct Answer to Problem 8

Fact. To prove or disprove this assertion you would compare side by side the party of all Presidents, increases in the income tax rate, and outbreak of war. However, it should be remembered that although two events may occur at the same time, e.g., a person is elected President and war breaks out, it does not mean that one event caused the other.

Correct Answer to Problem 9

Fact. The phrase "disposable income" is quite specific and refers to data which are generally published in official volumes. Whether American workers earn higher disposable incomes than workers in other countries can be determined with relative ease. Note, however, that proof of this statement would not necessarily substantiate the assertion that American workers have a higher standard of living. The standard of living includes services which are free in some countries but have to be purchased in the United States (like medical care); it also involves value judgments of what is to be included in a "high" standard of living.

Correct Answer to Problem 10

Fact. Besides technical problems of getting information, the only problem would be deciding at what point someone supported a particular party (did voting for the Democrats 3 out of 5 times constitute support or would it have to be 4 out of 5 times?). However, since all standards can be employed simultaneously, this problem is a secondary one (you can say, for example, that 80 percent of Jews vote Democratic 65 percent of the time. 60 percent of Jews vote Democratic 70 percent of the time, etc.).

Correct Answer to Problem 11

Value. This statement is a prescriptive statement. Had it read "Many nations have copied the United States Constitution" or "Most Americans think other nations should copy the Constitution" or "Nations that have copied the Constitution have the same standard of living that the United States has," it would be a statement of fact. Although these statements are not identical with the original one, they can be proved or disproved.

Correct Answer to Problem 12

Value. The problem here is what constitutes "too much power." For some people any union power is "too much" power, while for others, unions could never have "too much" power. Factual versions of this assertion would include "Most workers in the United States belong to unions" or "There are no laws to stop a union from calling a strike regardless of the circumstances" or "Most people in America feel that unions are too powerful."

Correct Answer to Problem 13

Fact. All that would be necessary would be to compare the various lengths of tenure of Southern vs. non-Southern congressmen.

Correct Answer to Problem 14

Value. The proposition is of the comparative type, of value rather than of fact, because of the word "immoral." Immoral, like goodness and virtue, is a term with very imprecise meaning, and whatever meaning is given to the term largely depends on personal choice. If the statement had been "Most people today think that there is more immorality than in 1776" or "More people today are concerned with immorality than were concerned with it in 1776" or "There is a higher crime rate in America today than in 1776," it would have been a factual statement. In proving or disproving this last statement, there would be two related problems: (1) it may not be easy to get crime statistics for a period 175 years ago, and (2) there is no assurance that those statistics and present ones mean the same thing (definitions of crimes have changed, as well as methods of keeping track of crimes).

Correct Answer to Problem 15

Value. Here, as in statement 14, the problem lies in an imprecise word, "representation." Representation can mean a variety of things, e.g., whether a person acts for someone or is similar to someone else, and which definition you employ rests to a large degree on personal values. By spelling out the definition, one can change this value statement into a factual one. "Supreme Court judges have different opinions on important issues from those of most citizens," "Justices are not chosen from all ethnic and religious groups," or "Supreme Court justices have a wealthier family background than most Americans." If you decide that family background determines "representation" (people are representative if they are of the same background as those who elected them to office), then your analysis of the factual question also pertains to the original value question.

Chapter 6
THE INTERPRETATION OF TEXTUAL DATA

Much of the information we receive about political affairs is verbal; most of it comes from newspapers, magazines, and books. These sources present information to us in the form of factual propositions, but often such propositions are interspersed with value statements which are sometimes disguised as facts. In this chapter we shall examine the presentation of information in textual material—especially in the popular press—to alert you to the following problems:

1. the identification of sources
2. the identification of bias
3. the separation of fact from value propositions

THE IDENTIFICATION OF SOURCES

As with statistical data, it is important to identify the source of information in order to judge its reliability and the possible biases which may be associated with it. When we read a story about the plans of a political candidate, the _____ of the information may lead us to regard it as creditable or as sheer speculation. If we find that the reporter learned about such plans from the candidate's campaign manager, we might regard the source as _____ ; if he got the plans from the candidate's rival, we may wish to evaluate it as _____ . In many instances, however, the reporter cannot reveal his source because it is confidential; the story was given to him only on the condition that the reporter not name his source. In such instances, the story is likely to quote "a reliable source" or "an unimpeachable source." Such a phrase usually means that a high official has given a back-

    source

    reliable

    unreliable

114 The Basic Tools of Analysis

ground briefing to the reporter but is unwilling to be quoted by name. In such instances, the reader must guess the _____ of the information; he has no reliable guide. Compare, for instance, the following stories:

    Beirut, Lebanon, July 24, Tuesday [AP]—The hijackers of a Japanese jumbo jetliner blew it up today at Benghazi, the Libyan port on the North African coast, after evacuating the 137 persons, Egypt's Middle East News announced. [*Chicago Tribune*, July 24, p. 1. Reprinted courtesy of the *Chicago Tribune*.]

source

Underline the source of the story. The source is given as _____ . We may surmise (although we are not told directly) that the news agency's source was an eyewitness account of the evacuation of the airplane and its explosion. Consider the next story.

Egypt's Middle East News Agency

    St. Louis, July 23 [Special]—At least 36 persons were killed tonight when a twin-engine Ozark Air Lines plane carrying 45 persons crashed as it approached Lambert–St. Louis International Airport in a severe thunderstorm. Eight persons were injured in the crash and one is unaccounted for, according to Raymond J. Harris, St. Louis County assistant medical examiner. [*Chicago Tribune*, July 24, p. 1. Reprinted courtesy of the *Chicago Tribune*.]

The source is identified as _____ . We know both his name and his position; he is identified as someone with expertise in the field of accidental deaths, and therefore we may take at least the part of the story that deals with the number of fatalities as relatively reliable.

St. Louis County assistant medical examiner, Raymond J. Harris

However, consider the following story:

    Prime Minister Geogh Whitlam will meet President Nixon and Henry Kissinger next Monday in Washington to explain Australia's growing independence in the Pacific. . . . The President's invitation to Whitlam came as a pleasant surprise to Australian diplomats. Their overtures for a meeting between Whitlam and the President earlier this year had been met with a cool silence from the White House. Observers said the President had been angered by a strong letter of protest from Whitlam over U.S. bombing in Cambodia. [*Chicago Tribune*, July 24, p. 5. Reprinted courtesy of the *Chicago Tribune*.]

The source for President Nixon's feelings toward Whitlam is specified as _____ . From that description, we [know, do not know] who revealed the information and cannot easily judge its reliability.

observers
do not know

THE IDENTIFICATION OF BIAS

All news stories are biased. The biases come from many sources, and it is important that we identify them.

Bias most frequently comes from incompleteness. No newspaper reports all the news. Editors must select which stories they wish to print and which they will omit as if the events never occurred. The number and length of the stories they print any given day depend on the amount of advertising the newspaper has on that day. On Wednesdays and Thursdays, when most newspapers have many grocery ads, more news will be printed; on Monday's and Saturdays, when there are fewer advertisements, less news is printed. Some newspapers, however, print more of the news than others. Compare for instance, the coverage of the subpoenas issued to President Nixon by the Senate Committee on the Watergate scandal for the tape recordings of conversations in Nixon's White House office. The *Chicago Tribune* gave the story 43 ½ column inches the next day; the *San Francisco Chronicle* gave it 51 ½ column inches; the *Atlanta Journal* gave the story 32 column inches. Using the rough yardstick of column inches as an indicator of thoroughness of coverage, there was least bias by omission of information in the _____ and most bias in the _____ . In addition, the *New York Times* reprinted the texts of the President's letter to the Senate Committee, but none of the other newspapers reprinted all of them. However, even the most comprehensive coverage is only a *selection* of the available information. Newspapers friendly to President Nixon may present quite different selections of the information than those opposed or neutral to him. Such bias, resulting from the _____ of news, can only be identified by relying on several competing news media and comparing the information which each presents.

A second frequent source of bias is the use of *loaded* words or phrases. Such words subtly lead the reader to a value-laden conclusion without alerting him to that danger. For instance, a defendant in a criminal case may be described as a drug addict, leading the reader to associate the crime with drug use. In this

San Francisco
Chronicle
Atlanta Journal

selection

instance, the term _____ is the loaded phrase. In other instances, an unpopular label may be placed on a person or country—e.g., communist, fascist, dictator, homosexual, divorcee, or drunk. Each of these terms is _____ with a value preference espoused by the editors of the newspaper but not made explicit in the story.

drug addict

loaded

For instance, consider the following headlines:

President Refuses to Release Tapes; Senate and Cox Serve Subpoenas; White House Expected to Ignore Them [*New York Times,* July 24, 1973]

Senate Panel and Cox Issue Subpoenas for Nixon Tapes [*Los Angeles Time,* July 24, 1973]

Fight over Nixon Tapes Heads for Supreme Court [*Chicago Daily News,* July 24, 1973]

Nixon Battles Subpoena of Watergate-Talk Tapes [*Atlanta Journal,* July 24, 1973]

Eventual Court Decision to Decide Subpoena Fight [*Denver Post,* July 24, 1973]

The *Los Angeles Times* and the *Denver Post* used relatively neutral words to headline the news; the other newspapers used more loaded phrases: "refuses to"; "Nixon Battles"; "Fight over Nixon Tapes." Although all reported a conflict between the President and Congress and Special Prosecutor Cox, we might consider the headline in the *Atlanta Journal* [more, less] biased than that in the *Denver Post.*

more

Look at the next group of headlines:

Terrorists Blow Up Airliner [*Washington Star-News,* July 24, 1973]

Washington Star-News

Hijackers Seized as They Free 137 and Blow Up Jet [*New York Times,* July 25, 1973]

Hijackers Blow Up Jumbo Jet: Passengers Safe [*Denver Post,* July 24, 1973]

Air Hijackers Free 137, Then Blow Up Jet in Libya [*St. Louis Post Dispatch,* July 24, 1973]

Underline what you consider the most biased headline. Note that none of the headlines described the hijackers as Freedom Fighters or Palestinian Nationalists. Those would also be loaded phrases that _____ the reader in favor of the Palestinians. The terms used bias the reader [for, against] the Palestinian cause.

bias

against

SEPARATION OF FACTUAL FROM VALUE STATEMENTS

Readers are prepared to find value statements on editorial pages and in feature articles. These are the traditional forums for the statement of opinions in newspapers and magazines. However, one also often finds value statements in news stories. Consider, for instance, the following opening sentence of a news story on the rising cost of living.

> Anyone planning to buy lots of pork and eggs this week might want to think twice. [*Chicago Tribune*, July 24, 1973]

This is a [fact, value] statement. It is in the form of an [evaluative, prescriptive] statement which seeks to advise consumers about their prospective course of action. The remainder of the article describes the level of food prices. For instance, consider the next sentence from the same news story:

value
prescriptive

> The price of large eggs in several major food chains jumped from 75 cents to 84 cents a dozen. Fresh pork is up anywhere from 6 cents to 22 cents a pound, depending on the cut.

These sentences are [fact, value] statements. They [do, do not] give the source of the information. They [do, do not] provide precise measurements of the rise in the cost of living.

fact
do not
do

Value statements are often combined with loaded phrases which emphasize the author's perspective. Consider the following opening paragraph from a feature story:

> According to what I've been reading in magazines and newspapers and seeing and hearing on television documentaries and talk shows, the new liberal mecca and sacred cow is Communist China. Sacred even to the extent that it can smuggle heroin into the United States virtually without censure, protected by a largely liberal media who ironically tell us that the public has a right to know. [Mike LaVelle, *Chicago Tribune*, July 24, 1973, p. 14. Reprinted courtesy of the *Chicago Tribune*.]

These statements are [fact, value] statements. Underline the loaded phrases which indicate bias. These are descriptive terms which indicate a conclusion for which no supporting evidence is presented. Note also that relations with Communist China are dis-

value
liberal mecca,
sacred cow,
liberal media

cussed in the context of drug traffic ("smuggle heroin"), a topic which often arouses strong emotions.

The necessity of identifying sources, looking for loaded phrases which surreptitiously bias the reader, and separating fact from value statements is not limited to your reading of newspapers and magazines. The same problems occur in many books, even textbooks.

EXERCISES

1. Read the following two excerpts. Under each, indicate the words or phrases which provide the source of the information (or indicate the lack of such information). Indicate the words which show the bias of the author and the value statements included in the story.

When you have finished, compare your answers with those given on the page following the stories.

HALDEMAN DENIES COVERUP. FAILS TO REFUTE CHARGES BY WATERGATE WITNESSES. By Arthur Siddon. Chicago Tribune Press Service. Washington, July 31—H. R. Haldeman, once reputed to be the President's eyes and ears in the White House, found it difficult today to recall key events surrounding the Watergate affair, while claiming he knew nothing of the White House coverup before last March 21.

The onetime stern gatekeeper of the flow of White House information repeatedly failed today to recall under questioning by the Senate Watergate committee events cited by the key witnesses against him as proving his involvement in the Watergate affair.

Haldeman seldom denied outright the allegations made by Gordon Strachan, his former aide in the White House, and fired White House Counsel John Dean III. In some cases he even admitted they might be right, but he just did not remember the incident or conversation. [*Chicago Tribune,* August 1, 1973, p. 1. Reprinted courtesy of the *Chicago Tribune.*]

THE ANATOMY OF DECEPTION

It is ironic that the United States first publicly acknowledged a lie during the Eisenhower Presidency. Although to many Americans, Eisenhower, as frequently noted, was a "father figure," his face never lost the igenuous, open quality of a Kansas farm boy. His public personality was that of a Huckleberry Finn reluctantly and unexpectedly occupying the White House.

Eisenhower often liked to emphasize that America's "moral" and "spiritual" power was the true source of its strength. Yet this man, who projected such a persuasive image of personal honesty, was hopelessly impaled on a lie and finally forced to admit it publicly to the nation and the world. [David Wise, *The Politics of Lying* (New York: Random House, Inc., 1973), p. 33. Copyright, Random House, Inc. Reprinted by permission.]

Answers

Siddon Story:

Source: Not given although it reads as if reporter was eyewitness to event.
Indicators of bias: "onetime stern gatekeeper".
Value statements: "fails to refute charges by Watergate witnesses"—an evaluative statement.

Wise excerpt:

Source: Not given.
Indicators of bias: "Lie," "ingenuous, open quality," "Huckleberry Finn," "hopelessly impaled on a lie."
Value statements: "It is ironic. . . . His public personality was that of a Huckleberry Finn reluctantly and unexpectedly occupying the White House"; "hopelessly impaled on a lie."

2. Select a story in a current issue of *Time, Newsweek, U.S. News & World Report,* or from your local newspaper. Identify the sources of the story, the indicators of bias, and the value statements in the story.

120 The Basic Tools of Analysis

3. Select a recent prominent event and compare news coverage of it in five different newspapers, magazines, or other media. If your library has videotapes of television news programs or transcripts of radio newscasts, include those in your analysis. Summarize, in the table below, your findings about the sources of the coverage, the indicators of bias, and the use of value statements in reportage of events.

	Magazine, Newspaper, TV, or Radio Broadcast				
	No. 1	No. 2	No. 3	No. 4	No. 5
Sources:	____	____	____	____	____
	____	____	____	____	____
	____	____	____	____	____
	____	____	____	____	____
Indicators of bias	____	____	____	____	____
	____	____	____	____	____
Value statements	____	____	____	____	____
	____	____	____	____	____
	____	____	____	____	____
	____	____	____	____	____

Part Two
Political Analysis

Chapter 7
PUBLIC OPINION

The relationship between citizen and government has long been of great interest to many people. For some philosophers, the only "good" government is government that obeys the will of the people. The idea that people ought to govern themselves has been a very old and persistent thought in the history of the Western world. Although the democratic belief in self-government is widespread in America, it has had its critics. On the one hand are those who believe in a natural elite. According to these critics, there are certain people who, by virtue of their intelligence or racial superiority, are the natural leaders of the "masses." A more popular criticism of self-government is that, while it is fine in theory, the average person lacks the ability or knowledge necessary for self-government; so any talk of democracy contains more myth than reality.

This chapter's problem deals with a part of this broad question:

"In the United States, the government reflects public opinion."

To assist you in your analysis, this chapter is divided into different sections. Complete instructions for each section are found at the beginning of the section.

I. REFORMULATING THE PROBLEM

The first step in analyzing an ambiguous political statement is reformulating it into a more precise statement. Unless this is done, the problem cannot be correctly analyzed. This section presents four reformulations of this chapter's problem. Some are acceptable; others are unacceptable; more than one may be adequate. An acceptable reformulation meets the following criteria:

1. Reformulations must be factual, not value statements, i.e., they can be proved or disproved with empirical data.

2. Terms and concepts in a reformulation must be concrete and specific. You must know what to look for in obtaining data.

3. Reformulations must not be single-variable oversimplifications. They must take into account the relevant aspects of a problem and make no unwarranted assumptions about what is most important.

4. Finally, the reformulation must be relevant to the original problem. An analysis of the reformulation should be an answer to the original problem.

Indicate whether each of the reformulations below is *acceptable* or *not acceptable*. Where unacceptable, briefly explain why. When you have given answers for all four reformulations, compare your answers with the correct ones that follow your answers.

Original Statement

"In the United States, the government reflects public opinion."

Reformulations

1. Most Americans want policies that are good for the national welfare, and oppose unfair policies.

2. A majority of the public favors those policies the government has enacted, and policies opposed by majorities are changed.

3. On the whole, public officials in America try their best to be responsive to public needs.

4. Government in the United States has always satisfied its citizens, as evidenced by the great loyalty of its citizens.

Your Answers

1.

2.

3.

4.

Now check your answers with the following correct ones.

Correct Answers

1. Unacceptable. This reformulation is irrelevant, since it says nothing about what specific policies the public wants and what government activity ensues. Furthermore, whether most Americans desire policies that are good for the "national welfare" cannot be determined until you define what the national welfare is. Any such analysis hinges on personal values. The national welfare for one person may be national disaster for another.

2. Acceptable. This reformulation is clear and specific ("A majority of the public favors those policies . . .") and is relevant to the original problem (the relationship between public wants and government activity).

3. Unacceptable. In the first place, the phrase "try their best to be responsive" is not clear and specific. How can we know if officials are "trying their best" or are "responsive"? It may be possible to clarify these concepts, but this reformulation does not do it. Second, testing this reformulation would not provide an answer to the original problem. Knowing that officials were "trying their best" does not say whether they did what the public wanted. An analysis on the basis of this reformulation would be irrelevant to the problem.

4. Unacceptable. This reformulation is inadequate because the fact that American citizens are loyal is no proof that their government does what they

126 *Political Analysis*

want. Showing that Americans are loyal citizens does not demonstrate that citizen opinion is consistent with government action. Loyalty and government action may be related, but they are not identical.

II. SELECTING THE NECESSARY DATA

In section I you selected a modification of the original problem so that it could be tested with data. The next step is to decide on the specific data necessary for such a test. You decide on the needed data in advance, because without some concrete idea of what you need, you would waste much time in examining information that will later prove to be irrelevant.

Below the correct reformulation is a list of different kinds of data. Only some of these data are necessary to test the reformulation. In deciding which data are necessary, keep in mind the following rules:

1. Avoid looking for vague and general kinds of data. What you need should be as specific and concrete as possible.

2. Choose data that are probably available. You do not know in advance exactly what is available, but try to limit yourself to things that either are of public record or are frequently researched by political scientists.

3. The data you need must be related to the reformulation. Data that are not related to the reformulation are useless.

4. The data should be sufficient to test the reformulated problem and provide an adequate answer to the original problem.

Below each item, indicate whether the data are necessary or unnecessary. Briefly explain why the information is needed or not needed. When you finish, compare your answers with the correct ones at the end of this section.

Reformulation

"A majority of the public favors policies the government has enacted, and policies opposed by majorities are changed."

What Data Are Needed To Analyze This Reformulation?

1. Information on the social background (e.g., race, social class, etc.) of important government decision makers.
These data are [necessary, unnecessary] because:

2. Data on who benefits the most and least from various government policies. These data are [necessary, unnecessary] because:

3. Public opinion polls on political issues.
These data are [necessary, unnecessary] because:

4. An explanation of how important public officials make their decisions. These data are [necessary, unnecessary] because:

5. Information on the kinds of policies enacted by local, state, and national government.
These data are [necessary, unnecessary] because:

6. Data on the effectiveness of the average person's participation in government decisions.
These data are [necessary, unnecessary] because:

Correct Answers

1. Unnecessary. The statement to be tested deals with what the public wants and what government does. Social backgrounds of officials are irrelevant to this definition of representation. Suppose you found, for example, that all government officials were white, upper- and middle-class Protestants. Such information would not show that these officials were responsive or unresponsive to public desires.

2. Unnecessary. Knowing who benefits or loses in government decisions is irrelevant to your operationalization of the problem. Knowing the distribution of benefits is quite different from knowing the distribution of preferences. For instance, it is quite conceivable that many people will favor policies that do not benefit them directly.

3. Necessary. In order to know if most Americans approve or disapprove of government policies, you need the results of opinion polls on political issues. Not every such poll will suffice, however. The poll must be on a well-defined issue relating to public policy.

4. Unnecessary. In the first place, information on how officials made their decisions is difficult to obtain. More important, this kind of information is not relevant to the reformulation. Knowing how a decision was reached does not tell you if the public wanted that decision. The reformulation asks whether a majority of Americans favor government policies, not how those decisions are made.

5. Necessary. To test the reformulation, you not only need opinion polls on public issues but also the government's decisions on such issues.

6. Unnecessary. The effectiveness of the average person's political participation is irrelevant to the problem. The reformulation deals with the citizen's approval or disapproval of government decisions, not his influence in making them. Furthermore, the concept of "effectiveness" would have to be made more specific and concrete before you could look for this kind of information.

The Data

In the following pages are some of the data you need to analyze this chapter's problem. Some of the data may be relevant to the problem; other data may be irrelevant. After you have examined each table and decided whether it is necessary to test the reformulation, turn to section III, which immediately follows the data.

TABLE 7.1-A PUBLIC OPINION ON GUN REGISTRATION

"Would you favor or oppose a law which would require a person to obtain a police permit before he or she could buy a gun?"

Year	Favors Firearms Controls	Opposes Firearms Controls	No Opinion
1959	75%	21%	4%
1964	78	17	5
1965	73	23	4
1966	68	29	3
1967	73	24	3
1971	71	25	4
1972	71	25	4

SOURCE: Gallup Poll. Cited in "The Polls: Gun Control," compiled by Hazel Erskine, *Public Opinion Quarterly,* vol. 36, p. 460, 1972.

TABLE 7.1-B CHRONOLOGY OF GUN-CONTROL LEGISLATION

Federal government actions on gun-control laws.

Date	Action
1927	Pistols and other concealable firearms are disallowed from the mails.
1928–1963	No action taken. All gun-control legislation defeated.
1963	Major effort to pass gun-registration law in wake of President Kennedy's assassination is defeated.
1968	Interstate shipment of mail-order firearms is prohibited.
1972	Senate passes bill outlawing manufacture of cheap, handguns. As of 1973 this legislation is still pending.

Note: Many states have gun-control laws, but these vary tremendously in degree of regulation.

SOURCE: *Editorial Research Reports,* pp. 541—560, July 19, 1972.

TABLE 7.2-A PUBLIC ATTITUDE TOWARD THE DEATH PENALTY

"Are you in favor of the death penalty for murder?"

Year	For Capital Punishment	Against	No Opinion
1936	62%	33%	5%
1937	60	33	7
1953	68	25	7
1960	51	36	13
1965	45	43	12
1966	42	47	11
1969	51	40	9
1970	50	41	9
1972	57	32	11
1973*	59	31	10

* The 1973 figure is from Harris Survey data. The Harris question was "Do you believe in capital punishment (death penalty) or are you opposed to it."

SOURCE: Gallup Poll. Cited in "The Polls: Capital Punishment," compiled by Hazel Erskine, *Public Opinion Quarterly,* vol. 34, p. 291, 1970.

TABLE 7.2-B GOVERNMENT POLICY ON CAPITAL PUNISHMENT

State Action

1846-1917—Five states abolish (and do not reinstate) capital punishment.
1964-1969—Oregon, West Virginia, Iowa, Vermont, New York, and New Mexico eliminate or virtually eliminate capital punishment.
1972—California Supreme Court invalidates the use of capital punishment.
1973—Several states move to write legislation regulating capital punishment to abide by Supreme Court ruling that capital punishment is unconstitutional except where specifically mandated or punishment for a specific crime.

Federal Action

1972—In *Furman* v. *Georgia* Supreme Court rules that capital punishment violates the Constitution. This decision is interpreted to mean that states can reinstate capital punishment only if it is mandated (not left to judge's discretion) for specific offenses.
1973—Nixon proposes reinstatement of capital punishment for certain federal crimes.

History of Executions

1930-1967: 3,859
1967-1972: 0

SOURCE: *Congressional Digest*, January, 1973.

TABLE 7.3 PUBLIC OPINION ON ANTI-POLLUTION TAX INCENTIVES

Year	For	Against	No Opinion
1967	63%	25%	12%
1968	57	29	14
1970	58	34	8

SOURCE: Opinion Research Corporation. Cited in "The Polls: Pollution and Industry," compiled by Hazel Erskine, *Public Opinion Quarterly,* vol. 36, p. 279, 1972.

POLICY: On December 23, 1970, the U.S. Treasury Department ruled that companies can write off pollution-control equipment in five years if equipment was installed or acquired in 1970 or after. In effect, this policy provides a tax incentive to install antipollution equipment.

TABLE 7.4 PUBLIC OPINION ON AMNESTY

Public opinion on amnesty for those who left the country to avoid the draft.

Year	Favor Amnesty	Oppose Amnesty	No Opinion
1972 (June)	36%	60%	4%
1973 (Feb.)	29	67	4

SOURCE: Gallup Poll.
POLICY: As of July, 1973, amnesty to draft evaders had not been granted.

TABLE 7.5-A PUBLIC SUPPORT FOR GOVERNMENT ASSISTANCE IN HEALTH CARE

Year	Support Government Assistance*
1936	79%
1937	80
1938	81
1942	78
1956	68
1960	75
1964	64
1968	67

*Percentages exclude those without opinions or those who give qualified answers. Questions varied somewhat from year to year, but all involve government assistance to those in need of assistance.

SOURCE: 1936 to 1942 figures are from Michael E. Schlitz, *Public Attitudes towards Social Security 1935–1965* (Washington: U.S. Government Printing Office, 1970), p. 128. Other data are from the Survey Research Center, University of Michigan.

TABLE 7.5-B FEDERAL GOVERNMENT POLICY ON HEALTH CARE ASSISTANCE

Year	Action Taken
1935	Roosevelt considers federally operated national health insurance program, but does not submit it to Congress.
1943	Wagner-Dingell bill proposing payroll tax based on compulsory national health insurance introduced but is defeated by Congress.
1945	Truman proposes comprehensive health insurance based on Social Security. No action taken.
1949	After bitter congressional fight, Truman proposals are defeated. Social Security Act is amended to provide federal grants to states for some payments of medical expenses for people on public assistance.
1954	Forand Bill raising Social Security payments to provide old-age health insurance is defeated by Congress.
1960	Kerr-Mills bill passed extending 1949 matching-grants program.
1962	Kennedy proposals for federally subsidized old-age health care insurance defeated by Senate.
1963–1964	Medicare, government medical insurance for the aged, passes Senate.
1965	Medicare, which provides medical assistance for the aged, passes House and is signed into law. Medicaid program in which federal government contributes to states for medical assistance to needy (regardless of age) is also enacted.
1971	Nixon and others introduce various government assisted health care programs, but no action taken.
1974	Comprehensive medical insurance program proposed by Nixon administration. It would combine public and private financing.

TABLE 7.6-A PUBLIC SUPPORT FOR FEDERAL INTERVENTION IN SCHOOL INTEGRATION

"Some people say that the government in Washington should see to it that white and Negro children are allowed to go to the same schools. Others claim that this is not the government's business."

Year	Favors Federal Government Involvement	Opposes Federal Government Involvement	Don't Know
1956	46.6%	51.9%	1.5%
1960	49.9	46.9	3.2
1964	49.7	46.3	4.0
1968	45.7	52.5	1.8
1970	56.5	41.8	1.7
1972	44.5	53.7	1.8

SOURCE: Survey Research Center, University of Michigan.

TABLE 7.6-B FEDERAL GOVERNMENT ACTIONS IN INTERVENING IN SCHOOL DESEGREGATION

Year	Action Taken
1954–5	Supreme Court rules in *Brown* v. *Board of Education* that schools must be racially integrated with "all deliberate speed."
1954–1963	Attorney General files *amicus curiae* ("friend of the court") briefs in desegregation cases in support of racial integration.
1964	Civil Rights Act of 1964 is passed which prohibits discrimination in federally assisted programs and also allows Attorney General to intervene directly in desegregation cases.
1965	Department of Health, Education and Welfare issues guidelines under which nonintegrated schools would lose federal funds.
1966	HEW approves desegregation plans in which individual students are given "freedom of choice" in deciding which school to attend
1968	Supreme Court rejects "freedom of choice" plans unless they lead to desegregation. HEW rejects "freedom of choice" alternative.
1968	Federal funds terminated in 123 Southern school districts by HEW. 1970 deadline is set for racial integration.
1969	Supreme Court rules that racially dual school systems must be terminated "at once."
1970	HEW reacts to banning of dual systems by formulating more aggressive desegregation guidelines.
1972	HEW relaxes demands on immediate school integration. Nixon administration wins mild ban on school busing, but Senate kills total ban on busing to achieve racial integration.

TABLE 7.7-A PUBLIC SATISFACTION WITH LEVELS OF DEFENSE SPENDING*

Year	Increase Spending	Decrease Spending	Keep Same	No Opinion
1952	29%	26%	25%	20%
1953	22	20	45	12
1960	21	18	45	16
1971	11	50	31	8
1972	9	35	40	9[†]

*In 1952 the question was "Do you think the Government should spend more money or less money for defense purposes." In other years the questions were along the lines of whether what the federal government in Washington spends for national defense should be increased, kept about the same, or reduced.

[†]In 1972 the alternative "ended altogether" was offered, and 5% agreed with this position.

SOURCE: Gallup Poll.

TABLE 7.7-B   FEDERAL EXPENDITURES FOR NATURAL DEFENSE (1952 to 1973)

Year	Expenditure for National Defense (in billions)	Total Federal Expenditures (in billions)
1952	44.0	65.4
1953	50.4	74.3
1954	46.9	67.8
1960	45.7	77.2
1961	51.1	88.4
1971	77.7	211.4
1972	78.0	236.6
1973	81.7	280.4

SOURCE: U.S. Bureau of the Census, *Statistical Abstract of the United States,* 1973; U.S. Bureau of the Census, *Historical Statistics of the United States, Colonial Times to 1957 and Construction to 1962 and Revisions.*

TABLE 7.8-A   PUBLIC SATISFACTION WITH FEDERAL INCOME TAX LEVELS

"Do you regard the income tax that you will have to pay this year as fair?"

	Fair	Unfair
1943 (Feb.–Mar.)	85%	15%
1944 (Feb.)	90	10
1945 (March)	85	15
1946 (Feb.–Mar.)	62	38

"Do you consider the amount of Federal income taxes which you have to pay too high, about right, or too low?"

	Too High	About Right	Too Low	No Opinion
1948 (Mar.)	57	38	1	4
1949 (Mar.)	43	52	1	4
1950 (Feb.)	56	40	—	4
1951 (Feb.)	52	43	1	4
1952 (Feb.)	71	26	—	3
1957 (Apr.)	61	31	—	8
1959 (Mar.)	51	40	1	8
1961 (Feb.)	46	45	1	8
1962 (Feb.)	48	43	—	9
1966 (Feb.)	52	39	—	9
1967 (Mar.)	58	38	1	3
1969 (Mar.)	69	25	—	6
1973 (Mar.)	65	28	1	6

SOURCE: Gallup Poll.

TABLE 7.8-B FEDERAL INDIVIDUAL INCOME TAX RATES, 1944 to 1972

Taxable Income*	1944-1945	1948-1949	1952-1953	1954-1963	1964	1965-1967	1968	1969	1970	1971-1972 single	1971-1972 joint
2001–4000	25	19	25	22	20	19	21	21	20	19	19
4001–6000	29	23	29	26	24	22	24	24	23	21	22
6001–8000	33	26	34	30	27	25	27	28	26	24	25
8001–10,000	37	30	38	34	31	28	30	31	29	25	28
10,001–12,000	41	33	42	38	34	32	34	35	33	27	32
12,001–14,000	46	38	48	43	38	36	39	40	37	29	36
14,001–16,000	50	41	53	47	41	39	42	43	40	31	39

*Income after exclusions, deductions, and exemptions.
SOURCE: U.S. Bureau of the Census, Statistical Abstract of the United States, 1973, Washington, D.C., p. 391.

TABLE 7.9-A PUBLIC OPINION ON VIETNAM INVOLVEMENT

"In view of the developments since we entered the fighting in Vietnam, do you think the United States made a mistake sending troops to fight in Vietnam?

Year	Yes	No	No Opinion
1965 (Aug.)	24%	61%	15%
1966 (Sept.)	35	48	17
1967 (July)	41	48	11
1968 (Aug.)	53	35	12
1969 (Sept.)	58	32	10
1970 (May)	56	36	8
1971 (May)	61	28	11
1973 (Jan.)	60	29	11

SOURCE: Gallup Poll.

TABLE 7.9-B GOVERNMENT POLICY IN VIETNAM (1965 to 1973)

Date	Action
1965 (Feb.)	Bombing of North Vietnam begins.
1965 (June)	U.S. troops engage directly in fighting.
1966 (Mar.)	Senate attempt to repeal Tonkin Gulf Resolution is defeated.
1967 (Sept.)	Johnson promises to end bombing when productive peace talks begin.
1968 (Jan.)	Major Communist offensive begins (Tet offensive).
1968 (Mar.)	Johnson announces he will not run for reelection and is ordering a bombing halt over 75 percent of North Vietnam.
1968 (May)	Peace talks begin in Paris.
1968 (Oct.)	Bombing totally halted.
1969 (Nov.)	Nixon announces that all U.S. troops will be withdrawn according to a secret timetable.
1970 (Apr.)	United States invades Cambodia.
1970 (Oct.)	Nixon proposes in-place ceasefire.
1972 (Mar.)	Nixon suspends Paris talks after his proposal is rejected.
1972 (Mar.)	Major North Vietnamese invasion of South begins.
1972 (May)	United States mines North Vietnam harbors.
1972 (July)	Paris peace talks resume.
1973 (Jan.)	Vietnam settlement reached.

TABLE 7.9-C AMERICAN INVOLVEMENT IN VIETNAM FIGHTING

Year	Troops Killed	Military Assistance (millions of dollars)	Number of Troops (as of Dec. 31 of each year)
1965	1,369	268.9	184,300
1966	5,008	861.8	385,300
1967	9,378	1,203.5	485,600
1968	14,592	1,054.4	536,100
1969	9,414	1,608.2	475,200
1970	4,221	1,689.4	334,600
1971	1,380	1,856.9	156,800
1972	300	1,849.4	24,100

SOURCE: *Congressional Quarterly,* January 27, 1973, for 1965–1972. *Congressional Quarterly,* May 11, 1974.

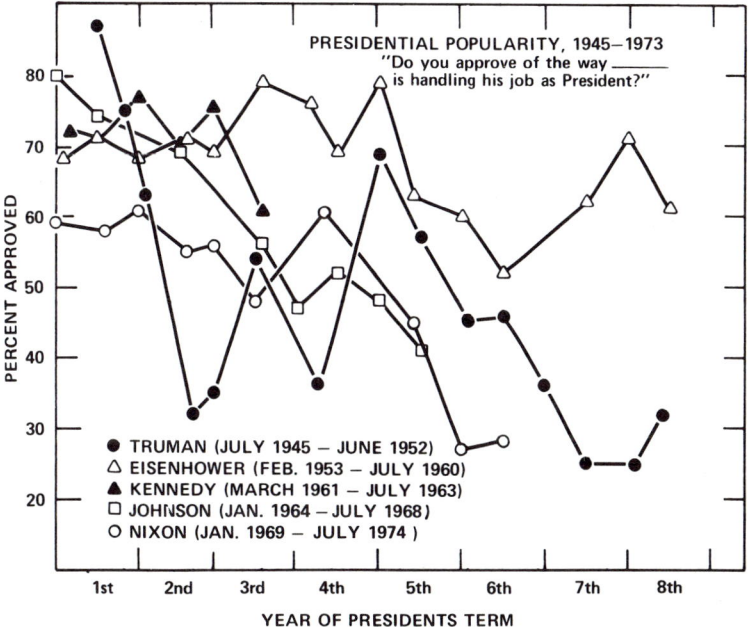

FIG. 7.1 Presidential popularity by year in office, 1945–1973. (Source: Gallup Poll.)

For further information:

You may wish to obtain more recent information about public opinion or governmental action. The best sources for current information are:

Gallup Opinion Index. Monthly reports of Gallup polls available from 1946 to 1950 and 1960 to the present. Individual Gallup polls and the polls by the Harris and Roper organizations are listed by year in *The Reader's Guide* and the *New York Times Index*.

Public Opinion Quarterly. Published quarterly and each issue since 1960 contains a section bringing together polls conducted by various organizations on a particular subject.

Congressional Quarterly Almanac (published yearly) and *Congressional Quarterly Special Reports* give congressional and presidential decisions on particular bills, as well as more general governmental policy decisions. *Congress and the Nation 1945–1964* and *Congress and the Nation 1965–1968* (Washington: *Congressional Quarterly,* 1965 and 1969) provide extensive summaries of government policy.

Statistical Abstract of the United States. (Published annually by the U.S. Government Printing Office) offers a wealth of information on such matters as tax policy, education, and housing.

Additional material on other issues may be found in the following:

Public Opinion Poll Data

Chandler, Robert: *Public Opinion* (New York: R. R. Bowker Company, 1972). Presents the findings of numerous polls on a variety of political topics during the late 1960s.

Free, Lloyd A., and Hadley Cantril: *The Political Beliefs of Americans* (New Brunswick, N.J.: Rutgers University Press, 1963).

The Gallup Poll: Public Opinion 1935–1971 (3 vols.) (New York: Random House, Inc., 1971). Lists all polls from 1935 to 1971 with an excellent index in vol. 3.

The Harris Survey Yearbook of Public Opinion 1970 (New York: Random House, Inc., 1971).

Polls. Published quarterly from 1965 to 1968 and reports a large number of foreign and American opinion surveys, including those conducted by American polling organizations.

Public Opinion 1935–1946. Edited by Hadley Cantril. (Princeton, N.J.: Princeton University Press, 1951).

Stouffer, Samuel: *Communism, Conformity and Civil Liberties* (Garden City, N.Y.: Doubleday & Company, Inc., 1955). Focuses on attitudes toward civil liberties during the early 1950s.

Analyses of American Public Opinion

Bogart, Leo: *Silent Politics* (New York: Wiley-Interscience, 1972).

Dawson, Richard E.: *Public Opinion and Contemporary Disarray* (New York: Harper & Row, Publishers, Incorporated, 1973).

Devine, Donald J.: *The Attentive Public: Polyarchial Democracy* (Chicago: Rand McNally & Company, 1970).

Erikson, Robert S., and Norman Luttbeg: *American Public Opinion: Its Origins, Content and Import* (New York: John Wiley & Sons, Inc., 1973).

Lane, Robert E., and David O. Sears: *Public Opinion* (Englewood Cliffs, N.J.: Prentice-Hall, Inc., 1964).

Data on Government Decisions

The Book of the States (published annually by the Council of State Governments, Lexington, Ky.) lists detailed information on state government policy.

III. ANALYZING THE DATA

We have presented a very large quantity of information dealing with public opinion and government policy. To help you analyze these data, we have prepared questions on specific tables and graphs. Answer only those questions (or parts of questions) that are directly relevant to your analysis of the reformulation. Correct answers to each question are found on page 142.

Question 1

Tables 7.1-A and 7.1-B show public opinion on a law requiring a police permit for purchasing a gun and a brief history of federal legislation in this area. Did a majority of the public favor such controls during the time period described in Table 7.1-A? What was the federal government's actual policy during this period?

Your Answer

Question 2
Do the data in Table 7.2-A show that between 1936 and 1973 majorities of citizens have always oppose the death penalty for murder? To what extent during this period has capital punishment been completely prohibited by law?

Your Answer

Question 3
Tables 7.3 and 7.4 present opinion data on the issues of tax incentives for antipollution equipment and amnesty for draft evaders. What has been the public's position on these issues? In which cases has the government enacted laws consistent with popular preference?

Your Answer

Question 4
Do the data in Table 7.5-A showing public support for government medical assistance to the needy indicate that such support has emerged only recently? According to the information in Table 7.5-B, when did the federal government decide to help those in need of medical assistance?

Your Answer

Question 5
How would you describe the overall thrust of public opinion on the question of federal intervention in school desegregation (Table 7.6-A)? Is the public in favor? opposed? largely undecided? Do the data in Table 7.6-B indicate that the federal government maintains a "hands-off" policy on this question?

Your Answer

Question 6
On the whole, do the data in Table 7.7-A indicate a consistent public desire to increase defense spending? Has defense spending increased during the period described in Table 7.7-B?

Your Answer

Question 7
How has the public viewed income tax levels since 1943 (Table 7.8-A)? Have tax rates been judged too high? about right? or too low? Do the income tax rates described in Table 7.8-B indicate overall increases or decreases in income tax rates?

Your Answer

142 Political Analysis

Question 8

According to the data in Table 7.9-A, at what time did public opinion come to believe that the Vietnam war was a mistake? Did the actions of the government (Tables 7.9-B and 7.9-C) change noticeably when public opinion shifted to thinking the war a mistake?

Your Answer

Question 9

Figure 7.1 depicts presidential popularity from 1945 to 1974. Has the American public generally been satisfied with the way Presidents have conducted themselves? What does this say about the policies enacted by these Presidents?

Your Answer

Correct Answers

1. From 1959 to 1972 a clear majority of the public endorsed requiring a police permit for ownership of a gun. Table 7.1-B indicates, however, that the only federal action during this period was the prohibiting of interstate shipment of firearms through the mails. Nevertheless, as Table 7.1-B notes, many states do regulate gun ownership. Thus at least in some places public sentiment on gun control is followed, but there certainly is no national gun-registration policy.

2. Except in 1965 and 1966, majorities of the American public have favored the death penalty for murder, although from 1960 to 1970 opinion was generally more closely divided than for the other years for which data are presented. Nevertheless, in 1972 the Supreme Court ruled that the imposition of capital punishment was to be severely limited in *Furman* v. *Georgia*. The number of prisoners executed also dropped dramatically.

3. The data in Tables 7.3 and 7.4 show majorities in favor of tax reductions for antipollution equipment and against amnesty for draft evaders. In the case of a tax credit for antipollution equipment, government action is in accordance with opinion. The same is true with the amnesty issue, although here it is government inaction that produces the congruency between opinion and policy.

4. Data on support for government assistance in health care show that majorities favored such assistance from 1936 to 1968. Table 7.5-B shows that it was not until 1949 that some, and then only very limited, federal government medical assistance to the needy was authorized. With the passage of Medicare and Medicaid legislation in the 1960s such assistance was greatly extended.

5. The data on the public's desire for federal government intervention in school desegregation do not show a clear, overtime pattern. In 1970 a majority favored national government action; in 1956, 1968, and 1972 majorities opposed such action. A larger proportion favored intervention than noninvolvement in 1960 and 1964, but no majority preference existed. The events described in Table 7.6-B indicate greater government involvement in the 1960s and early 1970s, but the trend is not always clear. For example, in 1966 HEW approved "freedom of choice plans" as a desegregation alternative. These plans, which typically lead to racial segregation, were subsequently prohibited by HEW. Overall, the government has been involved in implementing racial integration, but the strength of this effort has varied considerably.

6. Table 7.7 clearly shows a widespread public reluctance to increase defense spending during the indicated years. Note, however, that only in 1971 did a majority exist for any other alternative. On the whole, the data in Figure 7.1 show that defense spending has increased from 1952 to 1973 though not as rapidly as total federal expenditures. A careful analysis of Table 7.7 and Figure 7.1 shows that in three of the five years we have data for (1952, 1960, 1972) an increase in spending occurred, though no majority desired that policy. Defense spending fell between 1953 and 1954, a policy favored by only 20 percent in 1953. Finally, 50 percent of the people in 1971 desired a decrease in spending, but it remained about the same.

7. Table 7.8-A shows that between 1943 and 1946 most people accepted the income tax they paid as "fair." However, between 1948 and 1973, only once (1949) did a majority consider their federal income taxes "about right." Except for 1961 and 1962 the tax rate has been considered too high. The evidence on tax rates (Table 7.8-B) does not reveal a clear trend. Except for 1952–1953, tax rates declined from 1944 to 1967; they increased in 1968 and 1969, and then started to decline again in 1970. Of course, during this time period income levels increased so one's tax bracket changed, and this

meant paying more money in taxes (even if tax rates declined). In sum, no obvious parallel exists between public satisfaction with tax rates and the rates themselves.

8. The public opinion data in Table 7.9-A show that by August, 1968, a majority came to believe that our involvement in Vietnam was a mistake. We can also see in Tables 7.9-B and 7.9-C that 1968 was the turning point in government policy. For example, in March of 1968 Johnson ordered a bombing halt over 75 percent of North Vietnam, and peace talks in Paris were begun in May of 1968. Table 7.9-C shows our troop commitment (and number of casualties) declined from 1968 onward after having increased in each of the preceding three years.

9. Figure 7.1, which shows presidential popularity from 1945 to 1974, indicates that on most occasions the President is viewed as doing a good job. Ratings of presidential competence fell below the 50 percent level only in 14 of 58 instances (24.1 percent). We cannot, however, infer that these ratings indicate that Presidents enact programs desired by the public. The question in these polls concerned the way a President handled his job, not the popularity of Presidential policy. It is possible for the public to give high ratings where Presidents completely disregarded popular sentiment. Note also the precipitous decline in President Nixon's popularity as the Watergate scandal unfolded. This decline appears more closely related to public confidence in the integrity of the administration rather than a reflection of dismay with particular domestic or foreign policies of the Nixon administration.

Chapter 7
Public Opinion

Name _____

Section _____

IV. CONCLUSION

You have now completed the preliminary steps in the analysis of this chapter's problem. The final step consists of writing a memorandum on the relationship between public opinion and government policy. Wherever possible use specific data to support your conclusions. Do not merely repeat your answers to the short questions in section III; combine individual pieces of data into a coherent essay on public opinion and public policy.

Original Problem

"In the United States, the government reflects public opinion."

Memorandum

Chapter 8
POLITICAL SOCIALIZATION

For some people there is a close connection between democracy and education. They argue that a democracy cannot work unless the population of a nation is well educated. If people cannot read and write, discuss things knowledgeably, and know how a government works, the chances for democracy are not good. For these people, one of the most urgent tasks in the developing nations of Africa and Asia is to build an extensive educational system so that people will know how to participate in politics and not be influenced by false arguments of demagogues and would-be dictators.

Though this reasoning may seem convincing at first, critics of it have pointed to many countries which are not democracies but have well-educated citizens. The Soviet Union and East Germany, for example, have attained high educational levels; yet both are dictatorships. These critics claim that the amount of education itself is not as important as the content of the instruction. It is not the "three R's" and other kinds of factual knowledge which lead to democracy but discussions of "citizenship training" and the "democratic environment" in the classroom which make the crucial difference.

This chapter's problem is:

"A democratic and politically active citizenry depends on our system of public education."

To assist you in your analysis, this chapter is divided into different sections. Complete instructions for each section are found at the beginning of the section.

I. REFORMULATING THE PROBLEM

The first step in analyzing an ambiguous proposition is reformulating it into a more precise statement. Unless that is done, the problem cannot be correctly analyzed. This section presents four reformulations of the chapter's problem. Some are acceptable; others are unacceptable. An acceptable reformulation meets the following criteria:

1. Reformulations must be factual, not value statements; i.e., they can be proved or disproved with empirical data.

2. Terms and concepts in a reformulation must be concrete and specific. You must know what to look for in obtaining data.

3. Reformulations must take into account all the relevent aspects of a problem, and not oversimplify into a one-variable solution.

4. Finally, the reformulation must be relevant to the original problem. An analysis of the reformulation would be an answer to the original problem.

Indicate whether each of the reformulations below is *acceptable* or *unacceptable*. Where unacceptable, briefly explain why. When you have given answers for all four reformulations, compare your answers with the correct ones that follow your answers.

Original Statement

"A democratic and politically active citizenry depends on our system of public education."

Reformulations

1. Relatively well-educated citizens (high school graduates and above) show greater support for traditional democratic values (e.g., freedom of speech, the right to hold unpopular opinions, and the right to advance peacefully one's political cause) than those with less education. Well-educated citizens are also more politically active than those with less education, as measured by activities such as voting or belonging to political organizations.

2. Wherever we find examples of faulty civic education we are also likely to find a lack of democratic and civic responsibility among citizens.

3. The essence of democratic education should be the development of strong character and a sense of fair play. Because American education emphasizes these traits, we have a citizenry tolerant of traditional democratic values (e.g., free speech) and willing to share the responsibilities of government (e.g., vote and belong to organizations).

4. Those citizens who have received "civics training" in school (i.e., instruction in politics and history) are more appreciative of traditional democratic values (e.g., free speech) and more politically active (e.g., vote more often) than those without such exposure.

Your Answers
1.

2.

3.

4.

Correct Answers

1. Acceptable. This reformulation transforms the original assertion that a democratic and politically active citizenry depends on education into a relationship between these citizen characteristics and the amount of education an individual receives. Thus, the more schooling, the greater the extent of democratic beliefs and political activism. Note that all important terms (e.g., "relatively well-educated," "politically active") are concretely defined (or clarified by specific examples).

2. Unacceptable. This reformulation contains numerous undefined and vague terms. What do we mean by "faulty" education? What is "civic responsibility"? These terms must be defined more clearly before this reformulation would be useful.

3. Unacceptable. This reformulation begins with a value statement—". . . democratic education *should* be . . ." Also, terms such as "strong character" and "sense of fair play" remain undefined. Finally, it is asserted that American education emphasizes strong character and sense of fair play. This assertion must be demonstrated before claiming that American education produces democratic and active citizens because of its stress on the values.

4. Acceptable. This reformulation approaches the original problem in terms of the content, as opposed to the amount, of education. While the first reformulation distinguishes between well-educated and less well-educated, this reformulation suggests that *what* is taught makes the difference in democratic values and activism. As in the first reformulation, terms like "political activism" are clearly defined.

This section, unlike the one in Chapter 7, contains two adequate reformulations. Each approaches the original problem from a different perspective, yet each is a valid interpretation of the original problem. Given the broad, unspecific character of many statements about politics it should be clear that researchers can (and do) focus on different aspects of the identical problem. Depending on one's interests, these two adequate reformulations can be kept distinct or combined into a broader, more encompassing one dealing with both the amount of schooling and the impact of "civics courses" on democratic values and political participation.

II. SELECTING THE NECESSARY DATA

In section I you modified the original problem so that it could be tested with data. The next step is deciding on the specific data necessary for such a test. You decide on the needed data in advance, because without some concrete idea of what you need, you would waste much time in examining data which will later prove to be irrelevant.

Below the correct reformulations is a list of different kinds of data. Only some of these data are necessary to test the reformulations. In deciding which data are necessary, keep in mind the following rules:

1. Avoid looking for vague and general kinds of data. What you need should be as specific and concrete as possible.

2. Choose data that are probably available. You do not know in advance exactly what is available, but try to limit yourself to things that are either of public record or are frequently researched by political scientists.

3. The data you need must be related to the reformulation. Data that are not related to the reformulation are useless.

4. The data should be sufficient to test the reformulated problem and provide an adequate answer to the original problem.

Below each item, indicate which data are necessary and which are unnecessary. Briefly state your reasons for evaluating the data as you do. When you finish, compare your answers with the correct ones following your answers.

Reformulations

A. Relatively well-educated citizens (high school graduates and above) show greater support for traditional democratic values (e.g., freedom of speech, the right to hold unpopular opinions, and the right to advance peacefully one's political cause) than those with less education. Well-educated citizens are also more politically active than those with less education, as measured by activities such as voting or belonging to political organizations.

B. Those citizens who have received "civics training" in school (i.e., instruction in politics and history) are more appreciative of traditional democratic values (e.g., free speech) and more politically active (e.g., vote more often) than those without such exposure.

What Data Are Needed to Analyze Your Reformulation?

1. Data on the relationship between educational effort (e.g., school expenditures, pupil-teacher ratios, etc.) and scholastic achievement.
These data are [necessary, unnecessary] because:

2. Data on the impact of "civics courses" on students' attitudes toward democratic values and their political participation.
These data are [necessary, unnecessary] because:

3. Analysis of the importance of certain types of schools in the careers of important American political leaders.
These data are [necessary, unnecessary] because:

4. Data on educational levels, rates of political activism, and extent of support for democratic values for a number of nations including the United States.
These data are [necessary, unnecessary] because:

5. Public opinion polls on support for traditional democratic values subdivided according to level of education.
These data are [necessary, unnecessary] because:

6. Political-participation data (e.g., percent of the population belonging to a political club) subdivided according to level of education.
These data are [necessary, unnecessary] because:

Correct Answers

1. Unnecessary for either reformulation. Both reformulations deal with support for democratic values and political activism, so information on scholastic achievement is irrelevant. Such data could be relevant for a different reformulation that linked democratic politics to citizen competence (defined as scholastic achievement [e.g., mathematical proficiency]).

2. Necessary for the second, but not the first, reformulation. Such data would compare students who have taken civics course with those who have not, or measure support for democratic values and political activism before and after taking civics.

3. Unnecessary for either reformulation. It may be necessary to have the "right" education to attain political prominence in the United States, and this fact may say something about American democracy, but such information is irrelevant to this chapter's problem.

4. Unnecessary for either reformulation. Neither reformulation makes crossnational comparisons. However, an alternative reformulation could be: "Nations with lower educational levels than the United States are less democratic and have lower levels of citizen political participation than the United States. If this were the reformulation, these data would be necessary.

5. Necessary for the first, but not the second, reformulation.

6. Necessary for the first, but not the second, reformulation. The need for these data, and the data on support for democratic values, is self-evident from the reformulation. This is one characteristic of a well-conceived reformulation—the required data are easily specified.

The Data

On the following pages are some of the data you need to analyze this chapter's problem. Some of the data may be relevant to the problem; other data may be irrelevant. After you have examined each table and decided whether it is necessary to test the reformulation, turn to section III, which immediately follows the data.

TABLE 8.1 EFFECT OF SEMESTER COURSE IN CIVIC EDUCATION ON POLITICAL ATTITUDES OF HIGH SCHOOL STUDENTS IN THREE CITIES

	Before Course	After Course
City of "Alpha"*		
Political Attitude		
Support of democratic creed[†]	62%[‡]	89%
Political chauvinism[§]	23	8
Support of political participation	70	72
City of "Beta"*		
Political Attitude		
Support of democratic creed[†]	56%[‡]	74%
Political chauvinism[§]	31	19
Support of political participation	55	56
City of "Gamma"*		
Political Attitude		
Support of democratic creed[†]	47%[‡]	59%
Political chauvinism[§]	29	10
Support of political participation	32	29

* The names used here are pseudonyms for three cities in the Boston metropolitan area. "Alpha" is an upper-middle-class town, "Beta" a lower-middle-class town, and "Gamma" a working-class community.

† Democratic creed as used here refers to the belief in the rights of citizens and minorities to attempt to influence government through nontyrannical procedures.

‡ Each figure is the percentage of the sample strongly holding the political attitude.

§Political chauvinism is the glorification of American political institutions, procedures, and public figures. It is the belief that America has a monopoly on democracy and "good government."

SOURCE: Adapted from Edgar Litt, "Civic Education, Community Norms, and Political Indoctrination," *American Sociological Review*, vol. 28, no. 1, February, 1963.

TABLE 8.2 RELATIONSHIP BETWEEN NUMBER OF CIVICS COURSES TAKEN AND GOOD CITIZENSHIP ATTITUDES AMONG NEGRO AND WHITE HIGH SCHOOL STUDENTS

Students were asked the question: "People have different ideas about what being a good citizen means. We're interested in what you think. Tell me how you would describe a good citizen in this country—that is, what things about a person are most important in showing that he is a good citizen."

Number of Civics Courses Taken	Negroes Stressing:			
	Loyalty	Participation	Total	N
0	51%	49	100%	41
1 or more	75%	25	100%	85

Number of Civics Courses Taken	Whites Stressing:			
	Loyalty	Participation	Total	N
0	46%	54	100%	395
1 or more	39%	61	100%	803

SOURCE: By permission from Kenneth P. Langton and M. Kent Jennings, "Political Socialization and the High School Civics Curriculum in the United States," *American Political Science Review,* vol. 62, p. 863, September, 1968.

TABLE 8.3 NUMBER OF CIVICS COURSES TAKEN AND PERCENTAGE GIVING CORRECT RESPONSES TO QUESTIONS ON THE IDEOLOGICAL POSITIONS OF THE DEMOCRATIC AND REPUBLICAN PARTIES AMONG NEGRO AND WHITE HIGH SCHOOL STUDENTS

Number of Civics Courses Taken	Percent Giving Correct Responses		N
	Negro	White	
0	0%	29%	543
1 or more	19	31	1,184

SOURCE: By permission from Kenneth P. Langton and M. Kent Jennings, "Political Socialization and the High School Civics Curriculum in the United States," *American Political Science Review,* vol. 62, p. 863, September, 1968.

TABLE 8.4 EFFECTS OF TWO DIFFERENT KINDS OF COLLEGE INTRODUCTORY POLITICAL SCIENCE COURSES ON STUDENT ATTITUDES TOWARD PERSONAL POLITICAL PARTICIPATION

Year of Course	Kind of Course	No. of Students	Average Initial Score	Average Final Score
1953-1954	Standard*	60	72.5[†]	72.1
	Participation-oriented (a)[‡]	17	76.1	74.2
1954-1955	Standard	95	70.8	72.0
	Participation-oriented (b)	45	69.3	70.5
1955-1956	Standard	24	74.1	74.9
	Participation-oriented (c)	22	64.9	70.3
	Participation-oriented (d)	35	68.9	71.3

* The "standard" course is the traditional introductory course, which places a major stress on American government, with some attention to political theory and foreign political institutions.

[†] Each figure is the mean score for the entire class on a political-participation scale; the higher the score, the more a student favors participation.

[‡] "Participation-oriented" classes contained much of the same factual information as the "standard" course, but in addition, students heard talks by actual political leaders and were given many opportunities to participate in actual groups and campaigns. Each of the four courses was somewhat different.

SOURCE: By permission from Alber Somit, Joseph Tanenhaus, Walter H. Wilke, and Rita W. Cooley, "The Effect of the Introductory Political Science Course on Student Attitudes toward Personal Political Participation," *American Political Science Review*, vol. 52, p. 1130, December, 1958.

TABLE 8.5 THE DEVELOPMENT OF SUPPORT FOR DEMOCRATIC VALUES BETWEEN 6TH AND 12TH GRADES IN TWO CALIFORNIA COMMUNITIES

| | Grade | | |
Democratic Value	6th	9th	12th
1. Freedom of speech	1.82*	2.23	2.40[†]
2. Majority rule	2.00	2.06	2.11
3. Importance of elections	2.26	2.47	2.76
4. Minority rights	2.75	3.09	3.13

* Numbers are mean scores.

[†] On freedom-of-speech questions, scores ranged from 1 to 3, with the higher score indicating greater support for freedom of speech. For the other democratic values the scores ranged from 1 to 4, the latter being the most democratic.

SOURCE: By permission from Richard M. Merelman, *Political Socialization and Educational Climates* (New York: Holt, Rinehart and Winston, Inc., 1971) p. 77.

TABLE 8.6 PERCEPTION OF QUALITIES OF GOOD ADULT CITIZENS BY GRADE

Grade Level	Qualities of Good Citizens		
	Votes and Gets Others To Vote	Helps Others	Interested in Way Country Is Run
4	26.4%*	47.8%	28.2%
5	29.8	42.1	41.8
6	35.8	35.4	50.5
7	35.9	34.2	52.7
8	44.6	26.3	65.0

* Percentages are proportion of children choosing each alternative. More than one choice was permitted so percentage could add to more than 100%.
SOURCE: By permission from Robert D. Hess and Judith V. Torney, *The Development of Political Attitudes in Children* (Chicago: Aldine Publishing Co., 1968), p. 46.

TABLE 8.7 PARTICIPATION IN POLITICAL DISCUSSION AND READING ABOUT POLITICS, BY GRADE

Grade	Activity			
	Talked with Parents about Country's Problems	Talked with Parents about Candidate	Talked with Friends about Candidate	Read about Candidate
3	57%	52%	49%	60%
4	59	62	57	75
5	66	77	76	88
6	71	80	81	92
7	73	84	87	95
8	72	85	89	95

SOURCE: By permission from Robert D. Hess and Judith V. Torney, *The Development of Political Attitudes in Children* (Chicago: Aldine Publishing Co., 1968), pp. 81 and 100.

TABLE 8.8 "DEMOCRATIC" RESPONSES TO BASIC PRINCIPLES OF DEMOCRACY

Attitude	Total	Education* High	Low
Disagree that only informed should vote	49.0%	61.7%	34.7%
Disagree that Negro should be barred from office	80.6	89.7	68.6
Agree to allow antireligious speech	63.0	62.9	46.5
Agree to allow communist speech	44.0	62.9	23.5
N =	244	137	106

* "High education" means more than 12 years schooling; "low education" is 12 or less.

SOURCE: James W. Prothro and Charles M. Gregg, "Fundamental Principles of Democracy," *Journal of Politics,* vol. 22, 1960. The sample consisted of 144 voters in Ann Arbor, Michigan, and 100 voters in Tallahassee, Florida.

TABLE 8.9 TOLERANCE OF PROTEST AND CIVIL DISOBEDIENCE, BY EDUCATION (1972)

Political Action	Education			
	Grade School	Some High School	High School Graduate	Some College
1. Approve participating in protest marches permitted by local authorities	10.3%	9.1%	16.0%	33.0%
2. Approve of person going to jail to protest unfair law	10.5	12.4	16.3	23.4
3. Approve use of demonstrations to disrupt government activity	4.3	4.9	6.8	13.3

SOURCE: Survey Research Center, University of Michigan. Based on 1972 random sample of Americans of voting age.

TABLE 8.10 POLITICAL PARTICIPATION, BY EDUCATION (1972)

Activity	Education			
	Grade School	Some High School	High School Graduate	Some College
Voted	57.8%	60.8%	75.3%	86.6%
Attended political meetings	2.6	3.7	6.4	13.3
Displayed campaign button or bumper sticker	5.6	9.6	10.3	17.6
Ever wrote to public official	8.4	12.9	21.7	37.1
Interested in public affairs	43.4	49.4	58.8	75.5
Tried to influence other people's vote	14.2	22.6	22.8	38.6

SOURCE: Survey Research Center, University of Michigan. Based on random sample of Americans of voting age in 1972.

For further information you may wish to consult one of the following references:

Early Political Learning

Easton, David, and Jack Dennis: *Children in the Political System* (New York: McGraw-Hill Book Company, 1969).

Gallatin, Judith, and Joseph Adelson, "Legal Guarantees of Individual Freedom," *Journal of Social Issues,* vol. 27, 1971.

Greenstein, Fred I.: *Children and Politics* (New Haven, Conn.: Yale University Press, 1965).

Hess, Robert D., and Judith V. Torney: *The Development of Political Attitudes in Children* (Chicago: Aldine Publishing Co., 1968).

Langton, Kenneth: *Political Socialization* (New York: Oxford University Press, 1969).

Remmers, H. H., and Richard D. Franklin: "Sweet Land of Liberty," in *Anti-Democratic Attitudes in American Schools* (Evanston, Ill.: Northwestern University Press, 1963).

Zellman, Gail L., and David O. Sears: "Childhood Origins of Tolerance of Dissent," *Journal of Social Issues* vol. 27, 1971.

The Impact of School

Almond, Gabriel, and Signey Verba: *The Civic Culture* (Princeton, N.J.: Princeton University Press, 1963), chap. 12 (chap. 11 in paperback edition).

Ehrman, Lee H.: "An Analysis of the Relationship of Selected Educational Variables with the Political Socialization of High School Students," *American Educational Research Journal,* vol. 6, pp. 559—580, 1969.

Jacob, Philip E.: *Changing Values in College* (New York: Harper and Row, Publishers, Incorporated, 1957).

McClintock, C. G., and Henry A. Turner: "The Impact of College upon Political Knowledge Participation and Values," *Human Relations,* vol. 15, pp. 163–176, 1959.

Newcomb, Theodore M.: *Personality and Social Change: Attitude Formation in a Student Community* (New York: The Dryden Press, Inc., 1943).

Stember, C. M., *Education and Attitude Change.* (New York: Institute of Human Relations Press, 1961).

Differences among Educational Groups with Various Educational Levels

Most book-length studies of American public opinion and politcal participation give some attention to educationally related differences. Among others, see:

Campbell, Angus, Philip E. Converse, Warren E. Miller, and Donald Stokes, *The American Voter* (New York: John Wiley & Sons, Inc., 1960).

Key, V. O., Jr.: *Public Opinion and American Democracy* (New York: Alfred A. Knopf, Inc., 1963), chap. 13.

Milbrath, Lester: *Political Participation* (Chicago: Rand McNally & Company, 1965).

Verba, Sidney, and Norman H. Nie: *Participation in America* (New York: Harper & Row, Publishers, Incorporated, 1972).

III. ANALYZING THE DATA

To help you analyze these data on political socialization, we have prepared questions on specific tables. Answer only those questions (or parts of questions) that are directly relevant to your analysis of the reformulation. Correct answers to each question are found on p. 163.

Question 1

Tables 8.1 to 8.3 show the results of high school civics courses on different kinds of attitudes and knowledge.

A. In Table 8.1, what was the influence of the civics course on the three political attitudes in the three cities?

B. According to the data in Table 8.2, what was the influence of the civics course on the opinions of Negroes regarding what makes a good citizen? What were the results with white students?

C. Table 8.3 shows the impact of civics courses on whites' and Negroes' knowledge of the ideological differences between the Democratic and Republican parties. How much of an impact did the civics courses have?

Yours Answers

Question 2
Do the data in Table 8.4 demonstrate any impact of basic political science courses in attitude toward political activism?

Your Answer

Question 3
Table 8.5 shows the extent of support for certain democratic values in 6th, 9th, and 12th grades in two communities. Do children become more democratically oriented the longer they remain in school?

Your Answer

Question 4
Children's political beliefs and pre-adult political activity are depicted in Tables 8.6 and 8.7. To what extent do they become more participation oriented between 4th and 8th grades? To what extent does the school play a role in this change?

Your Answer

Question 5
Do the data in Table 8.8 show a consistent relationship between education and support for democratic values? Is there a similar pattern in Table 8.9 which shows tolerance for civil disobedience?

Your Answer

Question 6
According to Table 8.10, does political activity increase with education? Is this true for different types of political activity?

Your Answer

Correct Answers

1A. The data in Table 8.1 show that in all three cities the civics course increased support for democratic values and decreased political chauvinism, but had very little or no effect on support for political participation. The data also show that the students in "Alpha"—the upper-middle-class city—began with more support for democratic values, less chauvinism, and more support for political participation than the students in the other cities (this pattern is also true after the civics class).

1B. Negroes who had taken no civics courses were about evenly divided on what makes a good citizen: half stressed loyalty, half stressed participation. Among those having taken one or more civics courses, 75 percent stressed loyalty compared with 25 percent emphasizing participation. The white students who had taken no civics courses were about evenly divided. However, among those having taken one or more courses, 61 percent stressed participation compared with 39 percent stressing loyalty.

1C. No Negroes who had not taken a civics course could correctly identify the ideological positions of the two parties. Among those who had taken one or more such courses, 19 percent gave the correct answer. Among whites, however, those who took civics courses did little better than those who had not. Notice that while the civics courses had a greater value for Negroes, the courses did not eliminate the initial differences between whites and Negroes. Notice also that only 31 percent of the white students knew the ideological differences between the two parties.

2. The data in Table 8.4 show that in six of seven cases, the introductory political science course had little or no influence on attitudes toward participation, regardless of whether the course was "standard" or "participation oriented." The only exception is one participation-oriented class in 1955–1956. Here there was a difference of 5.4 between the initial and final scores. In other participation-oriented classes there was little difference in scores.

3. Each of the four democratic values shows an increase between 6th and 12th grade. Table 8.5 also shows a considerable range of support for these values. For example, at all three grade levels support for minority rights is much closer to the democratic end of the continuum than is support for freedom of speech.

4. Tables 8.6 and 8.7 show a consistent trend toward participatory beliefs and behavior between 4th and 8th grade. However, this is not to say that the schools are responsible for these changes. Additional schooling may result in these attitudinal and behavioral shifts, but more data are required before such a conclusion can be verified.

5. The data in Table 8.8 show that a greater proportion of well-educated people supports the democratic values presented in the table. . While 61.7 percent of the well-educated disagree with the idea that only the "informed" should vote, only 34.7 of the less well-educated disagree. More than three-fifths of the well-educated (62.9 percent) would allow an antireligious speech, compared with fewer than half of those with less than 12 years schooling (46.5 percent). Notice, however, that even among the well-educated, there are relatively large numbers (almost 40 percent in two cases) who give the "undemocratic" response. A similar pattern exists in Table 8.9. With only a single, small exception, support for various forms of civil disobedience increases with the number of years of schooling.

6. Table 8.10 clearly shows that as education increases so do rates of political involvement. Regardless of the measure of participation, better-educated citizens are more active than those with less education.

Chapter 8
Political Socialization

Name _____

Section _____

IV. CONCLUSION

Having reformulated the original statement and analyzed the relevant data, you can now return to the original problem. In the space below, write a short memorandum on education and support for democracy and political activism. Where possible, support your conclusions with specific data. Do more than repeat your answers to the short questions in section III. Combine individual pieces of data into a coherent essay and, when relevant, use information from additional souces. If you use additional sources of data, indicate the source.

Original Problem

"A democratic and politically active citizenry depends on our system of public education."

Memorandum

Chapter 9
POLITICAL PARTIES

A subject that has received much attention in recent years is the apparent similarity of American political parties. Some observers of American politics claim that the Republican and Democratic parties cannot be distinguished from one another. For them it makes no difference which party is in office or controls Congress, since both represent the same thing. On the other hand, there are others who insist that the two parties are different. The Republican and Democratic parties, they argue, may not differ on everything or differ as sharply as some would want, but they are far from identical.

The statement to be examined deals directly with that issue:

"The Democratic and Republican parties are so similar that citizens are offered no meaningful choices."

As in the preceding chapters, this chapter contains a number of sections which guide the analysis of the statement to be examined.

I. REFORMULATING THE PROBLEM

The first step in analyzing an ambiguous statement about politics is to reformulate it into a more precise one. Below are four reformulations of this chapter's proposition; some of them are acceptable and others are not. If you do not remember the criteria for acceptable reformulations, refer to p. 147 in the previous chapter. If you understand the criteria, examine the following reformulations and indicate why each is acceptable or unacceptable. Then check your answers with the correct ones on p. 169.

Original Statement:
"The Democratic and Republican parties are so similar that citizens are offered no meaningful choices."

Reformulations

1. Leaders of both parties as well as partisan supporters all endorse basic American values and the political status quo.

2. Democratic and Republican public officials do not differ in terms of the policies they pursue. Democratic officials such as congressmen or state governments dominated by Democrats are no different than their Republican counterparts on such policies as public welfare payment, tax rates, and other policies perceived as liberal or conservative by political organizations.

3. The fundamental similarity of the two parties is demonstrated by the fact that whatever party controls the national government (i.e., the Presidency and Congress) there is no shift either to socialism or free enterprise capitalism.

4. There is no difference between the two parties since both appeal to the same types of people and the same policy interests. Thus, those identifying themselves as Democrats do not differ from Republicans in terms of social class, religion, race, and other social characteristics or in terms of policy preferences on such issues as civil rights or government intervention in the economy.

Your Answers
1.

2.

Political Parties   169

3.

4.

Correct Answers

1.   Unacceptable. For this reformulation to be of use, key terms such as "basic American values" must be made more specific and concrete. What data would you need to test whether Democrats and Republicans differed on "basic American values"? The phrase "political status quo" is also too vague. This could be an acceptable reformulation if these terms were made much more specific and concrete.

2.   Acceptable. This reformulation focuses on the policies enacted by the two parties and how groups with well-known political points of view rate party behavior. The areas of policy agreement/disagreement are specifically spelled out—policies relating to welfare expenditures, tax rates, or those on which political organizations have taken a stand. These types of data are also either public record (e.g., legislation, public expenditures) or are readily available, as in the case of organization ratings of government actions.

3. Unacceptable. Like the first reformulation, this one could be made acceptable if certain key terms were better defined. Specifically "socialism" and "free enterprise capitalism" have to be spelled out in greater detail.

4. Acceptable. This reformulation approaches partisan similarities in terms of the characteristics and policy preferences of those identifying with the two parties. These types of characteristics are specifically listed and are the type of information frequently asked on public opinion polls.

As in the previous chapter (Political Socialization) we have two different reformulations of the same problem. Each approaches the basic issue from a different perspective, yet each is a valid interpretation of this problem. These differing reformulations can, of course, be kept separate or combined into a broader, more encompassing reformulation dealing with both party policies and characteristics and preferences of partisan supporters.

II. SELECTING THE NECESSARY DATA

The next step in your analysis is selecting appropriate information. You should list the data you need before beginning your search for it, because you will otherwise search aimlessly and are likely to collect irrelevant or redundant information.

Below are listed some of the data you might consider obtaining for your analysis. If you are uncertain about the criteria for selecting appropriate data, review p. 151 of the previous chapter. Then examine each of the data sets listed below and indicate why you think they would be necessary or unnecessary for your analysis. First, however, write down the reformulation you will analyze.

Your Reformulation

Required Data

What Data Are Needed To Analyze Your Reformulation?

1. A comparison of Republican and Democratic supporters according to such personal and social characteristics as social class, race, and religion. These data are [necessary, unnecessary] because:

2. Data on the organizational structure and activities of the Democratic and Republican parties.
These data are [necessary, unnecessary] because:

3. Comparisons of public policies (e.g., welfare expenditures) in Democratic and Republican controlled states.
These data are [necessary, unnecessary] because:

4. Political organizations' ratings of congressional votes divided according to political party.
These data are [necessary, unnecessary] because:

5. Data on the policy preferences (e.g., positions on foreign involvement) of Democratic and Republican supporters.
These data are [necessary, unnecessary] because:

Political Parties 173

6. Long-term voting data for presidential and congressional elections divided according to voter partisan identification.
These data are [necessary, unnecessary] because:

Correct Answers
1. Necessary for the second, but not the first, reformulation. Note, however, that certain terms in this data list must be further defined. What, for example, is a Democratic "supporter"? Someone who *votes* for the party or someone who considers himself to be a Democrat? A similar problem occurs with specifying "social class"? Do we use income or a person's own perceptions of social status as the indicator of social class? If you were collecting original data, these important questions would have to be concretely answered before gathering any data. However, in searching for existing data, some degree of imprecision may have to be tolerated in order to take into account differing definitions employed by other researchers.

2. Unnecessary for either reformulation. The organization nature and behavior of the two parties are irrelevant to these reformulations. Had the reformulation stated that the two parties were organizationally similar, then these data would be necessary.

3. Necessary for the first, but not the second, reformulation. As in the first set of data, further specification is necessary. Thus, the meaning of control has to be spelled out. Does control mean that one party has 51 percent (or 60 percent, etc.) of the legislative seats in both houses of a state legislature plus control of the governorship? As before, however, these details usually must wait until examining the actual data.

4. Necessary for the first, but not the second, reformulation. A number of organizations with clear-cut policy preferences (e.g., Americans for Democratic Action, Americans for Constitutional Action) rate the voting behavior of individual congressmen, and these ratings are readily available either through these groups' publications or in studies of Congress.

5. Necessary for second, but not first, reformulation. These data plus the ones in the first data set above are the two indicators of "similarity" of the second reformulation.

6. Unnecessary for either reformulation. Such data would not say whether either reformulation was true or false. Would knowing that in the last 30 years the Democrats have won more votes than the Republicans say anything meaningful about party differences?

The Data

In the following pages are some of the data you need to analyze this chapter's problem. Some of the data may be relevant to the problem; other data may be irrelevant. After you have examined each table and graph and decided whether it is necessary to test the reformulation, turn to section III, which immediately follows the data.

TABLE 9.1 VOTE FOR PRESIDENT BY SOCIAL GROUPS IN 1964, 1968, AND 1972

	Percent Favoring Democrats		
Social Group	1964 (Johnson)	1968 (Humphrey)	1972 (McGovern)
Entire nation	61%	43%	38%
Race			
Whites	59	38	32
Nonwhites	94	85	87
Education			
College	52	37	37
High school	62	42	34
Grade school	66	52	49
Occupation			
Professional and business	54	34	31
White collar	57	41	36
Manual	71	50	43
Farmers	53	29	—
Religion			
Protestants	55	35	30
Catholics	76	59	48

SOURCE: Gallup Poll.

TABLE 9.2 POLITICAL PARTY PREFERENCE
BY SOCIAL GROUPS, 1968 AND 1972

	Percent Favoring Democrats*	
Social Group	1968	1972
Race		
White	42.5	40.1
Black	88.5	66.1
Education		
Some college	30.6	35.0
High school graduate	48.6	41.8
Some high school	58.6	49.8
Grade school	67.6	56.6
Religion		
Protestant	48.7	40.7
Catholic	55.5	53.5
Jewish	57.9	57.4

* Percent based on those giving partisan preference and claiming to be Independents.

SOURCE: Survey Research Center, University of Michigan.

TABLE 9.3 PARTISAN AFFILIATION AND SUPPORT FOR
WITHDRAWAL FROM VIETNAM WAR, 1968 AND 1972

	1968		1972	
Issue Position	Democrats	Republicans	Democrats	Republicans
Favors withdrawal	47.5%	44.4%	70.3%	43.8%
Favors greater military action	52.5	55.6	29.7	56.2
Total	100.0%	100.0%	100.0%	100.0%
N =	440	225	717	381

SOURCE: Survey Research Center, University of Michigan.

TABLE 9.4 PARTISAN AFFILIATION AND SUPPORT FOR GOVERNMENT ASSISTANCE IN MEDICAL CARE, 1968 AND 1972

	1968		1972	
Issue Position	Democrats	Republicans	Democrats	Republicans
Supports government assistance	80.0%	45.4%	57.9%	38.4%
Opposes government assistance	20.0	54.6	42.1	61.6
Total	100.0%	100.0%	100.0%	100.0%
N =	676	293	390	237

SOURCE: Survey Research Center, University of Michigan.

TABLE 9.5 PARTISAN AFFILIATION AND POSITION ON FEDERAL GOVERNMENT'S ROLE IN SCHOOL INTEGRATION, 1968

	1968	
Issue Position	Democrats	Republicans
Favors federal enforcement of school integration	59.7%	39.6%
Opposes federal enforcement	40.3	60.4
Total	100.0%	100.0%
N =	673	298

SOURCE: Survey Research Center, University of Michigan.

TABLE 9.6 PARTY AFFILIATION AND PERCENTAGE LIBERAL RESPONSE OF DELEGATES TO 1968 NATIONAL PARTY CONVENTION

	Democrats	Republican	Difference
1. Public employees should not have the right to strike for higher wages.	69% (N = 185)	28% (N = 165)	40%
2. The best way to deal with people who break the law is to punish them so they fear the consequence of breaking it again.	49 (185)	18 (166)	31
3. Law-enforcement agencies should be allowed limited eavesdropping by wiretapping and other devices.	50 (187)	21 (166)	29
4. The United States should give help to countries even if they are not as much against communism as we are.	79 (185)	52 (159)	27
5. People who advocate radical changes in our way of life are overprotected by our laws.	63 (185)	39 (166)	24
6. School children should be bused to achieve racial balance in elementary and secondary schools.	33 (179)	10 (168)	23
7. Communism today has changed greatly, and we must recognize that most wars and revolutions are not communist inspired.	38% (184)	17 (169)	21
8. One has a moral responsibility to disobey laws he believes are unjust.	17 (186)	4 (169)	13
9. Vietnam is historically and geographically an Asian country and should be allowed to develop autonomously within the Asian sphere of power.	64 (181)	71 (155)	-7

SOURCE: John W. Soule and James W. Clark, "Issue Conflict and Consensus: A Comparative Study of Democratic and Republican Delegates to the 1968 National Conventions," *Journal of Politics,* Vol. 33 p. 78, February, 1971.

DEMOCRATIC—1972 PLATFORM—*Economic Policy*

Jobs, Income and Dignity. Full employment—a guaranteed job for all—is the primary economic objective of the Democratic Party. The Democratic Party is committed to a job for every American who seeks work. Only through full employment can we reduce the burden on working people. We are determined to make economic security a matter of right. This means a job with decent pay and good working conditions for everyone willing and able to work and an adequate income for those unable to work. It means abolition of the present welfare system.

To assure jobs and economic security for all, the next Democratic Administration should support:

—A full employment economy, making full use of fiscal and monetary policy to stimulate employment.

—Tax reform directed toward equitable distribution of income and wealth and fair sharing of the cost of government.
—Full enforcement of all equal employment opportunity laws, including federal contract compliance and federally regulated industries and giving the Equal Employment Opportunity Commission adequate staff and resources and power to issue cease and desist orders promptly.
—Vastly increased efforts to open education at all levels and in all fields to minorities, women and other under-represented groups.
—An effective nationwide job placement system to enhance worker mobility.
—Opposition to arbitrarily high standards for entry to jobs.
—Overhaul of current manpower programs to assure training—without sex, race of language discrimination—for jobs that really exist with continuous skill improvement and the chance for advancement.
—Economic development programs to ensure the growth of communities and industry in lagging parts of the nation and the economy.
—Use of federal depository funds to reward banks and other financial institutions which invest in socially productive endeavors.
—Improved adjustment assistance and job creation for workers and employers hurt by foreign competition, reconversion of defense-oriented companies, rapid technological change and environmental protection activities.
—Closing tax loopholes that encourage the export of American jobs by American-controlled multinational corporations.
—Assurance that the needs of society are considered when a decision to close or move an industrial plant is to be made and that income loss to workers and revenue loss to communities does not occur when plants are closed.
—Assurance that, whatever else is done in the income security area, the social security system provides a decent income for the elderly, the blind and the disabled and their dependents, with escalators so that benefits keep pace with rising prices and living standards.
—Reform of social security and government employment security programs to remove all forms of discrimination by sex, and race.
—Adequate federal income assistance for those who do not benefit sufficiently from the above measures.

REPUBLICAN—1972 PLATFORM—Economic Policy

The Road Ahead. We will continue to pursue sound economic policies that will eliminate inflation, further cut unemployment, raise real incomes, and strengthen our international economic position.

We will fight for responsible Federal budgets to help assure steady expansion of the economy without inflation.

We have already removed some temporary controls on wages and prices and will remove them all once the economic distortions spawned in the late 1960's are repaired. We are determined to return to an unfettered economy at the earliest possible moment.

We affirm our support for the basic principles of capitalism which underline the private enterprise system of the United States. At a time when a small but dominant faction of the opposition Party is pressing for radical economic schemes which so often have failed around the world, we hold that nothing has done more to help the American people achieve their unmatched standard of living than the free enterprise system.

It is our conviction that government of itself cannot produce the benefits to individuals that flow from our unique combination of labor, management and capital.

We will continue to promote steady expansion of the whole economy as the best route to a long-term solution of unemployment.

We will devote every effort to raising productivity, primarily to raise living standards but also to hold down costs and prices and to increase the ability of American producers and workers to compete in world markets.

In economic policy decisions, including tax revisions, we will emphasize incentives to work, innovate and invest; and research and development will have our full support.

We are determined to improve Federal manpower programs to reduce unemployment and increase productivity by providing better information on job openings and more relevant job training. Additionally, we reaffirm our commitment to removing barriers to a full life for the mentally and physically handicapped, especially the barriers to rewarding employment. We commit ourselves to the full educational opportunities and the humane care, treatment and rehabilitation services necessary for the handicapped to become fully integrated into the social and economic mainstream.

We will press on for greater competition in our economy. The energetic antitrust program of the past four years demonstrates our commitment to free competition as our basic policy.

DEMOCRATIC—1972 PLATFORM—Defense

We propose a program of national defense which is both prudent and responsible, which will retain the confidence of our allies and which will be a deterrent to potential aggressors.

Military strength remains an essential element of a responsible international policy. America must have the strength required for effective deterrence.

But military defense cannot be treated in isolation from other vital national concerns. Spending for military purposes is greater by far than federal spending for education, housing, environmental protection, unemployment insurance or welfare. Unneeded dollars for the military at once add to the tax burden and pre-empt funds from programs of direct and immediate benefit to our people. Moreover, too much that is now spent on defense not only adds nothing to our strength but makes us less secure by stimulating other countries to respond.

Needless projects continue and grow, despite evidence of waste, military ineffectiveness and even affirmative danger to real security. The "development" budget starts pressure for larger procurement budgets in a few years. Morale and military effectiveness deteriorate as drugs, desertion and racial hatreds plague the armed forces, especially in Vietnam.

The Democratic Party pledges itself to maintain adequate military forces for deterrence and effective support of our international position. But we will also insist on the firm control of specific costs and projects that are essential to ensure that each defense dollar makes a real contribution to national security. Specifically, a Democratic Administration should:

—Plan military budgets on the basis of our present needs and commitments, not past practices or force levels.

—Stress simplicity and effectiveness in new weapons and stop gold-plating and duplication which threaten to spawn a new succession of costly military white elephants; avoid commitment to new weapons unless and until it becomes clear that they are needed.

—Reduce overseas bases and forces.

By these reforms and this new approach to budgeting, coupled with a prompt end to U.S. involvement in the war in Indo-China, the military budget can be reduced substantially with no weakening of our national security. Indeed a leaner, better-run system will mean added strength, efficiency and morale for our military forces.

Workers and industries now dependent on defense spending should not be made to pay the price of altering our priorities. Therefore, we pledge reconversion policies and government resources to assure jobs and new industrial opportunities for all those adversely affected by curtailed defense spending.

REPUBLICAN—1972 PLATFORM—Defense

For the Future. We will continue the sound military policies laid down by the President—our policies which guard our interests but do not dissipate our resources in vain efforts to police the world. As stated by the President:

—We will maintain a nuclear deterrent adequate to meet any threat to the security of the United States or of our allies.

—We will help other nations develop the capability of defending themselves.

—We will faithfully honor all of our treaty commitments.

—We will act to defend our interests whenever and wherever they are threatened.

—But where our vital interests or treaty commitments are not involved our role will be limited.

We are proud of the men and women who wear our country's uniform, especially of those who have borne the burden of fighting a difficult and unpopular war. Here and now we reject all proposals to grant amnesty to those who have broken the law by evading military service. We reject the claim that those who fled are more deserving, or obeyed a higher morality, than those next in line who served in their places.

In carrying out our defense policies, we pledge to maintain at all times the level of military strength required to deter conflict, to honor our commitments to our allies, and to protect our people and vital interests against all foreign threats. We will not let America become a second-class power, dependent for survival on the good will of adversaries.

We will continue to pursue arms control agreements—but we recognize that this can be successful only if we maintain sufficient strength and will fail if we allow ourselves to slip into inferiority.

DEMOCRATIC—1972 PLATFORM—Crime

So that Americans can again live without fear of each other the Democratic Party believes:

—There must be equally stringent law enforcement for rich and poor, corporate and individual offenders.

—Citizens must be actively involved with the police in a joint effort.

—Police forces must be upgraded, and recruiting of highly qualified and motivated policemen must be made easier through federally assisted pay commensurate with the difficulty and importance of their job, and improved training with comprehensive scholarship and financial support for anyone who is serving or will contract to serve for an appropriate period of police service.

—The complex job of policing requires sensitivity to the changing social demands of the communities in which police operate.

—We must provide the police with increased technological facilities and support more efficient use of police resources, both human and material.

—When a person is arrested, both justice and effective deterrence of crime require that he be speedily tried, convicted or acquitted, and if convicted, promptly sentenced. To this end we support financial assistance to local courts, prosecutors, and independent defense counsel for expansion, streamlining, and upgrading, with trial in 60 days as the goal.

—To train local and state police officers, a Police Academy on a par with the other service academies should be established as well as an Academy of Judicial Administration.

—We will support needed legislation and action to seek out and bring to justice the criminal organizations of national scope operating in our country.

—We will provide leadership and action in a national effort against the usage of drugs and drug addiction, attacking this problem at every level and every score in a full scale campaign to drive this evil from our society. We recognize drug addiction as a health problem and pledge that emphasis will be put on rehabilitation of addicts.

—We will provide increased emphasis in the area of juvenile delinquency and juvenile offenses in order to deter and rehabilitate young offenders.

—There must be laws to control the improper use of handguns. Four years ago a candidate for the presidency was slain by a handgun. Two months ago, another candidate for that office was gravely wounded. Three out of four police officers killed in the line of duty are slain with handguns. Effective legislation must include a ban on sale of handguns known as Saturday night specials which are unsuitable for sporting purposes.

REPUBLICAN—1972 PLATFORM—Crime

Our goal is justice—for everyone.

We pledge a tireless campaign against crime—to restore safety to our streets, and security to law-abiding citizens who have a right to enjoy their homes and communities free from fear.

We pledge to:

—Continue our vigorous support of local police and law enforcement agencies, as well as Federal law enforcement agencies.

—Seek comprehensive procedural and substantive reform of the Federal Criminal Code.

—Accelerate the drive against organized crime.

—Increase the funding of the Federal judiciary to help clear away the logjam in the courts which obstructs the administration of justice.

—Push forward in prison reform and the rehabilitation of offenders.

—Intensify efforts to prevent criminal access to all weapons, including special emphasis on cheap, readily-obtainable handguns, retaining primary responsibility at the State level, with such Federal law as necessary to enable the States to meet their responsibilities.

—Safeguard the right of responsible citizens to collect, own and use firearms for legitimate purposes, including hunting, target shooting and self-defense. We will strongly support efforts of all law enforcement agencies to apprehend and prosecute to the limit of the law all those who use firearms in the commission of crimes.

—We pledge to seek further international agreements to restrict the production and movement of dangerous drugs.

—We pledge to expand our programs of education, rehabilitation, training, and treatment. We will do more than ever before to conduct research into the complex psychological regions of disappointment and alienation which have led many young people to turn desperately toward drugs.

—We firmly oppose efforts to make drugs easily available. We equally oppose the legalization of marijuana. We intend to solve problems, not create bigger ones by legalizing drugs of unknown physical impact.

—We pledge the most intensive law enforcement war ever waged. We are determined to drive the pushers of dangerous drugs from the streets, schools, and neighborhoods of America.

DEMOCRATIC—1972 PLATFORM—Environment

Choosing the Right Methods of Environmental Protection. The problem we face is to choose the most efficient, effective and equitable techniques for solving each new environmental problem. We cannot afford to waste resources while doing the job, any more than we can afford to leave the job undone.

—We must enforce the strict emission requirements on all pollution sources set under the 1970 Clean Air Act.

—We must support the establishment of a policy of no harmful discharge into our waters by 1985.

—We must have adequate staffing and funding of all regulatory and enforcement agencies and departments to implement laws, programs and regulations protecting the environment, vigorous prosecution of violators and a Justice Department committed to enforcement of environmental law.

—We must fully support laws to assure citizen's standing in federal environmental court suits.

—Where appropriate, taxes need to be levied on pollution to provide industry with an incentive to clean up.

—Strict interstate environmental standards must be formulated and enforced to prevent pollution from high-density population areas being dumped into low-density population areas for the purpose of evasion of strict pollution enforcement.

—The National Environmental Policy Act should be broadened to include major private as well as public projects, and a genuine commitment must be made to making the Act work.

—Our environment is most threatened when the natural balance of an area's ecology is drastically altered for the sole purpose of profits. Such practices as "clear cut" logging, strip mining, the indiscriminate destruction of whole species, creation of select ocean crops at the expense of other species, and the unregulated use of persistent pesticides cannot be justified when they threaten our ability to maintain a stable environment.

—Where appropriate, taxes need to be levied on pollution, to provide industry with an incentive to clean up.

We also need to develop new public agencies that can act to abate pollution —act on a scale commensurate with the size of the problem and the technology of pollution control.

Expanded federal funding is required to assist local governments with both the capital and operating expenses of water pollution control and solid waste management.

REPUBLICAN—1972 PLATFORM—Environment

We call upon the Congress to act promptly on the President's environmental proposals still stalled there—more than 20 in all. These include:

—Legislation to control, and in some cases prohibit, the dumping of wastes into the oceans, estuaries and the Great Lakes.

—A federal Noise Control Act to reduce and regulate unwanted sound from aircraft, construction and transportation equipment.

—Authority to control hundreds of chemical substances newly marketed each year.

—Legislation to encourage the States to step up to pressing decisions on how best to use land. Both environmentally critical areas such as wetlands and growth-inducing developments such as airports would have particular scrutiny.

—A proposal to provide for early identification and protection of endangered wildlife species. This would, for the first time, make the taking of endangered species a Federal offense.

   —Establishment of recreational areas near metropolitan centers such as the Gateway National Recreational Area in New York and New Jersey and the Golden Gate National Recreation Area in and around San Francisco Bay.

The nostalgic notion of turning the clock back to a simpler time may be appealing but is neither practical nor desirable. We are not going to abandon the automobile, but we are going to have a clean-burning engine.

We are not going to give up electric lighting and modern industry, but we do expect cleanly-produced electric power to run them.

We are not going to be able to do without containers for our foods and minerals, but we can improve them and make them reusable or biodegradable.

We pledge a workable balance between a growing economy and environmental protection. We will resolve the conflicts sensibly within that framework.

We commit ourselves to comprehensive pollution control laws, and rigorous research into the technological problems of pollution control. The beginnings we have made in these first years of the 1970's are evidence of our determination to follow through.

We intend to leave the children of America a legacy of clean air, clean water, vast open spaces and easily accessible parks.

TABLE 9.7   PARTY UNITY SCORES* IN CONGRESS, 1968–1972

	Year				
	1968	1969	1970	1971	1972
Democrats	57%	62%	57%	62%	57%
Republicans	63	62	59	66	64

* Party Unity Scores are the proportion of times the average Democrat and Republican voted with his party against a majority of the other party.

SOURCE: *Congressional Quarterly Weekly Report,* p. 3018, November 18, 1972.

TABLE 9.8 PARTISAN CONTROL AND PUBLIC POLICY WITHIN THE STATES

	Partisan Control*			
Policy Area	Democratic Control	Mixed but Democratic Stronger	Mixed but Republican Stronger	Republican Control
1. Average (mean) aid for Dependent Children payment per recipient (as of June 1971)	$ 33.95	$ 48.91	$ 51.00	$ 51.49
2. Average (mean) Public Assistance payment per recipient (fiscal year 1970–1971)	17.13	23.18	19.14	22.25
3. Average (mean) Unemployment benefit per recipient (fiscal year 1971–1972)	44.70	46.99	48.86	31.18
4. Per capita state tax revenue (1971) (1971)	248.73	258.83	230.67	261.34
5. Per capita state expenditure for higher education (fiscal year 1971–1972)	37.17	35.80	40.88	40.81
Number of states	16	12	9	10

* Partisan control was based on party control of the two houses of the state legislature and the governorship in 1970. Where a party controlled only one of these three institutions, the state was considered "mixed." Nebraska which has a unicameral state legislature was not included as was Michigan where partisan control was evenly divided.

SOURCE: The Council of State Governments: *The Book of States 1972–1973*, vol. 19, pp. 238, 327, 383, 384, 539, Lexington, Ky., 1973.

TABLE 9.9 THE RELATIONSHIP BETWEEN DEMOCRATIC PARTY CONTROL AND STATE POLICY OUTCOMES, CONTROLLING FOR LEVEL OF ECONOMIC DEVELOPMENT (1961)

	Democratic Control					
	Lower Houses		Upper Houses		Governorship	
Policy	Simple Correlation	Partial* Correlation	Simple Correlation	Partial* Correlation	Simple Correlation	Partial* Correlation
Per pupil expenditures in education	-.47	-.06	-.43	.06	-.58	-.18
Per capita welfare expenditure	.01	-.08	.06	.02	-.12	-.23
Unemployment benefits	-.51	-.13	-.51	-.11	-.53	.00
Old-age Assistance benefits	-.64	-.49	-.64	-.44	-.59	-.28
Adi to Dependent Children benefits	-.64	-.55	-.65	-.47	-.68	-.44

* The partial correlation coefficients control for the effects of urbanization, industrialization, income and education levels within the states. Where the coefficients approach zero, there is no relationship between Democratic control and the policy indicators. Where a substantial correlation coefficient persists in the partials, the control variables account for only part of the relationship.

SOURCE: Adapted from Thomas R. Dye: *Politics, Economics and the Public* (Chicago: Rand McNally & Company, 1966), p. 244.

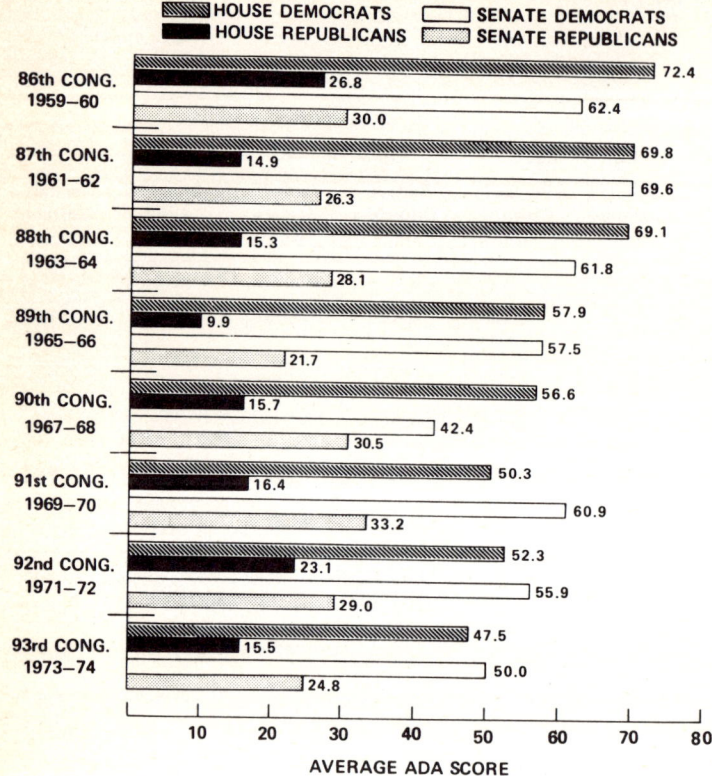

For further information you may wish to consult one of the following references:

Party in the Electorate
Alford, Robert R.: *Party and Society* (Chicago: Rand McNally & Company, 1963).
Campbell, Angus, Philip E. Converse, Warren E. Miller, and Donald E. Stokes: *The American Voter* (New York: John Wiley & Sons, Inc., 1960).
———: *Elections and the Political Order.* (New York: John Wiley & Sons, Inc., 1966).
Flanigan, William H.: *Political Behavior of the American Electorate,* 2d ed. (Boston: Allyn and Bacon, Inc., 1972).
Free, Lloyd A., and Hadley Contril: *The Political Beliefs of Americans* (New Brunswick, N.J.: Rutgers University Press, 1967), chap. 9 (Political Identification).
Key, V. O., Jr.: *The Responsible Electorate* (Cambridge, Mass.: The Belknap Press of Harvard University Press, 1966.
Ladd, Everett, C., Jr., and Charles D. Hadley: "Party Definition and Party Differentiation," *Public Opinion Quarterly,* vol. 37, pp. 21–34, 1973.
McClosky, Herbert, Paul Hoffman, and Rosemary O'Hara: "Issue Conflict and Con-

sensus among Party Leaders and Followers," *American Political Science Review,* vol. 54, pp. 406–427, 1960.

Party in the Legislature

Bone, Hugh A.: *American Politics and the Party System,* 4th ed. (New York: McGraw-Hill Book Company, 1971), chap. 8 (The Party in Legislative and Judiciary).

Jewell, Malcolm E., and Samuel C. Patterson: *The Legislative Process in the United States,* 2d ed. (New York: Random House, Inc., 1973), chap. 17 (Legislative Voting Behavior).

Matthews, Donald R.: *U.S. Senators and Their World* (New York: Vintage Books, Alfred A. Knopf, Inc., 1960), chap. 2 (The Men) and chap. 3 (The Politicians).

Mayhew, David R.; *Party Loyalty among Congressmen* (Cambridge, Mass.: Harvard University Press, 1966).

Rieselbach, Leroy N.: *Congressional Politics* (New York: McGraw-Hill Book Company, 1973), chap. 4 (Political Parties in Congress).

Ripley, Randall B.: *Party Leaders in the House of Representatives* (Washington: The Brookings Institution, 1967), chap. 6 (Party Loyalty) and appendix C (Analysis of Party Loyalty Scores).

Sorauf, Frank J.: *Party Politics in America* (Boston: Little, Brown and Company, 1968), chap. 14 (Party and Partisans in the Legislature).

Congressional Quarterly Weekly Reports and *Congressional Quarterly Almanac* (published yearly) both provide data on party voting and programs.

Party Programs

Ginsberg, Benjamin: "Critical Elections and the Substance of Party Conflict: 1844–1968," *Midwest Journal of Political Science,* vol. 16, pp. 603–625, 1972.

Pomper, Gerald M.: *Elections in America* (New York: Dodd, Mead & Company, 1970), chap. 7 ("If Elected, I promise") and chap. 8 (The Fulfillment of Platforms).

National Party Platforms, 1840–1964 and *National Party Platforms: Supplement 1968* compiled by Kirk H. Porter and Donald Bruce Johnson (Urbana: University of Illinois Press, 1966 and 1969).

III. ANALYZING THE DATA

We have presented a considerable amount of data on political parties. To help you analyze these data, we have prepared questions on specific tables and graphs. Answer only those questions (or parts of questions) that are directly relevant to your analysis of the reformulation. Correct answers to each question are found on page 191.

Question 1

Tables 9.1 and 9.2 show support for the Democratic party among various population groups using two different indicators of support (presidential vote and identification). Do the Democrats draw their support equally from all segments of the population? Among what groups is the Democratic party most successful?

Your Answer

Question 2

Tables 9.3 through 9.5 compare Democratic and Republican party identifiers on three policy issues in 1968 and 1972. What proportion of the time do Democrats and Republicans differ from one another on these issues? Are Democrats consistently more likely to adhere to the liberal position on these policy questions?

Your Answer

Question 3

Of the nine questions asked of delegates to the 1968 party conventions (Table 9.6), in how many are the Democratic delegates more liberal than their Republican counterparts? On what proportion of questions do a majority of Democrats oppose a majority of Republicans (i.e., 50+ percent of the Democrats agree with a statement and less than 50 percent of the Republicans agree with the statement).

Your Answer

Question 4A
An examination of the 1972 Democratic party platform in the area of economic policy shows a stress on the role of the federal government in creating work for everyone and eliminating unfair discrimination in hiring. Does the Republican party share these two policy goals?

Your Answer

Question 4B
When we compare the 1972 party platform in defense spending, does one party favor increasing our military spending while the other advocates cutbacks?

Your Answer

Question 4C
On the issue of crime control, do the platforms suggest that the Republicans advocate a highly punitive solution to crime while Democrats focus on social and economic roots of crime?

Your Answer

Question 4D
As indicated in their respective platforms, how much disagreement exists between the two parties in their environmental policy goals?

Your Answer

Question 5
Figure 9.1 displays the ratings given Democrats and Republicans in the House and the Senate. Within each legislative chamber are the Democrats always the more liberal?

Your Answer

Question 6
Congressional parties are sometimes accused of having little or no cohesion. Is this contention supported by the data in Table 9.7 showing party unity scores?

Your Answer

Question 7
Table 9.8 indicates the relationship between five different types of policies and partisan control of state government. Is it true that the greater the Democratic control the greater the expenditures for various policies such as public assistance and higher education? Do Democratic-dominated states also tax more?

Your Answer

Question 8
Table 9.9 shows some of the same data as did Table 9.8 though with different measures and for a different year. In how many instances is there a sizable relationship (greater than .30) between Democratic control and expenditures? When the effects of urbanization, industrialization, income, and educational levels are controlled for, how many of these sizable relationships remain above .30? What does this say about the effects of party control of state government on policy decisions?

Your Answer

Correct Answers
1. The data in Tables 9.1 and 9.2 show that whether the indicator of support is presidential voting or identification, the two parties differ in the types of people they attract. We see in Table 9.1, for example, that Democrats in 1964, 1968, and 1972 did comparatively better among nonwhites, the grade school educated, manual workers, and Catholics. A very similar pattern is exhibited in Table 9.2 except that Jews are the most supportive religious group.

2. The data in Tables 9.3 through 9.5 overall show differences between Democrats and Republicans in their issue positions. For example, in both 1968 and 1972 Democrats were more likely to favor American withdrawal from Vietnam though the difference in 1968 was very small. Moreover, if we

consider the positions of withdrawal from Vietnam, government assistance for medical care, and federal enforcement of school integration as the liberal choices, Democrats tend to be more liberal.

3. The data in Table 9.6 show Democratic convention delegates to be more liberal on eight of the nine questions (the exception being question 9). However, only on questions 1, 3, and 5 do we find a majority of Democrats opposed by a majority of Republicans. On the other questions majorities of both parties are on the same side of the issue.

4A. While the Democratic party platform stresses the role of the national government in controlling unemployment and providing economic security, the Republican party places greater emphasis on private enterprise and economic competition. Also observe that the Democratic platform explicitly calls for efforts to create greater economic equality and spread the benefit of development to all groups and communities. On the other hand, the Republican platform makes no explicit mention of discrimination against women or minorities; only the issue of greater help to the mentally and physically handicapped is discussed.

4B. While the Democrats support a militarily strong defense establishment, they also claim that much of present spending is wasteful and counterproductive. Thus, if necessary reforms were made, defense spending could be reduced while maintaining a strong military position. The Republican platform makes no mention of possible reductions of defense spending. The Republicans stress the necessity of honoring our military commitments.

4C. The platforms on crime control are very similar for both parties. Neither party calls for drastic "get-tough" measures to handle crime nor do the two parties advocate long-term social and economic changes to eliminate the roots of crime. Both parties stress additional police training, firearm control, and more efficient administration of justice as the best means of reducing crime.

4D. The platform data on environmental protection indicate substantial agreement on the desirability of preserving our environment. However, the Democrats are specific in stating what harmful industrial practices should be banned while the Republicans are quick to acknowledge that greater environmental protection does not mean giving up the benefits of industrialized society.

5. Figure 1 shows that the Democratic party is rated more liberal in its voting than the Republican party in both the House and the Senate. We should realize, however, that the ADA ratings are averages for each party, and some Democratic legislators may be more conservative than some Republicans. Also, the ADA rating is based on only a small number of roll-call votes, and thus a different set of votes might produce different results.

6. The party unity scores reported in Table 9.7 show that the two parties tend to vote together against a majority of the other party. However, even when party unity is achieved, many congressmen vote with the other party. In addition, these figures show that from 1968 to 1972 party unity never exceeded 66 percent, which does not suggest a picture of two highly disciplined parties always on opposite sides of each issue.

7. Table 9.8, which depicts the relationship between partisan control and various public policies, does not show the Democratic-controlled states to be the most liberal in public expenditures. In fact, on the first three measures the Democratic controlled states have the lowest expenditure levels. On per capita expenditures for education these states are the second from the lowest (the "Mixed but Democrats Stronger" group spends the least). Nor do the Democratic-controlled states tax more—Republican-controlled and "Mixed but Democrats Stronger" states both have higher tax burdens per capita.

8. The data in Table 9.9 show that, except for per capita welfare expenditures, a sizable correlation exists between Democratic control and expenditures (Democratic control is associated with lower expenditures). However, when we take urbanization, industrialization, income, and educational levels into account, 7 of the 12 correlations drop below .30 and the remaining 5 are reduced in magnitude. This suggests that part of this relationship between expenditures and party control is due to urbanization, industrialization, income, and educational differences between states.

Chapter 9
Political Parties

Name _____

Section _____

IV. CONCLUSION

Having reformulated the original statement and analyzed the relevant data, you can now return to the original problem. In the space below, write a short memorandum on whether the two parties are so similar that they offer no meaningful choice. Where possible, support your conclusions with specific data. Do more than repeat your answer to the short questions in section III. Combine individual pieces of data into a coherent answer, and where outside materials are used, be sure to indicate their source.

Original Problem

"The Democratic and Republican parties as so similar that citizens are offered no meaningful choices."

Memorandum

Chapter 10
PRESIDENTIAL ELECTIONS

The election of the President is an event surrounded by considerable pageantry, frenzied activity, analysis, and political mythology. Much has been said not only about particular elections and candidates, but also about the entire process by which Americans select their chief executive. Defenders of the status quo see the presidential election as a magnificent example of the democratic process at work. Critics, on the other hand, sometimes argue that such circuslike methods as conventions and almost endless campaigning are ill-suited to produce the best person for the job. One contention, however, seems to be almost universally accepted—successful presidential aspirants must have a broad appeal. Put somewhat differently, no one can hope to be President by appealing solely to narrow, extreme interests or groups. This chapter's problem confronts this question directly:

"Presidential elections demonstrate that only "middle-of-the-road" politicians can be nominated and elected President."

I. REFORMULATING THE PROBLEM

In the previous three chapters you selected an acceptable reformulation from among a number of different reformulations. Beginning in this chapter, we shall provide guides for developing your own reformulation of the problem rather than offering a ready-made reformulation. First, important aspects of this chapter's problem will be discussed. This discussion will call your attention to issues that must be dealt with in order to create an acceptable reformulation.

A list of partial reformulations is then presented that can serve as the basis of your own and original reformulation.

Discussion

The first question to be confronted concerns how many presidential elections are to be examined. To analyze every contest is an enormous task. Furthermore, only since the 1930s have presidential elections been scientifically studied, so we must take into account time and data limitations in our reformulation. The last two or three elections are both well studied and analyzable within a reasonable period.

An important concept to be defined is "middle of the road." This is a frequently used, but ambiguous, term that can be defined in many ways. For example, is a middle-of-the-road candidate one who appeals to all groups and offends no one? Or is it someone who takes the "middle" position on all major issues. Or perhaps we mean someone adopting the majority (though not necessarily "middle") position on major issues. Additional ways of defining "middle of the road" exist, and we must be clear in advance on how we use this term.

Finally, an acceptable reformulation must distinguish between the fate of candidates for major party presidential nominations and the success or failure of the nominees in the presidential election itself. The original statement does not specify whether non–middle-of-the-road politicians do not become nominees or winners in the election. An acceptable reformulation must consider this distinction.

Partial Reformulations

1. Successful nominees and winning presidential candidates in the last two presidential elections were favorably perceived by all major social groups, e.g., blacks, Catholics. Unsuccessful nominees and candidates, however, lacked this broadly based appeal.

2. Well-known political figures who are viewed as being closest to the most popular position on political issues become their party's nominee. A similar process occurs among nominees—the one viewed as closest to the public's own set of issue positions is elected.

3. The winning presidential candidate is a moderate in his policy preferences. This is indicated by the fact the candidate appeals to all major interests in a way that gives something for everyone while threatening no sizable group.

4. The last two presidential elections show that no candidate can win either the party's nomination or the election if many citizens, i.e., about 30 percent, view him as taking the most extreme position on important issues of the day.

5. To become President one must capture a majority of the middle-of-the-road voters (i.e., those who do not favor the extreme positions on such issues as civil rights, foreign involvement, and socioeconomic policy).

Each of these reformulations considers an aspect of the original problem. However, your analysis will be more complete if more than one of these partial reformulations are combined into a broader, more complex reformulation. Your reformulation can also include aspects of this chapter's problem not mentioned in these partial reformulations. Recall from our previous chapters that an acceptable reformulation must be a factual rather than a value statement, define all terms clearly, take into account all aspects of the original problem, and be relevant to the original problem.

Your Reformulation

II. SELECTING THE NECESSARY DATA

In Chapters 7 through 9, you indicated which types of data were required for your analysis by selecting several from a list provided in the book. Having gained experience in specifying required information before reviewing actual data, you need no longer depend on prepared listings.

In the space below, make your own list of required data. If you are uncertain about the criteria for required data, review the following rules.

Data Selection Rules

1. Avoid looking for vague and general kinds of data. What you need should be as specific and concrete as possible.

2. Choose data that are probably available. You do not know in advance, of course, exactly what is available, but try to limit yourself to things that either are public record or are frequently researched by political scientists.

3. The data you need must be related to the reformulation. Data that are not related to the reformulation are useless.

4. The data should be sufficient to test the reformulated problem and provide an adequate answer to the original problem.

Data for Your Reformulation

The Data

On the following pages are some of the data you need to analyze this chapter's problem. Some of the data may be relevant to your reformulation; some of it may be irrelevant. After examining the data, turn to section III, which immediately follows the data.

TABLE 10.1 VOTING AND SOLUTION TO SOLVING PROBLEMS OF URBAN UNREST, 1968

Respondent's Vote	Respondent's Issue Position					
	Solve Problems of Poverty and Employment		In-between		Use All Available Force	
	1	2	3	4	5	
Humphrey	48.2	15.1	22.5	5.0	9.2	100.0% N = 444
	65.0	59.8	35.2	21.2	23.4	
Nixon	23.1	8.7	35.7	14.8	17.6	100.0% N = 459
	32.2	35.7	57.7	65.4	46.3	
Wallace	8.9	5.0	19.8	13.9	52.5	100.0% N = 101
	_2.7_	_4.5_	_7.0_	_13.5_	_30.3_	
Total N =	100.0% 329	100.0% 112	100.0% 284	100.0% 104	100.0% 175	

SOURCE: Survey Research Center, University of Michigan.

TABLE 10.2 VOTING AND VIETNAM WAR POLICY PREFERENCE, 1968

Respondent's Vote	Respondent's Issue Position						
	Immediate Withdrawal		In-between		Complete Military Victory		
	1	2	3	4	5		
Humphrey	28.0	9.9	32.2	9.7	20.2	100.0%	N = 435
	55.7	52.4	46.4	39.6	31.7		
Nixon	18.8	8.6	30.8	13.1	28.8	100.0%	N = 452
	38.8	47.6	46.0	55.7	46.8		
Wallace	12.0	0	23.0	5.0	60.0	100.0%	N = 100
	5.5	0	7.6	4.7	21.6		
Total	100.0%	100.0%	100.0%	100.0%	100.0%		
N =	219	82	302	106	278		

SOURCE: Survey Research Center, University of Michigan.

TABLE 10.3 VOTING AND POSITION ON VIETNAM WAR, 1972

	Respondent's Issue Position					
	Immediate Withdrawal		In-between		Complete Military Victory	
Respondent's Vote	1	2	3	4	5	
Nixon	15.3	13.6	28.5	22.8	19.8	100.0% N = 960
	33.6		73.7		90.0	
McGovern	55.0	14.2	18.5	6.6	5.7	100.0% N = 529
	66.4		26.3		10.0	
Total N =	100.0% 438	100.0% 205	100.0% 372	100.0% 254	100.0% 220	

SOURCE: Survey Research Center, University of Michigan.

TABLE 10.4 VOTING AND OPINIONS ON USING BUSING TO ACHIEVE RACIAL INTEGRATION OF SCHOOLS, 1972

	Respondent's Issue Position						
Respondent's Vote	Strongly Support Busing		In-between		Strongly Oppose Busing		
	1	2	3	4	5		
Nixon	1.4	1.1	4.0	10.9	82.6	100.0%	N = 982
	14.1	26.8	48.8	59.1	74.0		
McGovern	16.5	5.8	8.2	14.4	55.1	100.0%	N = 515
	85.9	73.2	51.2	40.9	26.0		
Total	100.0%	100.0%	100.0%	100.0%	100.0%		
N =	99	41	82	181	1094		

SOURCE: Survey Research Center, University of Michigan.

TABLE 10.5 VOTING AND OPINION ON INCREASING TAXES ON THE WEALTHY, 1972

	Increase Tax on Rich		In-between		Equal Tax for Everyone	
Respondent's Vote	1	2	3	4	5	
Nixon	28.9	12.2	17.9	12.1	28.9	100.0% N = 888
	56.6	60.0	70.0	72.3	70.2	
McGovern	40.5	14.8	13.9	8.4	22.4	100.0% N = 487
	43.4	*40.0*	*30.0*	*27.7*	*29.8*	
Total N =	100.0% 454	100.0% 180	100.0% 227	100.0% 148	100.0% 366	

SOURCE: Survey Research Center, University of Michigan.

TABLE 10.6 PUBLIC PERCEPTIONS OF PRESIDENTIAL HOPEFULS, BY SOCIAL GROUPS, 1968

	Wallace (AIP)	Humphrey (D)	Nixon (R)	McCarthy (D)	Regan (R)	Rockefeller (R)
Middle class*	26.9†	59.9	68.3	57.0	50.2	55.5
Working class	32.7	65.2	63.3	53.3	47.3	52.5
Protestant	32.9	60.9	67.4	53.5	50.1	53.3
Catholic	23.5	68.1	62.3	57.2	45.8	54.2
Jewish	7.0	77.4	47.0	64.5	33.8	61.0
White	33.6	58.6	67.3	54.3	49.6	53.3
Black	12.1	85.0	55.1	56.5	40.6	56.6

	Johnson (D)	Romney (R)	R. Kennedy (D)	Muskie (D)		
Middle class	55.9	49.5	67.2	62.4		
Working class	62.7	48.6	73.8	60.8		
Protestant	58.7	49.4	68.3	59.0		
Catholic	63.4	47.8	78.3	67.7		
Jewish	64.5	48.5	77.8	80.1		
White	55.5	48.9	66.8	60.2		
Black	81.5	49.0	90.0	69.3		

*Social class is based on the respondents' own perception of their class status.
†Each respondent rated every candidate on a scale of 0 to 100 with 0 indicating great dislike and 100 indicating a very positive evaluation. The scores in the table are mean ratings for each candidate.
SOURCE: Survey Research Center, University of Michigan.

TABLE 10.7 PUBLIC PERCEPTIONS OF PRESIDENTIAL HOPEFULS, BY SOCIAL GROUPS, 1972

	Wallace (AIP)	McGovern (D)	Nixon (R)	Lindsay (D)	Muskie (D)	E. Kennedy (D)	Jackson (D)
Middle class*	49.3†	47.1	66.7	48.9	50.7	51.8	50.1
Working class	47.2	50.0	64.6	46.7	49.0	58.2	46.5
Protestant	51.6	46.9	67.8	48.0	47.8	52.5	48.7
Catholic	48.9	51.4	64.6	47.4	54.4	61.6	49.2
Jewish	15.8	61.8	43.8	49.7	63.0	66.5	52.3
White	53.0	45.7	67.4	46.8	49.2	51.6	48.5
Black	19.8	76.4	49.2	58.7	58.1	86.4	48.2

*Social class is based on the respondents' own perception of their class status.
†Each respondent rated every candidate on a scale of 0 to 100 with 0 indicating great dislike and 100 indicating a very positive evaluation. The scores in the table are mean ratings for each candidate.
SOURCE: Survey Research Center, University of Michigan.

CHART 10.1 A COMPARISON OF POLICY STATEMENTS MADE IN NOMINATING-CONVENTION ACCEPTANCE SPEECHES, 1968 AND 1972

THE VIETNAM WAR (1968)

Nixon: And I pledge to you tonight the first priority foreign policy objective of our next administration will be to bring an honorable end to the war in Vietnam.

We shall not stop there. We need a policy to prevent more Vietnams. All of America's peace-keeping institutions and all of America's foreign commitments must be re-appraised. Over the past 25 years America has provided more than $150 billion in foreign aid and lent it to nations abroad. In Korea and now again in Vietnam, the United States furnished most of the money, most of the arms, most of the men to help the people of those countries defend themselves against aggression . . .

And I say the time has come for other nations in the Free World to bear their fair share of the burden of defending peace and freedom around this world.

Humphrey: Let those who believe that our cause in Vietnam has been right, or those who believe that it has been wrong, agree here and now, that neither vindication nor repudiation will bring peace or be worthy of this country.

The question is not the yesterdays but the question is what do we do now? No one knows what the situation in Vietnam will be when the next President of the United States takes that oath of office on Jan. 20, 1969.

But every heart in America prays that by then we shall have reached a cease-fire in all Vietnam and be in serious negotiation toward a durable peace.

Meanwhile, as a citizen, a candidate and Vice President, I pledge to you and to my fellow Americans that I will do everything within my power, within the limits of my capacity and ability to aid the negotiations and to bring a prompt end to this war!

FOREIGN AFFAIRS AND NATIONAL DEFENSE (1968)

Nixon: What I call for is not a new isolationism. It is a new internationalism, in which America enlists its allies and its friends around the world in those struggles in which their interest is as great as ours. And now to the leaders of the Communist world we say, after an era of confrontation, the time has come for an era of negotiations.

Where the world's superpower is concerned, there is no acceptable alternative to peaceful negotiation. Because this will be a period of negotiation, we shall restore the strength of America so that we shall always negotiate from strength and never weakness.

As we seek peace through negotiation, let our goals be made clear. We do not seek domination over any other country. . . . We shall never be belligerent but we shall be as firm in defending our system as they are in defending theirs. We believe this should be an era of peaceful competition not only in the productivity of our factories but in the quality of our ideas. We extend the hand of friendship to all peoples. To the Russian people, to the Chinese people, to all people of the world we shall work toward the goal of an open world, open sky, open city, open hearts, open minds . . .

I believe we must have peace. I believe that we can have peace, but I do not underestimate the difficulty of this task. Because, you see, the art of preserving peace is greater than that of waging war and much more demanding . . .

As we commit the new policies for America tonight, let me make one further pledge. For five years, hardly a day has gone by when we haven't read or heard a report of the American flag being spit on, an Embassy being stoned, a library being burned or an ambassador being assaulted someplace in the world. . . . And I say to you tonight that when respect for the United States of America falls so low that a fourth-rate military power like North Korea will seize an American Naval vessel in the high seas, it is time for new leadership to restore respect for the United States of America.

Humphrey: Last week we witnessed once again in Czechoslovakia the desperate attempt of tyranny to crush out the forces of liberalism by force and brutal power, to hold back change.

But in Eastern Europe as elsewhere the old era will surely end, and there, as here, a new day will dawn.

And to speed this day we must go far beyond where we've been—beyond containment to communication; beyond the emphasis of differences to dialogue; beyond fear to hope.

We must cross those remaining barriers of suspicion and despair. We must halt the arms race before it halts humanity . . .

Within the last few years we have made progress, we have negotiated a nuclear test ban treaty, we have laid the groundwork for a nuclear nonproliferation treaty . . .

And now we must take new initiative, new initiative with prudence and caution but with perseverance. We must find the way and the means to control and reduce offensive and defensive nuclear missile systems . . .

But the search for peace is not for the timid or the weak, it must come from a nation of high purpose—firm without being belligerent, resolute without being bellicose, strong without being arrogant. And that's the kind of America that will help build the peace of this world.

POVERTY (1968)

Nixon: For the past five years, we have been deluged by government programs for the unemployed, programs for the cities, programs for the poor, and we have reaped from these programs an ugly harvest of frustration, violence and failure across the land, and now our opponents will be offering more of the same. More billions for government jobs, government housing, government welfare. I say it's time to quit pouring billions of dollars into programs that have failed in the United States of America.

To put it bluntly, we're on the wrong road and it's time to take a new road to progress. . . . So it is time to apply the lessons of the American Revolution to our present problems. Let us increase the wealth of America so that we can provide more generously for the aged, for the needy and for all those who cannot help themselves.

But for those who are able to help themselves, what we need are not more millions on welfare rolls, but more millions on payrolls in the United States. Instead of government jobs and government housing and government welfare, let government use its tax and credit policies to enlist in this battle the greatest agent of progress ever developed in the history of man—American private enterprise.

Let us enlist in this great cause the millions of Americans in volunteer organizations who will bring dedication to this task that no amount of money can every buy.

Humphrey: And we have, we have awakened expectations. We have aroused new voices and new voices that must and will be heard.

We have inspired new hope in millions of men and women, and they are impatient—and rightfully so, impatient now to see their hopes and their aspirations fulfilled.

We have raised a new standard of life in our America, not just for the poor but for every American—wage earner, businessman, farmer, school child and housewife. A standard by which the future progress must be judged . . .

Now let me speak of other rights. Nor can there be any compromise with the right of every American who is able and who is willing to work to have a job—that's an American right, too.

Who is willing to be a good neighbor, to be able to live in a decent home in the neighborhood of his own choice.

Nor can there be any compromise with the right of every American who is anxious and willing to learn, to have a good education.

LAW AND ORDER (1968)

Nixon: And tonight it's time for some honest talk about the problem of order in the United States. Let us always respect, as I do, our courts and those who serve on them, but let us also recognize that some of our courts in their dissents have gone too far in weakening the police forces against the criminal forces of this country. Let those who have the responsibility to enforce our laws and our judges who have the responsibility to interpret them also recognize that the first civil right of every American is to be free from domestic violence—and that right must be guaranteed in this country . . .

Time is running out for the merchants of crime and corruption in American society. The wave of crime is not going to be the wave of the future in the United States of America. We shall re-establish freedom from fear in America so that America can take the lead in re-establishing freedom from fear in the world. And to those who say that law and order is the code word for racism, there and here is a reply. Our goal is justice, justice for every American. If we are to have respect for law and order in America we must have laws that deserve respect. Just as we cannot have progress without order, we cannot have order without progress.

Humphrey: Violence breeds more violence; disorder destroys, and only in order can we build. Riot makes for ruin; reason makes for solution. So from the White House to the courthouse to the city hall, every official has the solemn responsibility of guaranteeing to every American—black and white, rich and poor—the right to personal security—life.

Every American, black or white, rich or poor, has the right in this land of ours to a safe and decent neighborhood, and on this there can be no compromise.

I put it very bluntly—rioting, burning, sniping, mugging, traffic in narcotics, and disregard for law are the advance guard of anarchy, and they must and they will be stopped.

But may I say most respectfully, particularly to some who have spoken before, the answer lies in reasoned, effective action by state, local and Federal authority. The answer does not lie in an attack on our courts, our laws or our Attorney General . . .

We do not want a police state but we need a state of law and order, and neither mob violence nor police brutality have any place in America.

And I pledge to use every resource that is available to the Presidency, every resource available to the President, to end once and for all the fear that is in our cities.

VIETNAM (1972)

McGovern: As one whose heart has ached for 10 years over the agony of Vietnam, I will halt the senseless bombing of Indochina on Inauguration Day . . .

Within 90 days of my inauguration, every American soldier and every American prisoner will be out of the jungle and out of their cells and back home in America where they belong.

Nixon: We've gone the extra mile—in fact, we've gone tens of thousands of miles trying to seek a negotiated settlement of the war. We have offered a cease-fire, a total withdrawal of all American forces, an exchange of all prisoners of war, internationally supervised free elctions with the Communists participating in the elections and in the supervisions.

There are three things, however, that we have not and that we will not offer:
We will never abandon our prisoners of war.

And, second, we will not join our enemies in imposing a Communist government on our allies—the 17 million people of South Vietnam.

And we will never stain the honor of the United States of America.

Now, I realize that many—particularly in this political year—wonder why we insist on an honorable peace in Vietnam. From a political standpoint, they suggest that, since I was not in office when over a half a million American men were sent there, that I should end the war by agreeing to impose a Communist government on the people of South Vietnam and just blame the whole catastrophe on my predecessors.

This might be good politics. But it would be disastrous to the cause of peace in the world. If at this time we betray our allies, it will discourage our friends abroad and it will encourage our enemies to engage in aggression.

FOREIGN AFFAIRS AND NATIONAL DEFENSE (1972)

McGovern: America must be restored to her proper role in the world. But we can do that only through the recovery of confidence in ourselves. The greatest contribution America can make to our fellow mortals is to heal our own great but deeply troubled land. We must respond to that ancient command: "Physican, heal thyself."

It is necessary in an age of nuclear power and hostile ideologies that we be militarily strong. America must never become a second rate nation. As one who has tasted the bitter fruits of our weakness before Pearl harbor, 1941, I give you my sacred pledge that if I become President of the United States, America will keep its defenses alert and fully sufficient to meet any danger. We will do that not only for ourselves, but for those who deserve and need the shield of our strength—our old allies in Europe, and elsewhere, including the people of Israel, who will always have our help to hold their promised land.

Yet we know that for 30 years we have been so absorbed with fear and danger from abroad that we have permitted our own house to fall into disarray. We must now show that peace and prosperity can exist side by side—indeed, each now depends on the other.

Nixon: And, within the space of four years in our relations with the Soviet Union, we have moved from confrontation to negotiation and then to cooperation in the interest of peace . . .

We have laid the foundation for further limitations on nuclear weapons, and, eventually, of reducing the armaments in the nuclear area.

More than on any other single issue, I ask you, my fellow Americans, to give us the chance to continue these great initiatives that can contribute so much to the future of peace in the world . . .

But a note of warning needs to be sounded. We cannot be complacent. Our opponents have proposed massive cuts in our defense budget which would have the inevitable effect of making the United States the second strongest nation in the world. For the United States unilaterally to reduce its strength with the naive hope that other nations would do likewise would increase the danger of war in the world. It would completely remove any incentive of other nations to agree to a mutual limitation to reduction of arms, the promising initiatives we have undertaken to limit arms would be destroyed, the security of the United States and all the nations in the world who depend upon our friendship and support would be threatened.

Let's look at the record on defense expenditures. We have cut spending in our Administration. It now takes the lowest percentage of our national product in 20 years. We should not spend more on defense than we need, but we must never spend less than we need . . .

And so tonight, my fellow Americans, I say, let us take risks for peace, but let us never risk the security of the United States of America.

TAX POLICY (1972)

McGovern: Above all, honest work must be rewarded by a fair and just tax system. The tax system today does not reward hard work—it penalizes it. Inherited or invested welath frequently multiplies itself while paying no taxes at all. But wages earned on the assembly line, or laying bricks, or picking fruit—these hard-earned dollars are taxed to the last penny. There is a depletion allowance for oil wells, but no allowance for the depletion of man's body in years of toil.

Nixon: Now my fellow Americans, in pointing up those things we do not overlook the fact that our system has its problems. Our administration, as you know, has provided the biggest tax cut in history, but taxes are still too high. That is why one of the goals in our next administration is to reduce the property tax, which is such an unfair and heavy burden on the poor, the elderly, the wage earner, the farmer and those on fixed incomes.

EMPLOYMENT (1972)

McGovern: The highest domestic priority of my Administration will be to ensure that every American able to work has a job to do. This job guarantee will and must depend upon a reinvigorated private economy, freed at last from the uncertainties and burdens of war. But it is our commitment that whatever employment the private sector does not provide, the federal government will either stimulate, or provide itself. Whatever it takes, this country is going back to work.

Nixon: And as a result of the millions of new jobs created by our new economic policies, unemployment today in America is less than the peacetime average of the sixties, but we must continue the unparalleled increase in new jobs so that we can achieve the great goal of our new prosperity—a job for every American who wants to work, without war and without inflation.

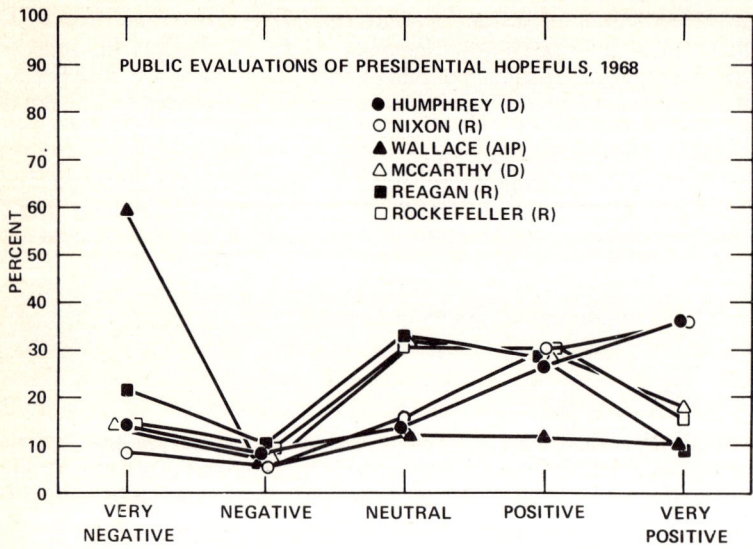

FIG. 10.1 Public evaluations of presidential hopefuls, 1968. (Source: Survey Research Center, University of Mich.)

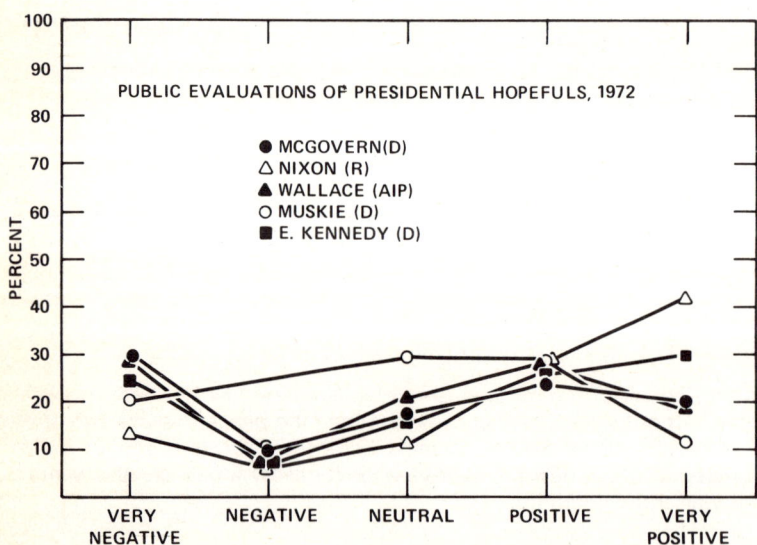

FIG. 10.2 Public evaluations of presidential hopefuls, 1972. (Source: Survey Research Center, University of Michigan.)

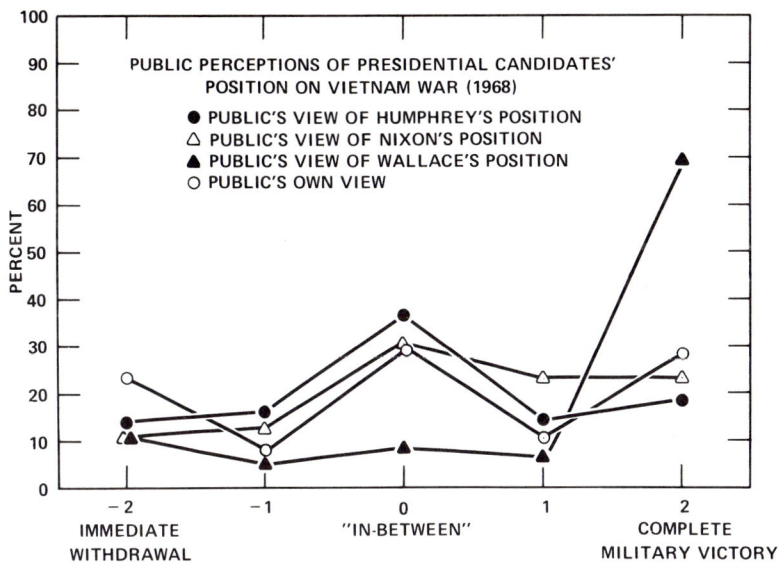

FIG. 10.3 Public perceptions of presidential candidates' position on the Vietnam war, 1968. (Source: Survey Research Center, University of Michigan.)

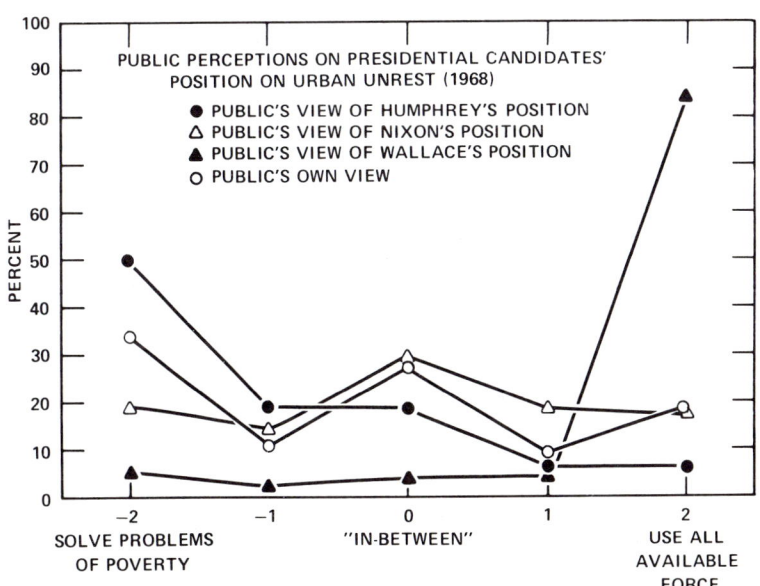

FIG. 10.4 Public perceptions of presidential candidates' position on urban unrest, 1968. (Source: Survey Research Center, University of Michigan.)

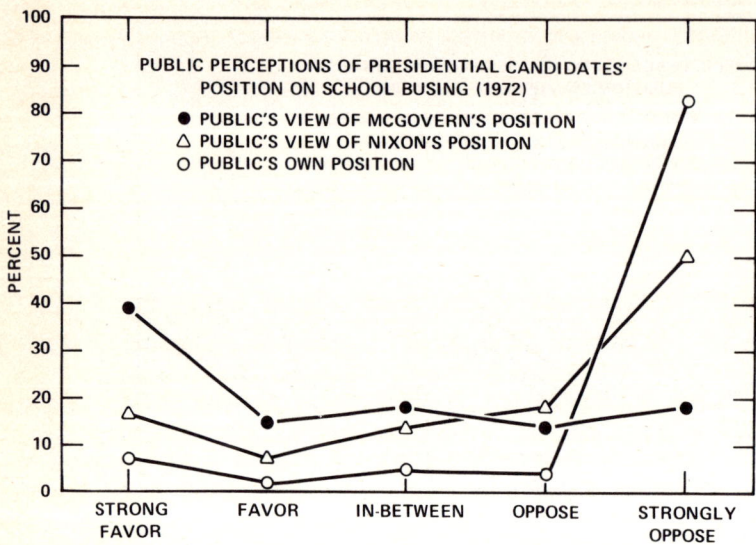

FIG. 10.5 Public perceptions of presidential candidates' position on school busing, 1972. (Source: Survey Research Center, University of Michigan.)

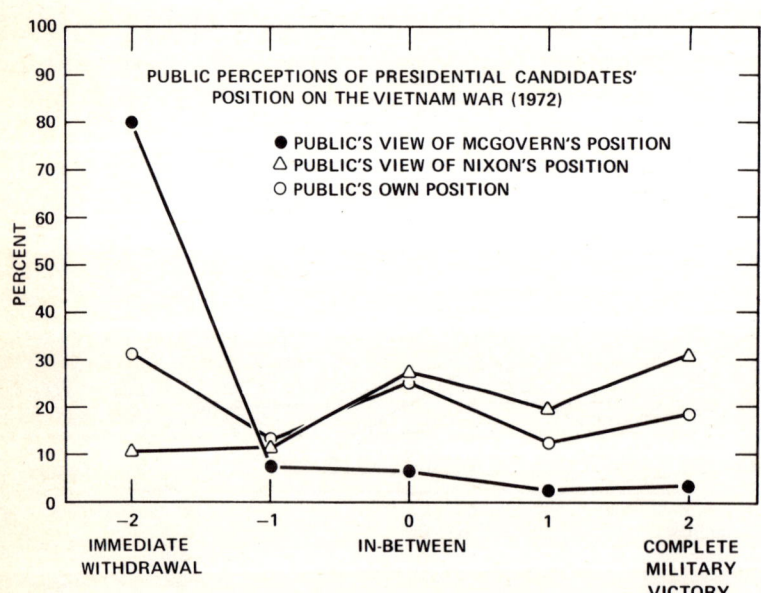

FIG. 10.6 Public perceptions of presidential candidates' position on the Vietnam war, 1972. (Source: Survey Research Center, University of Michigan.)

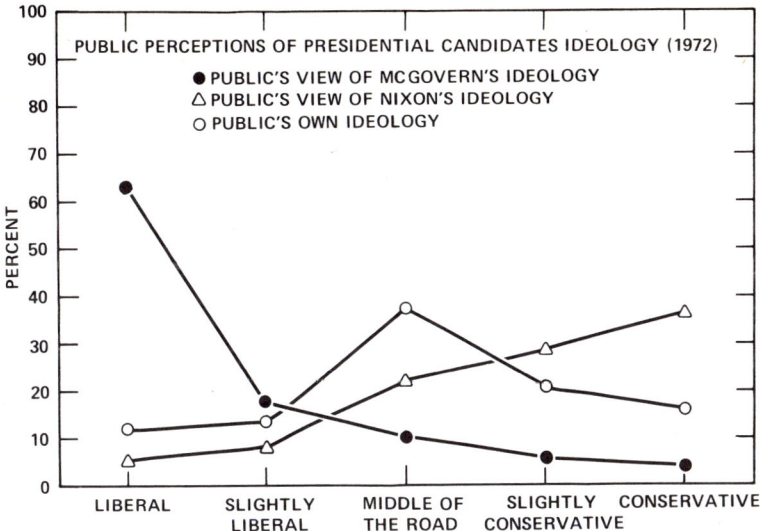

FIG. 10.7 Public perceptions of presidential candidates' ideology, 1972. (Source: Survey Research Center, University of Michigan.)

For further information—

If you need more information on recent elections, you can find the latest data in:

Gallup Opinion Index. Monthly reports of Gallup polls.

The New York Times Index. Cites references to recent Harris, Roper, and other polls.

Congressional Quarterly. Weekly reports on political developments, including positions taken by presidential candidates or nominees.

For more detailed analyses of past elections, you may wish to refer to the following:

The Nominating Process

David, Paul T., Ralph M. Goldman, and Richard C. Bain: *The Politics of National Party Conventions,* revised ed. (New York: Vintage Books, Random House, Inc., 1964).

Polsby, Nelson: "Decision-Making at the National Conventions," *Western Political Quarterly,* vol. 13, pp. 609–619, 1960.

Pomper, Gerald: *Nominating the President* (New York: W. W. Norton & Company, Inc., 1966), especially chap. 6 (Conventions and Presidential Candidates).

Presidential Elections and Voting

Campbell, Angus, Philip E. Converse, Warren E. Miller, and Donald E. Stokes: *The American Voter* (New York: John Wiley & Sons, Inc., 1960), especially chap. 8 (Public Policy and Political Preference).

Converse, Philip E., Aage R. Clausen, and Warren E. Miller: "Electoral Myth and Reality: The 1964 Election," *American Political Science Review,* vol. 59, 1965.

Converse, Philip E., Warren E. Miller, Jerrold G. Rusk, and Arthur C. Wolfe: "Continuity and Change in American Politics: Parties and Issues in the 1968 Elections," *American Political Science Review,* vol. 63, 1083–1105, 1969.

Field, John O., and Ronald E. Anderson: "Idealogy in the Public's Conceptualization of the 1964 Election," *Public Opinion Quarterly* vol. 33, 1969.

Page, Benjamin I., and Richard A. Brody: "Policy Voting and the Electoral Process: The Vietnam War Issue," *American Political Science Review,* vol. 66, 979–995, 1972.

Polsby, Nelson, and Aaron B. Wildavsky: *Presidential Elections,* 3d ed. (New York: Charles Scribner's Sons, 1971).

Pomper, Gerald M.: *Elections in America* (New York: Dodd, Mead & Company, Inc., 1970).

Scammon, Richard M., and Ben J. Wattenberg: *The Real Majority* (New York: Coward, McCann and Geoghegan, Inc., 1971), especially chap. 20 (Looking Ahead: To Move the Moving Center).

III. ANALYZING THE DATA

We have presented much material on presidential elections. Some of these data may be relevant, others irrelevant depending on your reformulation (and in particular how you defined "middle of the road"). Below are some specific questions on these data. Answer only those questions that pertain to your reformulation. As in previous chapters, the correct answers will be found at the end of this section.

Question 1

Figures 10.1 and 10.2 indicate public evaluations of political leaders in 1968 and 1972. Is it true that, within each political party, leaders who are strongly disliked by relatively large numbers cannot win their party's nomination? Among the Democratic and Republican contenders, does being disliked by a relatively large number of people preclude winning the Presidency?

Your Answer

Question 2
Figures 10.3 through 10.6 depict the public's own issue preferences and public perceptions of where candidates stood on these issues for both 1968 and 1972. First, in how many instances is the "in-between" position the most popular among the public? Second, in how many instances did half or more of the public perceive one of the candidates as standing for one of the two extreme positions on these different issues? Third, in how many cases did a majority of the public endorse one of the extreme positions?

Your Answer

Question 3
Tables 10.1 through 10.5 cross tabulate voting behavior with issue position in 1968 and 1972. Notice that both the row and column percentages are given. In each election, did Nixon receive a majority of the "in-between" voters on each issue? On each issue, did a majority of Nixon's vote come from the "in-between" voters?

Your Answer

218 Political Analysis

Question 4

Figure 10.7 shows the public's rating of itself and its perceptions of Nixon and McGovern on a liberal-conservative scale. Which of the two candidates' political image is most like the public's?

Your Answer

Question 5

In Tables 10.6 and 10.7 we see the public's ratings of a number of political leaders, many of whom sought their party's presidential nomination. These ratings are divided according to various social groupings. Is it true, as it is sometimes argued, that no political personality can win their party's nomination if they are disliked by a significant social group? Do all the successful nominees receive positive ratings within each group?

Your Answer

Question 6

Chart 10.1 compares policy statements made by successful party nominees in 1968 and 1972 when they accepted their party's nomination. It is sometimes argued that a successful candidate must straddle many diverse points of view and thus on each issue position either offer something to everyone or appear vague enough not to offend major interests. Are there any examples here in which this dictum is not followed? That is, does a candidate strongly support one position on an issue without conceding anything to the opposite position?

Your Answer

Correct Answers

1. Figure 10.1 shows that among Democrats both McCarthy, who did not gain his party's nomination, and Humphrey, who did win the nomination, received about the same number of "very negative" and "negative" evaluations. Note, however, that Humphrey received many more "very positive" evaluations than did McCarthy. In 1968, Reagan and Rockefeller, who fought Nixon for the Republican nomination, received many more "very negative" evaluations than did Nixon. In 1972, McGovern received many more "very negative" evaluations than any other leader including George Wallace. Unfortunately, no Republican leaders other than Nixon are rated in 1972 so we cannot say whether he received the fewest negative judgments. It is clear, however, that comparatively few people intensely disliked Nixon in 1972. Finally, both the 1968 and 1972 data show that the candidate intensely disliked by the greatest number of foes did not win the Presidency. All and all, Figures 10.1 and 10.2 suggest that being strongly disliked by a comparatively large group of the general population does not foreclose gaining a party's nomination; actually winning the Presidency, however, is a different matter.

2. In Figures 10.3 through 10.6 we find that the middle-of-the-road position was the most popular issue position only in the case of the Vietnam question in 1968. Even here, less than 30 percent of the public favored this position. Regarding the question of which candidate was perceived by a majority as advocating the most extreme position, Wallace in 1968 was considered to support the extreme position on Vietnam and urban unrest. A slight majority also saw Humphrey in 1968 as advocating one of the extreme positions on urban unrest. Similarly, 80 percent saw George McGovern as favoring the extreme position on the 1972 Vietnam question. Observe that in none of these instances did a majority of the public favor this extreme position. When a majority of the public did adopt the extreme position, as on the school busing issue, none of the candidates were perceived by the majority as also advocating this issue position (though Nixon was very close). This suggests that candidates perceived as advocating extreme positions not shared by the public do less well than those whose positions are considered more moderate.

3. An examination of the column percentages in the "in-between" category for Tables 10.1 through 10.5 shows that Nixon won a majority of this group in three out of five instances (urban unrest in 1968, Vietnam war in 1972, and tax policy in 1972.) However, in no instance did a majority of Nixon's vote come from this "in-between" group. This latter finding is not surprising since this middle group is frequently of very small size and thus unable to supply the majority of a candidate's votes. Hence, additional votes must come from voters favoring more extreme positions if a candidate is to be elected.

4. Figure 10.7 shows that when asked to classify themselves on liberal-conservative scale, most Americans fall between "slightly liberal" and "slightly conservative" points with middle of the road as the most popular (though not the majority) choice. Of the two candidates, McGovern was far more likely to be viewed outside this middle ground than Nixon though 36 percent of the public labeled Nixon as a conservative, about 64 percent viewed McGovern as a liberal (a position occupied by only about 12 percent of the American public).

5. Tables 10.6 and 10.7 show that even leaders who receive negative ratings from certain social groups can receive their party's nomination and win the Presidency. For example, Jews tended to rate Nixon unfavorably in 1968 and 1972, and McGovern was rated unfavorably by the middle class, Protestants, and whites in 1972. Observe that in 1968 a number of Democrats (McCarthy, Robert Kennedy, and Muskie) who did not receive the nomination were favorably rated in all groups. Similarly, in 1972 Edward Kennedy did better among all groups than did George McGovern. Thus, appealing to all social classes, religions, and races is no guarantee of being nominated and elected, and being disliked among these groups does not automatically result in defeat.

6. An examination of the various issue statements in Chart 10.1 shows that in most instances both candidates either offer assurances on both sides of an issue or phrase their position in such vague terms that it is unclear what particular policies are endorsed. For example, in foreign affairs and national defense for 1968 and 1972 everyone seems to favor reducing world tensions and bettering relations with Communists, on the one hand, and fully maintaining our military strength and national integrity on the other hand. Similarly on the issue of law and order in 1968 both Nixon and Humphrey stressed that strong enforcement of "law and order" would benefit all groups and interests. The clearest exception to this pattern is McGovern's stand on Vietnam withdrawal—he promises immediate withdrawal within 90 days of his inauguration. This is in sharp contrast to Nixon who mentions both his major peace initiatives and his unwillingness to "stain the honor of the United States." Other instances of one-sided policy preference can also be found, though perhaps not as clear as in the Vietnam issue. Nixon's great stress on private enterprise and no mention of government assistance (Poverty [1968]) and McGovern's emphasis on tax reform for workers but not for other groups (Tax Policy [1972]) could be classified as "unbalanced" advocacy. On the whole, however, most statements encompass differing policy positions or are too vague to give the impression of advocating a single controversial position.

Chapter 10
Presidential Power

Name _____

Section _____

IV. CONCLUSION

Having reformulated the original problem and analyzed the relevant data, you can now return to the original problem. In the space below, write a short memorandum on whether only middle-of-the-road candidates can be elected President. Your essay should integrate various kinds of data into a coherent statement on the problem. Where outside sources are used be sure to cite the source.

Original Problem

"Presidential elections demonstrate that only 'middle-of-the-road' politicians can be nominated and elected President."

Memorandum

Chapter 11
PRESIDENTIAL POWER

The Constitution originally intended the three branches of government to be equals. Congress, the President, and the courts each had great power, but all three were designed to be mutually interdependent to prevent tyrannical domination by a single interest. Thus, for example, congressional action frequently requires executive and judicial cooperation or at least acquiescence. With the emergence of a stronger, more centralized federal government, however, it frequently appears that the President has achieved the upper hand in relations with the other two branches. At various times in recent years Congress and the courts have given the impression of following along with presidential initiative rather than being co-equal partners. This trend, if appearances do indeed reflect real shifts in power, raises important questions about Constitutional constraints on the exercise of power. The question we consider is:

"Despite the intentions of those drafting the Constitution, the President is now unchecked in his power by the other branches of government."

I. REFORMULATING THE PROBLEM

This section follows the pattern established in the previous chapter on presidential elections. Instead of having you select from among a number of reformulations, you shall develop your own reformulations. To assist you we shall first discuss some important aspects of this chapter's problem and then suggest some partial reformulations that can be combined into a broader, more complex reformulation.

Discussion

Our first problem is the time span encompassed by the original problem. By "now" do we mean only the current President? the last five Presidents? Though we could try to analyze presidential power during the twentieth century, time and data limitations restrict our investigation to more recent Presidents. Let us confine our discussion to the last four Presidents—Eisenhower, Kennedy, Johnson, and Nixon.

 A far more complex problem concerns the measurement of "power," a concept that has posed many difficulties for political analysts. There are many different accepted meanings and measures of presidential power. For example, we may say that the President is more powerful than either Congress or the Supreme Court if presidentially supported legislation is rarely rejected by Congress or declared unconstitutional by the courts. This view of presidential power emphasizes legislation. Another conception could stress unequal resources available to the three branches, i.e., the monetary and personnel advantage enjoyed by the executive branch. A third notion of power could be based on the judgment of expert analysts who have studied the Presidency and its relation with the other branches of government. Of course, these experts might use the first two measures of presidential power to reach their conclusions, but reliance on experts provides a wide variety of data collected over many years by different scholars.

Partial Reformulations

1. Neither congressmen nor Supreme Court justices take issue with policies advocated by the President.

2. Legislation advocated by the President is almost always passed by Congress and only rarely vetoed by the courts.

2. The President is able to dominate the other two branches of government because of public opinion. When conflict arises on whose will is to prevail, the public overwhelmingly supports the President.

4. The shift from equality of power to presidential domination is clearly reflected in the resources available to each branch of government. In the last 20 years, even when we exclude expenditures for national defense, the executive branch has grown substantially, relative to the other branches in terms of expenditures and number of employees.

5. Expert scholars who have studied presidential power agree that in the last 20 years Congress and the Supreme Court have been unable to check the President's power.

Each of these reformulations considers only an aspect of the original problem. Your analysis will be more complete if more than one of these partial reformulations are combined into a broader, more complex reformulation. Your reformulation can also include aspects of this chapter's problem not discussed in these partial reformulations. Recall from our previous chapters that an acceptable reformulation must be a factual rather than a value statement, define all terms clearly, take into account all aspects of the original problem, and be relevant to the original problem.

Your Reformulation

II. SELECTING THE NECESSARY DATA

Before proceeding to the data on presidential power, it is first necessary to decide on what data are needed to test your reformulation. If you are uncertain about the criteria for required data, review the following rules. Then list the data necessary to test your own reformulation.

Data Selection Rules

1. Avoid looking for vague and general kinds of data. What you need should be as specific and concrete as possible.

2. Choose data that are probably available. You do not know in advance exactly what is available, but try to limit yourself to things that either are of public record or are frequently researched by political scientists.

3. The data you need must be related to the reformulation. Data that are not related to the reformulation are useless.

4. The data should be sufficient to test the reformulated problem and provide an adequate answer to the original problem.

Data for Your Reformulation

The Data

In the following pages are some of the data you need to analyze this chapter's problem. Some of the data may be relevant to the problem; other data may be irrelevant. After examining the data, turn to section III, which immediately follows that data.

TABLE 11.1 PUBLIC SUPPORT FOR PRESIDENTIAL LEADERSHIP

The President versus Congress	Percent Agree
"The President is an inspired leader; he has ideas of his own to help the country. He should be able to make the people and Congress work along with him..."	51.5%
"It is up to the people through their Congressmen to find solutions to the problems of the day. The President should stick to carrying out what the people and Congress have decided..."	39.6
Combination of presidential and congressional leadership preferred...	6.0
No answer	3.0
Total	100.1%

The President versus the People	
Suppose that fighting is breaking out somewhere abroad, and the President thinks it's *important* to send American troops there. He knows, however, that most Americans are *opposed* to sending our troops there. Now what do you think: Should he *send* these troops, which he may *legally* do as President?...	75.0%
Or should he *follow* public opinion and keep them home?	20.8
No answer	4.0
$N = 1342$	
Total	99.8%

NOTE: Respondents are all from Detroit, Michigan, and the interviews were conducted in 1960.

SOURCE: Adapted from Roberta S. Sigel: "Image of the American Presidency—Part II of an Exploration into Popular Views of Presidential Power," *Midwest Journal of Political Science,* vol. 10, pp. 123–137, 1966. Reprinted by permission of Wayne State University Press and the author.

TABLE 11.2 NUMBER OF BILLS VETOED BY PRESIDENTS

Presidents	Number of Bills Vetoed	Number of Vetoes Overridden
Franklin Roosevelt (1932–1945)	631	9
Harry Truman (1945–1952)	250	12
John Kennedy (1961–1963)	25	0
Lyndon Johnson (1963–1968)	30	0
Richard Nixon (1969–1973)	37	5

SOURCE: *Facts About the Presidents,* edited by Joseph N. Kane (New York: The H. W. Wilson Company, 1968), p. 353. Source for Lyndon Johnson: *Congress and the Nation,* vol. II, p. 92a, 1965–1968. Source for Nixon vetoes: *CCH Congressional Index.*

TABLE 11.3 CONGRESSIONAL SUPPORT FOR PRESIDENTIAL PROGRAMS, 1953 TO 1972

Year	President	Presidential Support Score*
1953	Eisenhower	89%
1954	Eisenhower	83
1955	Eisenhower	75
1956	Eisenhower	70
1957	Eisenhower	68
1958	Eisenhower	76
1959	Eisenhower	52
1960	Eisenhower	65
1961	Kennedy	81
1962	Kennedy	85
1963	Kennedy	87
1964	Johnson	88
1965	Johnson	93
1966	Johnson	79
1967	Johnson	79
1968	Johnson	75
1969	Nixon	74
1970	Nixon	77
1971	Nixon	75
1972	Nixon	66

*The presidential support score indicates the proportion of time Congress voted in accordance with the President's preferences.

SOURCE: *Congressional Quarterly 1970 Almanac,* pp. 1123–24.
Congressional Quarterly 1972 Almanac, p. 42.

TABLE 11.4 TRENDS IN NUMBER OF FEDERAL GOVERNMENT EMPLOYEES, 1950-1972

Year	Branch		
	Executive (excluding Defense Dept.)	Legislative	Judicial
1950	1,181,000*	23,000*	4,000
1952	1,237,000	23,000	4,000
1954	1,173,000	22,000	4,000
1956	1,192,000	22,000	4,000
1958	1,258,000	22,000	5,000
1960	1,324,000	23,000	5,000
1962	1,415,000	24,000	6,000
1964	1,440,000	25,000	6,000
1966	1,588,000	27,000	6,000
1968	1,703,000	29,000	7,000
1970	1,691,000	31,000	7,000
1972	1,681,000	32,000	8,000

*Figures have been rounded to the nearest thousand.

SOURCES: *Historical Abstract of the United States to 1957. Historical Abstract of the United States to 1957—Continuation to 1962. Statistical Abstract of the United States,* 1972.

EXPERT OPINION 1
JAMES M. BURNS: *Presidential Government*

The Presidency today is at the peak of its prestige. Journalists describe it as the toughest job on earth, the presiding office of the free world, the linchpin of Western alliance, America's greatest contribution to the art of self-government. Foreigners are fascinated by the Presidency, just as they are appalled by Congress and perplexed by party and election shenanigans. Scholars describe it as the most popular and democratic—and withal the most elevated and even most elitist—part of American government. They lovingly dissect the Presidency, slicing up its essentially indivisible power into that of Chief Executive, Chief of State, Chief Legislator, and so on. And they worry about its infirmities even as they marvel at its strength.

Even so, we may have underestimated the long-term impact of presidential government on the whole structure of American government. Past trends and current tendencies may permit some guarded speculations as to the future.

Conservatives have long held that the Presidency, as idealized and operated by liberals and internationalists, was imperialistic and exploitative and hence that it would eventually overpower the other branches of government. They are substantially right. For almost a century now, the Presidency has been warding off forays against its own constitutional domain and drawing other governmental and political institutions into the orbit of its influence. At least since the days of President Grant the defense and expansion of the office have been conducted not only by strong

SOURCE: *Presidential Government: The Crucible of Leadership* (Boston: Houghton Mifflin Company, 1965), pp. 313-335. Copyright © 1965 by James MacGregor Burns. Reprinted by permission of the publisher Houghton Mifflin Company.

Presidents but by "weak" ones; hence we can say that the growth of the Presidency has been in part an institutional tendency and not one turning merely on the accident of crisis and personality.

The President in recent decades has seemed to bring the Cabinet more certainly under his personal influence than was often the case in the nineteenth century. Lincoln's famous episode of "seven noes, one aye—the ayes have it" would be impossible today; Cabinet members would not dare risk such a posture of opposition to the chief. The Vice Presidency also has been tucked securely into the executive establishment. Some agencies, such as the Federal Bureau of Investigation, remain classic examples of the limitations of the President's control, but this independence is in part a product of unique personality and will probably diminish in time.

Presidential aggrandizement has been even more marked in the sphere of party politics. There was a time when conventions refused to renominate incumbent Presidents, when the national chairman was independent of presidential control, when the national party apparatus was dominated by competing leaders of factions. Things are very different now. The most important change affecting the nominating process since 1896 in the party in power, according to David, Goldman, and Bain, "has been the rising position of the Presidency and the increased recognition accorded the President as party leader. Other circles of influence continue to exist; but the group consisting of the President and his immediate associates has become the innermost inner circle; the others can now be regarded as a loose constellation of groups surrounding the White House as the center of power." Recently the national party chairman has been simply one more political lieutenant of the President's and one who often has less power than political aides in the White House. The President's party influence does not run much beyond the scope of the presidential party; but the scope of the presidential party may be expanding too, depending in part on the President's influence over other sectors of the whole government.

Perhaps the most extraordinary but least remarked expansion of presidential government lies in the extension of its influence to the Supreme Court. Prior to the modern presidential epoch, successive Presidents held sharply different doctrines and hence put men of varying viewpoints on the bench. Judicial appointees of a Theodore Roosevelt versus a Taft, of a Wilson versus a Harding, of a Hoover versus a Franklin Roosevelt, could hardly be expected to agree in their socioeconomic doctrine, and generally their decisions reflected their differences. This does not mean that Presidents always appointed men who slavishly expressed the presidential line. Indeed, they sometimes chose men who in time diverged widely from the President's basic doctrine, as in the case of Wilson's appointment of James C. McReynolds. But inescapably the type of appointment, and the appointee's social and economic doctrine on the bench, were affected by the general set of ideas, as well as by the political interrelationships, of a presidential administration. Thus it was not surprising that the Supreme Court of 1933–37, composed mainly of appointees of Republican Presidents, rejected major New Deal legislation. Since 1937, however, the Supreme Court has not invalidated a major piece of national social legislation. The Court is composed of men who respond to the same general ideas of freedom and equality as have recent Presidents. . . .

Federalism has also felt the impact of presidential government. Modern Presidents have overturned old doctrines and practices of states' rights by extending their policy-making power into the urban areas of the nation. Historically the growth of cities has brought more need for public regulation and control and hence the growth of government. This tendency has been evident in public health, public transportation, social welfare services, traffic and crime control, and many other sectors. These developments in turn have produced financial crises in many cities; as the burden on city government has increased, its fiscal resources have proved inadequate. City officials have had to go cup in hand to state legislatures. But the states too have been struggling with financial limitations, and rurally dominated state legislatures have not been eager to hand out money to their city brethren. So the cities have turned to Washington. But here too they often have met frustration, for Congress too is heavily influenced by the rurally based congressional party coalition, especially in the appropriations committees. So the mayors head for the White House. . . .

Thus the man in the White House has become the President of the Cities; he has become the Chief Executive of Metropolis. He has provided the main motive power for shaping legislation needed by the cities; he pushes through the federal money bills with their provision for matching grants; he commands the executive departments—Labor, Justice, Health, Education and Welfare—that work closely with metropolitan governments; he appoints the heads of promotional and regulatory agencies for housing, urban renewal, transportation, communication, that affect the city. The President of course extends aid to the cities with strings attached—strings in the form of presidentially approved standards, procedures, safeguards, and the like. But the community of doctrine and interest between presidential government and big-city government is so close that major conflicts of politics and policy do not arise. More often the President and the mayors are allied against hostile or indifferent officials in other parts of the "marble cake" of federalism—against state legislators, county officials, congressional appropriations committees and subcommittees, even Governors.

EXPERT OPINION 2

RICHARD E. NEUSTADT: Presidential Influence

The separateness of institutions and the sharing of authority prescribe the terms on which a President persuades. When one man shares authority with another, but does not gain or lose his job upon the other's whim, his willingness to act upon the urging of the other turns on whether he conceives the action right for him. The essence of a President's persuasive task is to convince such men that what the White House wants of them is what they ought to do for their sake and on their authority.

Persuasive power, thus defined, amounts to more than charm or reasoned argument. These have their uses for a President, but these are not the whole of his resources. For the men he would induce to do what he wants done on their own responsibility will need or fear some acts by him on his responsibility. If they share his authority, he has some share in theirs. Presidential "powers" may be inconclusive when a President commands, but always remain relevant as he persuades. The status and authority inherent in his office reinforce his logic and his charm.

Status adds something to persuasiveness; authority adds still more. When Truman urged wage changes on his Secretary of Commerce while the latter was administering the steel mills, he and Secretary Sawyer were not just two men reasoning with one another. Had they been so, Sawyer probably would never have agreed to act. Truman's status gave him special claims to Sawyer's loyalty, or at least attention. In Walter Bagehot's charming phrase, "No man can *argue* on his knees." Although there is no kneeling in this country, few men—and exceedingly few Cabinet officers—are immune to the impulse to say "yes" to the President of the United States. It grows harder to say "no" when they are seated in his oval office at the White House, or in his study on the second floor, where almost tangibly he partakes of the aura of his physical surroundings. In Sawyer's case, moreover, the President

SOURCE: *Presidential Power* (New York: John Wiley & Sons, Inc., 1960), pp. 33–46. Footnotes omitted. Reprinted by permission of John Wiley and Sons, Inc.

possessed formal authority to intervene in many matters of concern to the Secretary of Commerce. These matters ranged from jurisdictional disputes among the defense agencies to legislation pending before Congress and, ultimately, to the tenure of the Secretary, himself. There is nothing in the record to suggest that Truman voiced specific threats when they negotiated over wage increases. But given his *formal* powers and their relevance to Sawyer's other interests, it is safe to assume that Truman's very advocacy of wage action conveyed an implicit threat.

A President's authority and status give him great advantages in dealing with the men he would persuade. Each "power" is a vantage point for him in the degree that other men have use for his authority. From the veto to appointments, from publicity to budgeting, and so down a long list, the White House now controls the most encompassing array of vantage points in the American political system. With hardly an exception, the men who share in governing this country are aware that at some time, in some degree, the doing of *their* jobs, the furthering of *their* ambitions, may depend upon the President of the United States. Their need for presidential action, or their fear of it, is bound to be recurrent if not actually continuous. Their need or fear is his advantage.

A President's advantages are greater than mere listing of his "powers" might suggest. The men with whom he deals must deal with him until the last day of his term. Because they have continuing relationships with him, his future, while it lasts, supports his present influence. Even though there is no need or fear of him today, what he could do tomorrow may supply today's advantage. Continuing relationships may convert any "power," any aspect of his status, into vantage points in almost any case. When he induces other men to do what he wants done, a President can trade on their dependence now *and* later.

The President's advantages are checked by the advantages of others. Continuing relationships will pull in both directions. These are relationships of mutual dependence. A President depends upon the men he would persuade; he has to reckon with his need or fear of them. They too will possess status, or authority, or both, else they would be of little use to him. Their vantage points confront his own; their tempers his.

Persuasion is a two-way street. Sawyer, it will be recalled, did not respond at once to Truman's plan for wage increases at the steel mills. On the contrary, the Secretary hesitated and delayed and only acquiesced when he was satisfied that publicly he would not bear the onus of decision. Sawyer had some points of vantage all his own from which to resist presidential pressure. If he had to reckon with coercive implications in the President's "situations of strength," so had Truman to be mindful of the implications underlying Sawyer's place as a department head, as steel administrator, and as a Cabinet spokesman for business. Loyalty is reciprocal. Having taken on a dirty job in the steel crisis, Sawyer had strong claims to loyal support. Besides, he had authority to do some things that the White House could ill afford. Emulating Wilson, he might have resigned in a huff (the removal power also works two ways). Or emulating Ellis Arnall, he might have declined to sign necessary orders. Or, he might have let it be known publicly that he deplored what he was told to do and protested its doing. By following any of these courses Sawyer almost surely would have strengthened the position of management, weakened the position of the White House, and embittered the union. But the whole purpose of a wage increase was to enhance White House persuasiveness in urging settlement upon union and companies alike. Although Sawyer's status and authority did not give him the power to prevent an increase outright, they gave him capability to undermine its purpose. If his authority over wage rates had been vested by a statute, not by revocable presidential order, his power of prevention might have been complete. So Harold Ickes demonstrated in the famous case of helium sales to Germany before the Second World War.

The power to persuade is the power to bargain. Status and authority yield bargaining advantages. But in a government of "separated institutions sharing powers," they yield them to all sides. With the array of vantage points at his disposal, a President may be far more persuasive than his logic or his charm could make him. But outcomes are not guaranteed by his advantages. There remain the counter pressures those whom he would influence can bring to bear on him from vantage points at their disposal. Command has limited ulitility; persuasion becomes give-and-take. It is well that the White House holds the vantage points it does. In such a business any President may need them all—and more.

EXPERT OPINION 3

GLENDON A. SCHUBERT: The President and the Courts

The most significant aspect of judicial review of presidential orders is its ineffectiveness. If the courts are the most important bulwark of freedom and liberty in the United States, then we have every right to view with alarm the future security of the republic. And yet, the courts have an indispensable role to perform in ensuring that our government will afford in the future, as it already has ensured in such substantial measure in the past, a maximum of freedom under law, and that balance between the rights of the few and the many, of the individual and society, which has constituted the central problem of all liberal political philosophers. How is this seeming paradox to be explained?

First and most fundamentally, we should give up the myth that the judiciary either can or should resolve the critical questions of public policy that each generation must face anew. It is both unreasonable and antidemocratic for us to expect the judges to fulfill such a function. This is merely a way of saying that the elected representatives of the people—the President and the Congress—must decide the great questions of constitutional law. Obviously, this places a premium upon the efficacy of political processes, including the enormously expanding job of administering the manifold functions of modern government.

Deciding constitutional questions is a means of making law: law is the formal statement of public policy. If the courts are not to, and normally do not, attempt to second-guess the President on fundamental issues of public policy, what is left for them to do?

Much. There remains, for instance, the obligation of incumbent officials to comply with requirements and limitations imposed by the laws that they themselves, and their predecessors, have made. It is in this sense that "the Rule of Law" assumes its largest significance, and it is here that the courts are peculiarly well adapted to function and act. In truth, there is much evidence to suggest that this is precisely what is happening in the United States today. . . . For the courts to return to their historic role in Anglo-Saxon polities of enforcing, for citizen and official alike, the requirements of existing law is a large enough task. Our concern, therefore, should be with the extent to which the judiciary have fulfilled this responsibility, rather than with their inevitable failure to discharge the impossible function of substituting their judgment for that of the President in time of crisis. To speak of the federal judiciary alone, it simply is not true that in this sense and at such a time, three hundred heads are better than one.

SOURCE: *The Presidency in the Courts,* Minneapolis: University of Minnesota Press, 1957, pp. 347–354. By permission of the publisher and author.

Measured in terms of such criteria, what is the record of eight generations and eight hundred cases, in which constitutional questions concerning the exercise of presidential power have been raised before the courts?

When the President acts, literally, as Commander in Chief, his constitutional authority is on unimpeachable grounds. He may raise armies and send them where he wills. In addition to regular members of the armed forces, his authority extends (or has extended historically) to militiamen, volunteers, draftees, and conscientious objectors. Although a civilian Court of Military Appeals recently has been created near the apex of the system of military courts, the President continues to function as the highest reviewing authority and the agency of final determination. There are a number of Civil War cases which hold to the contrary, but the preponderance of judicial opinion has upheld and the unquestionable practice has been that the President can declare martial law when in his judgment the exigencies of military necessity make this step imperative; and at such a time and in such places, civilians generally are subject to the jurisdiction of military courts. The vanquished enemy, whether his role was that of professional soldier or politician, may be tried for "unlawful belligerency" or "crimes against humanity" before military commissions authorized by the President alone, or in cooperation with the governments of other states. The civilian residents of territory occupied by the military forces of the United States, as well as the American-citizen entourage of our occupying forces, are subject to the jurisdiction of special military government courts whose constitution lies, again, in the authority and powers of the President. None of these various types of military courts dispensing military justice is subject to the supervision and review of the regular federal judiciary; as to them, the President himself is the Supreme Court.

Alien enemies—a classification which includes, for various purposes, many citizens of the United States, both naturalized and natural-born—are subject to what amounts in practice to almost absolute presidential control—and he may deal with them in ways which unquestionably are contrary to the normal requirements of both permanent statutory law and the Bill of Rights, as these are usually interpreted. The alien enemy may be interned, either in a regular jail with common criminals, or in a special concentration camp specially constructed for thousands like himself. If not incarcerated, he may be placed under surveillance, licensed, restricted in his movement, and required to report periodically like a parolee. . . .

The regulatory authority in all these actions is the President; and it is he who in substantial measure makes the laws which determine the obligations of the alien enemy.

The President also legislates to license, prohibit, and otherwise to control the carrying on of commerce with the enemy in time of either civil or international war, whether it be war *de facto* or war *de jure*. Vessels and persons who violate his regulations may be seized; and in the case of property, may be confiscated, while in the case of persons, may be indicted on criminal charges. . . .

There are no apparent legal limitations upon the power of the President to proclaim the existence of a national emergency. Certainly, the courts will not substitute their judgment of the state of the Union for that of the Chief Executive. He may then claim the right to exercise, throughout the duration of his self-proclaimed emergency, extraordinary powers which would not be considered available for his use in time of "normalcy." Increasingly, Congress has adopted permanent legislation which is automatically invoked and revivified upon a presidential declaration of a national emergency. This state of emergency has no necessary relationship to the existence of war *de jure*. It may be occasioned by domestic crisis, as in the spring of 1933, or it may either precede the outbreak of war *de jure* (as during the period 1939–1941) or extend beyond the end of war *de jure* (as in the case of the continuing extension of the emergency declared by President Truman in December 1950 beyond the date of ratification of the peace treaty with Japan on April 28, 1952). The whole period of the Civil War was that of a presidentially declared emergency, although there was no war *de jure*. On the other hand, the United States was at war *de jure* throughout the decade extending from December 7, 1941, until April 28, 1952, and there was also the presidentially declared national emergency which includes this same period.

During the period of such a national emergency, the President may exercise such abnormal powers over private property as that of fixing prices for producers, manufacturers, wholesalers, retailers, and consumers; he may allocate raw materials and ration the consumption of finished goods; under his direction, public contracts may be made, modified, and broken, and rights under private contracts may be altered to the extent that they conflict with the requirements of the public contracting power. The President does all these things in the right of his constitutional status and authority as the Commander in Chief, although his constitutional powers are usually reinforced by almost unlimited delegation of statutory powers.

As the Chief of State, his power is, if anything, even more absolute and beyond the scope of challenge in the courts, because in this area, he does not share constitutional power as an equal of the Congress, as he does in the case of the war power of the national government. In the realm of foreign relations, he is either the primary or else the exclusive organ of governmental power. He is, in the words of the Supreme Court, the *sole* organ of the nation. It is he who recognizes, or refuses to recognize, the governments of foreign states. He may make agreements with them which have the same binding force and effect as treaties. He may extend the national *imperium* over new lands which are acquired through discovery, conquest, or—as in the case of the tidelands—as the result of his own assertion of title. His supplementary regulations may contribute substantially to the national policy governing immigration and admission to the United States. Similarly, he may act to place an embargo upon or to license trade by residents of the United States with foreign countries. Since the power to regulate foreign commerce is vested by the Constitution in the Congress in unequivocal terms, the President's action in this area is usually undertaken on the basis of statutory delegation of authority, but his own independent constitutional power is such that there are no apparent limitations on the power of Congress to transfer to him the power to legislate for the regulation of such foreign commerce.
. . .

As the Chief Administrator, his legal authority over the personnel and properties which constitute the executive branch of the government of the United States is limited, as a matter of administrative necessity, by statutory law, regulations of his own making, and rule-making power of his subordinates; but only to a very modest extent is he controlled by the power of the courts. His power of removal over his military and civil subordinates has been, throughout most of our history, practically unassailable. This was demonstrated anew in the most recently frictional aspect of this, administrative removals authorized by his own executive order on grounds of disloyalty. His power of administrative direction over his subordinates cannot be challenged by them in the courts, nor has it yet been successfuly forestalled before the courts by those outside the government who are indirectly affected by his power to thus control the activities of his subordinates. He may issue regulations, orders, directives, and instructions; he may transfer statutory responsibilities from one official to another; he may change the organizational status and composition of administrative agencies; and his subordinates may present their advice to him—which he of necessity is bound to follow in most instances—and all this without creating justiciable rights of a substantial enough nature for the judiciary to review his judgment.

Furthermore, the courts have since an early period recognized that he must be able to subdelegate his powers, and particularly his statutory powers, if he is to exercise more than a fraction of them, so his authority to act through his subordinates, irrespective of the language used in statutory acts of delegation to him, has been consistently recognized in hundreds of cases. This assumes importance from another point of view in that, when such a subordinate acts for him, in the eyes of the judiciary, it is still in law *the President* who has acted; consequently, the effect of this legal fiction is to expand the scope of executive discretion and judicial non-reviewability into impredictable depths of the administrative hierarchy where these doctrines are inapposite and should be inapplicable. If it is true that he is the Commander in *Chief,* it cannot follow, as the courts have in effect held, that every commander of a military district is in law the Commander in Chief too; if he is the "*Sole* Organ of the Nation," then certainly neither the Secretary of State nor the Attorney General, nor both of them together, can also be the Sole Organ at the same time; and if he is the *Chief* Administrator, or the "Chief Executive" to use the more common phrase, then neither the director of the Office of Price Stabilization, the Secretary of the Interior, nor a bureau chief in some other agency can also be the Chief Executive. For many purposes, however, they are such in the eyes of the judiciary.

In times past, the President has exercised considerable discretion over the disposition and uses to which the public lands have been put. In the absence of statutory authority, Presidents for more than a century made reservations of the public lands for military purposes, to conserve our natural resources, and for the resettlement of the aboriginal Americans, as well as for such other purposes as lighthouse reservations and bird sanctuaries. This is largely a closed chapter today save for the continuing activities of that recondite specialist, the Indian claims lawyer. Nevertheless, the subject is important to us because of the great liberality with which the courts have characteristically viewed the exercise of presidential authority in this area, creating precedents which are available, and which have been used, to justify an equally broad range of presidential discretion in other areas of substantive activity.

The sources of the President's power are various and in the view of the Supreme Court today it makes little difference whether they are clearly distinguished for purposes of justifying any particular order which is challenged. In quantitative terms, statutes are certainly the most important source, and there are today no apparent limitations upon the power of Congress to make such delegations of authority to the President, either prospectively or retroactively. Whatever the war power is, it is defined by the courts as being largely equivalent to military necessity; and it is constitutionally invested in the President fully as much as in the Congress. At least in some times and with respect to certain subjects, the Supreme Court and other courts have recognized the right of the President to act affirmatively in the public interest, even where there is no apparent authority for his action in either statute or the Constitution. This writer finds it most accurate and most useful to speak of this as the President's implied powers. Whatever they are to be called, they are a part of the panoply of authority of the presidential office. Statutes may occasionally be held unconstitutional where they conflict with or encroach upon the exclusive constitutional authority of the executive, just as presidential orders may occasionally be found unconstitutional where they conflict with valid acts of the Congress within the scope of its own exclusive constitutional authority.

Judicially determined standards of form and procedure for executive legislation are practically nonexistent. There is no necessary form for executive orders or proclamations other than that required by statute and executive order. The President probably should, but does not have to, refer to the source of his authority in his orders and regulations of general effect. He can amend or revoke his own ordinances and those of his predecessors. Statutory and executive law now determines when executive legislation goes into effect. The courts will take judicial notice of his ordinances, and are required by statute to notice the great bulk of them which are printed in the Federal Register. A proclamation or executive order is public law, just as are statutes.

When we turn to the mechanics of the exercise of judicial review, the full extent of the freedom of presidential action from judicial control becomes inescapably apparent. The courts will not review executive discretion: therefore, they will not intervene in presidential decisions of political questions; they must occasionally submit to superior force, or the threat of it, if the President chooses to take direct action to frustrate the judicial process; they compel him to act no matter what the nature or certainty of his obligation may be; they cannot compel him to divulge official information that he chooses to withhold; his formal statement that he has complied with statutory conditions to his action is accepted as binding; and with rare exceptions involving subordinates acting in his name, his findings of "facts" are accepted as conclusive and are not open to judicial re-examination.

It is the duty of the courts to uphold the constitutionality of the President's action, and they must give great weight to his own interpretation and construction of the scope of his own powers. Those who seek to challenge the President's action must assume the burden of proof and the courts will always assume that the President has complied with the requirements of law. The Chief Executive has not been and apparently cannot be forced to appear personally before any court; he is officially and personally immune from judicial process and prospective judicial control. The courts can neither force him to do anything, nor prevent him from doing anything he may decide to do, although they may, of course, decide (and on rare instances they have decided) that action he had already taken was unconstitutional.

EXPERT OPINION 4

V. O. KEY: Administrative Constraints on Presidential Power

Administrative Agencies Not Ciphers. Administrative agencies are not as clay in the hands of the President and his partisan associates. They tend to have a tradition, an outlook, and a policy inclination of their own. To budge them from their predetermined paths is not always easy. Vast aggregations of public servants, military and civil, organized into well-knit hierarchies and animated by common aims and spirit have a potency in the political process that is often underestimated or even ignored. Government departments and agencies at times act as spokesmen or representatives before legislative bodies and the public for segments of society that they serve. Through the prosecution of research that reveals public needs and points toward public action, administrative agencies often initiate movements leading to new public policy. In the management of programs of procurement and expenditure, agencies may affect significantly the fortunes of great industries. In the politics of appropriations almost every administrative bureau or department seeks to maintain or enlarge the scope of its operations.

In one respect administrative agencies are like pressure groups: they operate continually, in Republican and Democratic administrations alike, to advance their interests; indeed, often the closest working relations are maintained between a pressure organization and the governmental agencies in which it is interested. Pressure groups and administrative departments are elements in the pattern of politics that may be jarred and realigned by the results of an election but are seldom completely thrown from power. The administrative organization exerts its strength

SOURCE: *Politics, Parties and Pressure Groups* (New York: Thomas Y. Crowell Company, 1964), pp. 691–700. Footnotes omitted.

through transient department heads and Presidents, no matter what party is in power. With close relationships between its headquarters personnel in Washington and Congress it is able to make its wishes known to Congress either through the department head or through unofficial channels. Often with a personnel distributed over the nation, it is sometimes able to stir up, by discreet measures, pressure from home to bear on Congress. With almost a monopoly of information in the sphere of interest, the administrative organization is able to release or withhold data in such a fashion as to influence the course of legislative action.

Representative Role of Administrative Agencies. A factor that conditions the task of the President in the direction of administration is the representative role of administrative agencies. Pressure groups and administrative agencies themselves often contend that the agency has a duty to act in furtherance of the interests of the group it serves. This is a doctrine of bureaucratic representation: that the Department of Labor should speak for and represent the interests of labor in making recommendations for new legislation; that the Department of Agriculture should promote vigorously the interests of the farmer and ignore those of other groups; and so on. . . .

With agency after agency attached to the interests of particular groups and under pressure to promote partial interests, the President as administrative leader has no little difficulty in bringing about the operation of the government in accord with a party program dedicated to the general welfare. The prevailing practice is that the administrative agencies represent the interest they serve. Many of them owe their existence to the groups they serve. As new groups or classes rise to power and influence they are recognized through the establishment of governmental departments. The creation of the Department of Agriculture was the first recognition of an economic class in the administrative structure; later the departments of Commerce and Labor were established.

Administrative Agency and Its Congressional Allies. By their close communion with interests in society administrative agencies may gain a certain independence of presidential direction. By the same token they become beholden to those groups upon whose support they depend. These group relations often extend over into alliances involving the administrative agency, the pressure group, and Congress. Administrative agencies develop friends in Congress whose policy interests parallel those of the agency. At times a bureau or agency may become virtually independent of the President, so powerful is its support in Congress. These relationships make it difficult to bring the work of such agencies into line with the President's program, and insofar as it is a party program they tend to vitiate party responsibility. To the extent that a President fails as a legislative leader he is also likely to fail as chief administrator; when Congress has the whiphand in legislation, it also tends to undercut the President as Chief Executive.

Text of Judge Sirica's Ruling on the "Watergate Tapes"

On July 23, 1973, Watergate Special Prosecutor Archibald Cox, acting on behalf of the June 1973 grand jury empaneled by this court, caused to be issued a subpoena duces tecum to the President of the United States, Richard M. Nixon. The subpoena required the President, or any appropriate subordinate official, to produce for the grand jury certain tape recordings and documents enumerated in an attached schedule. The President complied with the subpoena insofar as it related to memoranda of Gordon Strachan and W. Richard Howard, but otherwise declined to follow the subpoena's directive. In a letter to the court dated July 25, 1973, the President advised that the tape recordings sought would not be provided, and by way of explanation wrote: " . . . I follow the example of a long line of my predecessors

SOURCE: *The New York Times,* August 30, 1973. Abridged and footnotes omitted. © 1973 by The New York Times. Reprinted by permission.

as President of the United States who have consistently adhered to the position that the President is not subject to compulsory process from the courts."

Therafter, the grand jury instructed Special Prosecutor Cox to apply for an order requiring production of the recordings. On July 26, the Special Prosecutor petitioned this court for a show cause order directed to the President. At the time of this application a quorum of the grand jury was polled in open court, and each juror expressed his or her desire that the court order compliance. Subsequently, the court ordered that the President or any appropriate subordinate official show cause "why the documents and objects described in [the subpoena] should not be produced as evidence before the grand jury."

In response to the show cause order, the President, by his attorneys, filed a special appearance contesting the court's jurisdiction to order the President's compliance with the grand jury subpoena. The court allowed for the filing of a response by the Special Prosecutor and reply by the President, and the matter came on for hearing on August 22.

The parties to the controversy have briefed and argued several issues including the court's jurisdiction in the matter of compulsory process, the existence and scope of "executive privilege" generally, applicability of "executive privilege" to the tape recordings subpoenaed, and waiver of privilege. The court has found it necessary to adjudicate but two questions for the present: (1) whether the court has jurisdiction to decide the issue of privilege, and (2) whether the court has authority to enforce the subpoena duces tecum by way of an order requiring production for inspection in camera. A third question, whether the materials are in fact privileged as against the grand jury, either in whole or in part, is left for subsequent adjudication. For the reasons outlined below, the court concludes that both of the questions considered must be answered in the affirmative.

I

A search of the Constitution and the history of its creation reveals a general disfavor of government privileges, or at least uncontrolled privileges. Early in the Convention of 1787, the delegates cautioned each other concerning the dangers of lodging immoderate power in the executive department. This attitude persisted throughout the convention, and executive powers became a major topic in the subsequent ratification debates. The framers regarded the legislative department superior in power and importance to the other two and felt the necessity of investing it with some privileges and immunities, but even here an attitude of restraint, as expressed by James Madison, prevailed: Mr. Pinckney moved a clause declaring "that each house should be the judge of the privilege of its own members."

Mr. Madison distinguished between the power of judging of privileges previously and duly established, and the effect of the motion which would give a discretion to each house as to the extent of its own privileges. He suggested that it would be better to make provision for ascertaining by *law*, privileges of each house, than to allow each house to decide for itself. He suggested also the necessity of considering what privileges ought to be allowed to the Executive.

The upshot of Madison's final suggestion regarding a definition of executive privileges was that none were deemed necessary, or at least that the Constitution need not record any. . . .

Are there, then, any rights or privileges consistent with, though not mentioned in, the Constitution which are necessary to the executive? One answer may be found in the Supreme Court decision, United States v. Reynolds, 354 U.S. 1 (1953). The Court recognized an executive privilege, evidentiary in nature, for military secrets. Reynolds held that when a court finds the privilege is properly invoked under the appropriate circumstances, it will, in a civil case at least, suppress the evidence. Thus, it must be recognized that there can be executive privileges that will bar the production of evidence. The court is willing here to recognize and give effect to an evidentiary privilege based on the need to protect Presidential privacy.

The court, however, cannot agree with respondent that it is the executive that finally determines whether its privilege is properly invoked. The availability of evidence, including the validity and scope of privileges, is a judicial decision.

Judicial control over the evidence in a case cannot be abdicated to the caprice of executive officers.

It is emphatically the province and duty of the judicial department to say what the law is. Those who apply the rule to particular cases must of necessity expand and interpret that rule. If two laws conflict with each other, the courts must decide on the operation of each.

In all the numerous litigations where claims of executive privilege have been interposed, the courts have not hesitated to pass judgment. Executive fiat is not the mode of resolution. As has been stated most recently in this circuit: "No executive official or agency can be given absolute authority to determine what documents in its possession may be considered by the court in its task. Otherwise the head of any executive department would have the power on his own say to cover up all evidence of fraud and corruption when a Federal court or grand jury was investigating malfeasance in office, and this is not the law."

II

If after judicial examination in camera, any portion of the tapes is ruled not subject to privilege, that portion will be forwarded to the grand jury at the appropriate time. To call for the tapes in camera is thus tantamount to fully enforcing the subpoena as to any unprivileged matter. Therefore, before the court can call for production in camera, it must have concluded that it has authority to order a President to obey the command of a grand jury subpoena as it relates to unprivileged evidence in his possession. The court has concluded that it possesses such authority.

Analysis of the question must begin on the well-established premises that the grand jury has a right to every man's evidence and that for purposes of gathering evidence, process may issue to anyone. . . .

The burden here, then, is on the President to define exactly what it is about his office that court process commanding the production of evidence cannot reach there. To be accurate, court process in the form of a subpoena duces tecum has already issued to the President, and he acknowledges that pursuant to Burr, courts possess authority to direct such subpoenas to him. A distinction is drawn, however, between authority to issue a subpoena and authority to command obedience to it. It is this second compulsory process that the President contends may not reach him. The burden yet remains with the President, however, to explain why this must be so. What distinctive quality of the Presidency permits its incumbent to withhold evidence? To argue that the need for Presidential privacy justifies it is not persuasive. On the occasions when such need justifies suppression, the courts will sustain a privilege. The fact that this is a judicial decision has already been discussed at length, but the opinion of Chief Justice Marshall on the topic deserves notice here. When deciding that a subpoena should issue to the President, the Chief Justice made it clear that if certain portions should be excised, it being appropriate to sustain a privilege, the court would make such a decision upon return of the subpoena.

To argue that it is the constitutional separation of powers that bars compulsory court process from the White House is also unpersuasive. Such a contention overlooks history. Although courts generally, and this court in particular, have avoided any interference with the discretionary acts of coordinate branches, they have not hesitated to rule on nondiscretionary acts when necessary. Respondent points out that these and other precedents refer to officials other than the President, and that this distinction renders the precedents inapplicable. Such an argument tends to set the

White House apart as a branch of government. It is true that Mississippi v. Johnson, 4 Wall. 475 (1866) left open the question whether the President can be required by court process to perform a purely ministerial act, but to persist in the opinion, after 1952, that he cannot would seem to exalt the form of the Youngstown Sheet & Tube Co. case over its substance. Though the court's order there went to the Secretary of Commerce, it was the direct order to President Truman that was reversed.

The special prosecutor has correctly noted that the framers' intention to lodge the powers of government in separate bodies also included a plan for interaction between departments. A "watertight" division of different functions was never their design. The legislative branch may organize the judiciary and dictate the procedures by which it transacts business. The judiciary may pass upon the constitutionality of legislative enactments and in some instances define the bounds of Congressional investigations. The executive may veto legislative enactments, and the legislature may override the veto. The executive appoints judges and justices and may bind judicial decisions by lawful executive orders. The judiciary may pass on the constitutionality of executive acts.

While the Constitution diffuses power the better to secure liberty, it also contemplates that practice will integrate the dispersed powers into a workable government. It enjoins upon its branches separateness but interdependence, autonomy but reciprocity.

That the court has not the physical power to enforce its order to the President is immaterial to a resolution of the issues. Regardless of its physical power to enforce them, the court has a duty to issue appropriate orders. The court cannot say that the executive's persistence in withholding the tape recordings would "tarnish its reputation," but must admit that it would tarnish the court's reputation to fail to do what it could in pursuit of justice. In any case, the courts have always enjoyed the good faith of the executive branch, even in such dire circumstances as those presented by Youngstown Sheet & Tube Co. v. Sawyer, 343 U.S. 579 (1952), and there is no reason to suppose that the courts in this instance cannot again rely on the same good faith. Indeed, the President himself has publicly so stated. . . .

In all candor, the court fails to perceive any reason for suspending the power of courts to get evidence and rule on question of privilege in criminal matters simply because it is the President of the United States who holds the evidence. The Burr decision left for another occasion a ruling on whether compulsory process might issue to the President in situations such as this. In the words of counsel, "This is a new question," with little in the way of precedent to guide the court. But Chief Justice Marshall clearly distinguished the amenability of the king to appear and give testimony under court process and that of this nation's chief magistrate. The conclusion reached here cannot be inconsistent with the view of the great Chief Justice nor with the spirit of the Constitution. . . .

In deciding whether these tape recordings or portions thereof are properly the objects of a privilege, the court must accommodate two competing policies. On the one hand, as has been noted earlier, is the need to disfavor privileges and narrow their application as far as possible. On the other hand lie a need to favor the privacy of Presidential deliberations; to indulge a presumption in favor of the President. To the court, respect for the President, the Presidency, and the duties of the office, gives the advantage to this second policy. This respect, however, does not decide the controversy. Such a resolution on the court's part, as Chief Justice Marshall observed, "would deserve some other appellation than the term respect." Nevertheless, it does not hurt for the courts to remind themselves often that the authority vested in them to delimit the scope and application of privileges and immunities of government is a trust. And as with every trust, an abuse can reap the most dire consequences. This court, then, enters upon its present task with care and with determination to exercise that judicial restraint that characterizes the conduct of courts.

The teaching of Reynolds is that a court should attempt to satisfy itself whether or not a privilege is properly invoked without unnecessarily probing into the material claimed to be privileged. A decision on how far to go will be dictated in part by need for the evidence. . . . .

The grand jury's showing of need here is well documented and imposing. The special prosecutor has specifically identified by date, time and place each of the eight meetings and the one telephone call involved. Due to the unusual circumstances of having access to sworn public testimony of participants to these conversations, the special prosecutor has been able to provide the court with the conflicting accounts of what transpired. He thus identifies the topics discussed in each instance, the areas of critical conflict in the testimony, and the resolution it is anticipated the tape recordings may render possible. The relative importance of the issues in doubt is revealed.

The point is raised that, as in Reynolds, the sworn statements of witnesses should suffice and remove the need for access to documents deemed privileged. Though this might often be the case, here, unfortunately, the witnesses differ, sometimes completely, on the precise matters likely to be of greatest moment to the grand jury. Ironically, need for the taped evidence derives in part from the fact that witnesses have testified regarding the subject matter, creating important issues of fact for the grand jury to resolve. It will be noted as well in contradistinction to Reynolds, that this is a criminal investigation. Rather than money damages at stake, we deal here in matters of reputation and liberty. Based on this indisputably forceful showing of necessity by the grand jury, the claim of privilege cannot be accepted lightly.

In his brief of support, the special prosecutor outlines the grand jury's view regarding the validity of the respondent's claim of privilege. Its opinion is that the right of confidentiality is improperly asserted here. Principally, the special prosecutor cites a substantial possibility, based on the sworn testimony of participants, that the privilege is improperly invoked as a cloak for serious criminal wrongdoings.

According to the testimony of John W. Dean, many of the conversations in which he participated were part and parcel of a criminal conspiracy to obstruct justice by preventing the truth from coming out about the additional participants in the original conspiracy to break into and wiretap the offices of the Democratic National Committee. He has testified that in the presence of H. R. Haldeman he told respondent on September 15, 1972, that "all [Dean] had been able to do was to contain the case and assist in keeping it out of the White House." Dean also told respondent that he "could make no assurances that the day would not come when this matter would start to unravel."

Respondent allegedly congratulated him on the "good job" he was doing on that task (S. Tr. 2229-30). Dean also has testified that on March 13, 1973, respondent told him that respondent had approved executive clemency for Hunt, and that there would be no problem in raising $1-million to buy the Watergate defendants' silence (S. Tr. 2324). In addition, there is uncontradicted testimony that respondent was briefed on Watergate on June 20, 1972, three days after the arrests by Haldeman, Ehrlichman and Mitchell, his closest political advisers (S. Tr. 5924, 3407-08). If these three told respondent all they allegedly knew, respondent would have been aware of details of the nascent cover-up. . . .

To paraphrase Chief Justice John Marshall, if it be apparent that the tapes are irrelevant to the investigation or that for state reasons, they cannot be introduced into the case, the subpoena duces tecum would be useless. But if this not be apparent, if they may be important to the investigation, if they may be safely heard by the grand jury, if only in part, would it not be a blot on the pages which record the judicial proceedings of this country, if, in a case of such serious import as this, the court did not at least call for an inspection of the evidence in chambers?

Bibliography

(Additional materials can also be found in the sources cited in this chapter's data.)

General Analyses of Presidential Power

Hirschfield, Robert S. (ed.): *The Power of the Presidency* (New York: Atherton Press, Inc., 1968), selections by Edward S. Corwin, "The Aggrandizement of Presidential Power"; Robert S. Hirschfield, "The Power of the Contemporary Presidency"; Owen S. Stratten, "The Weakness of the Presidency"; and Sidney Warren, "The Paradox of Presidential Power."

Liston, Robert A.: *Presidential Power* (New York: McGraw-Hill Book Company, 1971).

McConnell, Grant: *The Modern Presidency* (New York: St. Martin's Press, Inc., 1967).

Strum, Philippa: *Presidential Power and American Democracy* (Pacific Palisades, Calif.: Goodyear Publishing Company, 1972).

Wildavsky, Aaron: "The Two Presidencies," in *The Presidency,* edited by Aaron Wildavsky (Boston: Little, Brown and Company, 1969), pp. 230–243.

The President and the Public

Cornwell, Elmer E., Jr.: *Presidential Leadership of Public Opinion.* (Bloomington, Ind.: Indiana University Press, 1965).

———: "Presidential News: The Expanding Public Image," *Journalism Quarterly,* vol. 36, pp. 275–283, 1959.

Greenstein, Fred I.: "Popular Images of the Presidency," *American Journal of Psychiatry,* vol. 122, pp. 523–529, 1965.

Mueller, John E.: "Presidential Popularity from Truman to Johnson," *American Political Science Review,* vol. 64, pp. 18–34, 1970.

The President and Other Public Officials

Polsby, Nelson W.: *Congress and the Presidency,* 2d ed. (Englewood Cliffs, N.J.: Prentice-Hall, Inc., 1971), chap. 7 (Conflict and Cooperation).

Riker, William H., and William Bast: "Presidential Action in Congressional Nomination," in *The Presidency,* edited by Aaron Wildavsky (Boston: Little, Brown and Company, 1959), pp. 250–267.

Truman, David B.: *The Congressional Party* (New York: John Wiley & Sons, Inc., 1959), chap. 8 (Functional Interdependence).

Watergate and Its Aftermath

The Hearings and Reports of the Senate Watergate Committee are published by the Government Printing Office. A portion of these may be found in *Watergate Hearings: Break-in and Cover-up* (New York: Bantam Books, Inc., 1973). The most extensive listing of official reports, including public documents from the House Judiciary

Committee's impeachment proceedings, may be found in the Congressional Information Service's index to congressional materials.

An insightful analysis of the Presidency before Watergate which emphasizes the conditions leading to Watergate is: George E. Reedy, *Twilight of the Presidency* (New York: W. W. Norton & Company, Inc., 1970). Reedy was press secretary to President Lyndon B. Johnson.

III. ANALYZING THE DATA

In previous chapters we asked specific questions that were designed to help you interpret the data. Since you have now had considerable experience in analyzing data, this chapter will instead emphasize more general aspects of the data. Our goal is to help you understand not only what the data mean, but also some of the limitations of these data. This is done not to show you that all information is defective, but rather to make you more aware of what can and cannot be said about certain types of data. As in previous chapters, the correct answers will be found at the end of this section.

Question 1

Table 11.1 shows that considerable support for presidential power exists among the American public. Can these data be interpreted to mean that the President can do just about anything without causing public displeasure?

Your Answer

Question 2

We see in Table 11.2 that both the number of bills vetoed and vetoes overridden have declined substantially since the time of Roosevelt. One interpretation of this change is that the President has grown less able to resist congressional legislature initiatives. What could be offered as an alternative explanation of this trend?

Your Answer

Question 3

Table 11.3 shows that at least from 1953 to 1972 Congress has passed most legislation supported by the President. Can we infer that the President is likely to get almost any legislative request passed by Congress?

Your Answer

Question 4
The data in federal employment make clear that in terms of sheer personnel the executive branch completely overshadows the two other branches. Do such figures suggest something about the scope of the executive branch's activity? Do these figures also imply that the other branches are powerless against the executive branch because they are overwhelmingly outnumbered?

Your Answer

Question 5
The first three expert opinions on presidential power (Burns, Neustadt, and Schubert) all argue that the President possesses numerous opportunities and advantages in implementing his will. Do any of these experts claim that the President's power is completely unchecked? Do any authors show in their analyses that the President can win conflicts even when everyone opposes him?

Your Answer

Question 6

In expert opinion 4, V. O. Key discusses the problems a President might face in dealing with various executive agencies. In light of this argument, how might the increase in executive-branch employees depicted in Table 11.4 be related to presidential power? In other words, could he automatically equate more employees with increased control?

Your Answer

Question 7

Events surrounding the Watergate break-in and subsequent cover-up have raised an important Constitutional question about a President's power. Many of these questions emerged in the conflict between Special Prosecutor Cox and President Nixon on whether executive privilege and the doctrine of separation of powers enable the President to ignore requests that he surrender tapes of White House conversations. According to Judge Sirica's opinion presented on page 239, what Constitutional principles and related legal arguments compel the President to provide access to these tapes?

Your Answer

Correct Answers

1. The data in Table 11.1, while indicating considerable public willingness to go along with the President, cannot be construed as presenting the President with a blank check. If we carefully note the wording of the various statements we can see that people are not agreeing with unlimited, unchecked exercise of power. For example, the first statement refers to making the people and Congress work along with the President. "Work along" is not the same thing as to order around. Similarly, the statement on sending troops abroad despite public opinion stresses the facts that (1) such action is considered *important* by the President and (2) it is perfectly *legal* to take such action. Neither of these statements about presidential power thus asks the public to approve unconstitutional or blatantly dictatorial acts.

2. Though interpreting Table 11.2 as showing a slackening of presidential resistance to Congress is not incorrect, many other explanations are also plausible. For example it could be argued that the President has increasingly been able to stop unwanted bills before they are ever passed, thus eliminating the need for a veto. Alternatively, the changing nature of public policy debate may have eliminated significant clashes between Congress and the President so the number of vetoed bills declined regardless of changes in relative power. Many more data are required before one of these interpretations could be verified.

3. As we saw in our discussion of the decline in presidential vetoes (Table 11.2), data in the passage of legislation cannot always be unambiguously interpreted. The data in Table 11.3 do not tell us what legislation supported by the President passed Congress. It is not unreasonable to believe that in many instances little or no conflict existed between Congress and the President, so these scores do not indicate the exercise of power. Also, Presidents may not publicly advocate legislation that is likely to be opposed vehemently by Congress. In short, these data suggest that while Presidents are usually successful in getting Congress to agree with them, more data are required to determine whether the President can actually enforce his will on Congress.

4. Table 11.4 shows not only that the executive branch is of enormous size as compared to the other two branches, but that a half million new employees have been added since 1950. Since these figures exclude defense personnel, the magnitude of these numbers suggests considerable involvment in public policy. The presidential bureaucracy has obviously come a long way from being a handful of officials engaged only in the few tasks the states cannot do for themselves. Nevertheless, sheer numbers do not automatically imply actual power. To be sure, the existence of a vast bureaucratic apparatus may give the executive branch a potential advantage over the other branches of government, but these data say nothing about what all these employees do or even whether the President can actually use these employees in a conflict of wills with Congress or the courts.

5. Though Burns, Neustadt, and Schubert emphasize the President's power position, none of these authors implies that this power is unrestricted. For example, Burns in his analysis of the President and the cities argues that the President acts for the cities by shaping legislation and influencing Congress; that is, the President does not completely decide himself, but instead tries to influence the policy-making process. Such behavior may provide greater scope for presidential action, but no claim is made that a President can thus control mayors. Similarly, Neustadt stresses the importance of bargaining and persuasion in presidential action. Finally, Schubert's analysis suggests that the President's power vis-à-vis the courts is not based on usurpation of judicial prerogatives but rather derives from existing powers that are broadly interpreted. Schubert also notes that many of these presidential powers are explicitly granted by the courts or Congress and could readily be restricted. Finally, it is interesting to note that none of these experts speaks about situations in which the President prevailed even when opposed by everyone. This may have occurred, but these expert analyses are not based on such cases.

6. V. O. Key suggests that the existence of a large bureaucratic organization within the executive branch may constrain the President as well as promote potential power. In the light of analysis, the figures in Table 11.4 *could* be interpreted to mean that the Presidency is becoming increasingly unwieldy and difficult to control. Hence, the creation of new agencies and larger and larger staffs may create more points of friction for presidential policy making rather than extending control to every aspect of political life.

7. On the basis of a number of Constitutional and legal principles, Judge Sirica concludes that President Nixon cannot use the doctrine of executive privilege or separation of powers to resist surrendering the tapes. Sirica observes that the framers of the Constitution left the issue of privilege undefined and did not intend for each branch of government to be the sole judge of its privileges. As for the separation-of-power argument, Sirica claims that various Constitutional provisions, e.g., presidential veto power over legislation, clearly show that a "watertight" division between branches was not intended. Moreover, a variety of judicial rulings do not put the President beyond the reach of the usual legal process. Even though *United States* v. *Reynolds* recognizes executive privilege for suppressing of evidence, according to Sirica, it is to be decided by the courts, not the executive. In addition, the Youngstown Sheet and Tube case demonstrated that courts can require the President to perform certain duties. Finally, Chief Justice Marshall's opinion in the Burr case is referred to on a number of occasions as precedent-setting authority on the issuance of subpoenas requiring presidential cooperation in criminal proceedings.

Chapter 11
Presidential Power

Name _____

Section _____

IV. CONCLUSION

Having reformulated the original problem and analyzed the relevant data, you can now return to the original problem. In the space below, write a short memorandum on the extent to which the President now dominates the other branches of government. Your essay should integrate various kinds of data into a coherent statement on the problem. Where outside sources are used be sure to cite the source.

Original Problem

"Despite the intentions of those drafting the Constitution, the President is now unchecked in his power by the other branches of government."

Memorandum

Chapter 12
CONGRESSIONAL LEADERSHIP

The Founding Fathers originally intended Congress to be the branch of government closest to the people. Because congressmen, unlike judges, are popularly chosen and, unlike the President, are elected from relatively small districts, it is frequently assumed that congressmen do best represent the average citizen in government. Nevertheless, it is also sometimes argued that congressmen are more interested in seeing their own, as opposed to their constituents', opinions enacted into law. It is further argued that Congress is controlled by a small group of unrepresentative leaders who thwart other congressmen who might attempt to represent the average citizen. If only leaders were more representative, the argument goes, then Congress as a whole would better reflect the public will. The problem we shall consider is:

"Congress is not a representative institution, because not only are congressmen unrepresentative of the public, but congressional leaders, who are even more unrepresentative, dominate law making and thwart their colleagues."

I. REFORMULATING THE PROBLEM

To assist you in reformulating this chapter's problem we shall first discuss some of its important aspects and then offer a number of partial reformulations. These partial reformulations will then help you develop your own reformulation.

Discussion

This chapter's problem involves two assertions. First, it claims that congressmen and congressional leaders are unrepresentative of the American public. Second, it asserts that congressional leaders thwart other, more representative, congressmen from following public dictates. Let us briefly consider each of these assertions.

The first assertion—congressmen in general and leaders in particular are unrepresentative—requires greater elaboration of two points: who are congressional leaders and what do we mean by "representative." Determining who are congressional leaders can be done by reviewing the research of scholars who have examined congressional behavior. A consensus exists that important congressional leaders include floor leaders of both parties (including the House Speaker) and chairmen of key committees such as Appropriations, Armed Services, Rules (in the House), Ways and Means (House),

Judiciary, and Foreign Relations (in the Senate), and Labor and Public Welfare (in the Senate). The meaning of "representation" is a more difficult question. It can be interpreted to mean a similarity on certain social or physical characteristics, e.g., social class or sex. In this sense, male congressmen would not be "representative" of female constituents. On the other hand, we can also speak of representation in terms of similarity of policy preferences. Thus, for example, liberal leaders would represent other liberals. Yet a third meaning would picture representatives in terms of one person acting in behalf of another's interest. The way a lawyer represents a client is an illustration of this third meaning. Moreover, an acceptable reformulation would have to be specific on whether representation referred to the relationship between congressional leaders and other congressmen or the relationship between congressional leaders and the general public.

The second assertion—congressional leaders thwart the goals of other congressmen—is also fraught with complexities. How do we measure the sometimes subtle and hidden exercises of influence within Congress. No doubt much leadership pressure is exerted behind closed doors and is not part of the public record. A reasonable solution to this problem is reliance on expert judgment of those who have studied leadership influence on legislation. The role of leaders in the congressional process is well studied, and it should thus be possible to ascertain leaders' influence over congressional action.

The last question that must be dealt with concerns the time span of the reformulation. The original problem does not specify whether only the present Congress is unrepresentative or whether all Congresses exhibit this characteristic. An acceptable reformulation would have to be specific as to when Congress was unresponsive due to its leadership.

Partial Reformulations

1. Within the last five years congressional leaders (i.e., elected party floor leaders and chairmen of important committees) come from different types of districts than their colleagues. Areas represented by leaders are untypical with respect to such characteristics as regional location, proportions of population in urban areas, and racial composition. Leaders also differ on personal characteristics such as age, previous occupation, race, and sex.

2. With the last five years congressional leaders (i.e., elected party floor leaders and chairmen of important committees) are more conservative than their colleagues as indicated by their roll-call votes. By conservative we mean they tend to agree with positions taken by well-known conservative groups. Congressional leaders are also more obstructionist than their colleagues as indicated by their lower support for presidential programs.

3. Within the last five years, congressional leaders (i.e., elected party floor leaders and chairmen of important commitees) compared to their colleagues, admit to being less interested in what the public thinks ought to be done than in doing what they think is correct.

Congressional Leadership 255

4. Experts who have studied congressional leadership all agree that a strong tendency exists for the leaders to exercise autocratic power of their colleagues and thus prevent Congress from responding to any interests other than their own.

Each of these reformulations considers an aspect of the original problem. However, your analysis will be more complete if more than one of these partial reformulations are combined into a broader, more complex reformulation. Your reformulation can also include aspects of this chapter's problem not mentioned in these partial reformulations. Recall that an acceptable reformulation must be a factual rather than a value statement, define all terms clearly, take into account all aspects of the original problem, and be relevant to the original problem.

Your Reformulation

II. SELECTING THE NECESSARY DATA

Before examining information on congressional leaders, it is necessary to specify the data required to test your reformulation. Without a guide to the data you need, it will be difficult to sort through all the information within a reasonable time. If you wish to refresh your memory of the rules which may guide your selection of data, refer to p. 227.

Data Needed for Your Reformulation

The Data

On the following pages are some of the data you need to analyze this chapter's problem. Some of the data may be relevant to the problem; other data may be irrelevant. After examining the data, turn to section III, which immediately follows the data.

TABLE 12.1 PERSONAL CHARACTERISTICS OF CONGRESSMEN AND CONGRESSIONAL LEADERS, 90th (SECOND SESSION) AND 92nd CONGRESS (FIRST SESSION)

	Characteristics							
	Average Age (mean)		Percent Black		Percent Female		Percent from South‡	
	90th	92nd	90th	92nd	90th	92nd	90th	92nd
Representatives	51.6	51.9	1.7	3.0	2.6	2.8	27.3	27.0
House leaders*	65.7	68.2	0	0	0	0	50.0	50.0
Senators	58.7	53.0	1.0	1.0	1.0	1.0	22.0	22.0
Senate leaders†	67.6	63.7	0	0	0	0	55.5	55.5
U.S. population (1970)	28.1		11.1		51.3		24.6	

*House Leaders are elected party leaders—majority leader, majority whip, Speaker of the House, minority leader and minority whip—and chairmen of important committees. Most experts agree that the important House committees are Appropriations, Rules, Ways and Means, Judiciary, and Armed Services, and these are thus employed in our analysis.

†Senate leaders are the majority leader, majority whip, minority leader, and minority whip. The important Senate committees are Appropriations, Armed Services, Foreign Relations, Judiciary, and Labor and Public Welfare, and the chairmen of these committees are included in the leadership group.

‡Here, and in all of this chapter's analyses, the South includes Virginia, North Carolina, South Carolina, Georgia, Florida, Alabama, Mississippi, Louisiana, Texas, Arkansas, and Tennessee.

SOURCES: Data on the U.S Population (including population in the South) are from the *Statistical Abstract of the United States, 1972*. Age, sex, and race data for the 90th Congress are from *Congressional Quarterly 1968 Almanac*, pp. 31–37. 92nd Congress age data are reported in *Congressional Quarterly Weekly Report*, January 15, 1971, pp. 127–133.

TABLE 12.2 RELIGIOUS BACKGROUNDS OF CONGRESSMEN AND CONGRESSIONAL LEADERS, 90TH (SECOND SESSION) AND 92ND CONGRESS (FIRST SESSION)

Religion	Representatives		House Leaders		Senators		Senate Leaders		U. S. Population
	90th	92nd	90th	92nd	90th	92nd	90th	92nd	
Catholic	22.2%	23.3%	20.0%	40.0%	13.0%	12.0%	11.0%	11.0%	24.1%
Methodist	15.7	15.0	50.0	30.0	23.0	12.0	44.0	11.0	12.4
Presbyterian	14.8	15.4	0	0	12.0	16.0	0	11.0	6.5
Episcopal	11.8	11.3	20.0	10.0	15.0	17.0	22.0	11.0	2.7
Baptist	9.5	9.7	0	0	11.0	8.0	0	22.0	18.7
Other Protestant	21.3	21.6	0	10.0	23.0	25.0	22.0	33.0	30.1
Jewish	3.2	2.8	10.0	10.0	2.0	1.0	0	0	2.3
Greek Orthodox	.5	0	0	0	0	0	0	0	.2
Unspecified	1.0	.9	0	0	1.0	1.0	0	0	3.9
Total	100.0%	100.0%	100.0%	100.0%	100.0%	100.0%	99.0%	100.0%	100.0%

SOURCES: Data on the 90th Congress are from *Congressional Quarterly Weekly Report*, January 19, 1971. U.S. Population figures are from the 1972 national election study conducted by the Survey Research Center, University of Michigan. 92nd Congress data are from *Congressional Quarterly 1968 Almanac*, pp. 31–37.

TABLE 12.3 OCCUPATIONAL BACKGROUNDS OF CONGRESSMEN AND CONGRESSIONAL LEADERS, 90TH (SECOND SESSION) AND 92ND CONGRESS (FIRST SESSION)

Occupation	Representative 90th	Representative 92nd	House Leaders 90th	House Leaders 92nd	Senators 90th	Senators 92nd	Senate Leaders 90th	Senate Leaders 92nd
Public service	40.2%	40.9%	43.5%	43.5%	41.5%	44.0%	40.9%	45.0%
Law	26.6	26.6	39.1	34.8	29.1	28.9	31.8	35.0
Agriculture	4.2	4.1	4.3	4.3	7.7	5.8	4.5	5.0
Business	17.2	16.3	8.6	8.6	10.1	12.0	4.5	5.0
Journalism	4.2	3.4	0	4.3	4.3	3.1	0	0
Teaching	6.2	6.9	4.3	4.3	6.4	4.9	13.6	5.0
Other*	1.5	1.8	0	0	1.3	1.3	4.5	5.0

* "Other" includes professions such as engineering, the ministry, and labor official. Percentages do not add to 100% because many congressmen claim more than one previous occupation.
SOURCE: Same as Table 2.

TABLE 12.4 DISTRICT CHARACTERISTICS OF CONGRESSMEN AND CONGRESSIONAL LEADERS, 90TH (SECOND SESSION) AND 92ND CONGRESS (FIRST SESSION)

	District Characteristics					
	Competitiveness* (mean)		Percent Urban† (mean)		Percent Black and Other Minorities (mean)	
	90th	92nd	90th	92nd	90th	92nd
Representatives	64.3	69.4	68.6	73.5	11.1	11.1
House leaders	83.4	80.7	71.7	74.1	20.0	20.9
Senators	59.8	68.2	68.6	73.5	11.1	11.1
Senate leaders	65.5	61.0	65.1	56.8	19.7	16.8

* Competitiveness is measured by the congressman share of the vote in his most recent election. Hence, the higher the number, the greater the lack of competition.
† A person is considered urban if residing in a city of greater than 2,500 population or in a closely settled fringe.
SOURCE: Competitiveness index data for the 90th Congress are from *Congressional Quarterly Weekly Report,* April 5, 1965, and May 12th, 1967. For the 92nd Congress data are from *Congressional Quarterly 1967 Almanac* (pp. 1283–1308) *1968* (p. 958), and *1970,* (pp. 1085–92). Data on proportion urban and black and other minorities are from the *Congressional District Data Book: Districts of the 92nd Congress.*

TABLE 12.5 VOTING BEHAVIOR OF CONGRESSMEN AND
CONGRESSIONAL LEADERS, 90TH (SECOND SESSION) AND 92ND
CONGRESS (FIRST SESSION)

	Voting Index					
	Support for Conservative Coalition* (mean)		Presidential Support Score† (mean)		ADA Score‡ (mean)	
	90th	92nd	90th	92nd	90th	92nd
Representatives	45.9	50.0	58.8	58.0	38.5	38.7
House leaders	54.7	54.9	61.6	55.5	34.2	30.3
Senators	43.9	50.7	53.2	51.0	39.0	46.2
Senate leaders	53.1	53.6	47.3	56.2	12.7	38.5

* The Conservative Coalition exists where a majority of Republicans and Southern Democrats vote together in a major issue. Support scores are the proportion of times an individual votes with this bloc.

† The Presidential Support score is the proportion of times a congressman has voted for bills publically advocated by the President.

‡ The ADA (Americans for Democratic Action) is a well-known liberal organization that rates congressmen according to votes on a small number of bills. The higher the rating, the greater the agreement between the ADA and the congressmen's voting record.

SOURCES: Presidential Support scores, Conservative Coalition scores, and ADA scores for the 90th Congress (2d session) are from *Congressional Quarterly 1968 Almanac,* pp. 832, 824–826, and 870–871, respectively. ADA scores for the 92nd Congress are from the *Congressional Quarterly Weekly Report,* April 29, 1972, pp. 931–933. Conservative Coalition and Presidential Support scores are from the *Congressional Quarterly 1972 Almanac,* pp. 42–49, 66–70.

TABLE 12.6 SENIORITY OF
CONGRESSMEN AND CONGRESSIONAL LEADERS, 90TH
(SECOND SESSION) AND 92ND
CONGRESS (FIRST SESSION)

	Seniority (mean)	
	90th	92nd
Representatives	9.4	9.2
House leaders	30.3	30.8
Senators	11.1	11.1
Senate leaders	24.6	18.4

SOURCES: 90th Congress data are from the *Congressional Quarterly 1968 Almanac,* pp. 25–27. 92nd Congress data are from the *Congressional Quarterly Weekly Report,* January 15, 1971, pp. 127–133, 137–140.

TABLE 12.7 LEGISLATIVE ROLES AMONG LEADERS AND NONLEADERS IN THE HOUSE OF REPRESENTATIVES, 88TH CONGRESS (1963–1964 SESSION)

Legislative Role*	Leader†	Nonleader
Trustee	31%	27%
Politico	60	46
Delegate	10	27
Total	100%	100%
$N =$	42	71

†Leaders held one or more of the following positions: committee chairmanship and ranking minority member; chairman and ranking member of Appropriations subcommittee; Speaker, majority leader, and majority whip; and minority leader, minority whip, and Republican Conference Chairman.

*The legislative roles are defined as follows: Trustees view themselves as acting independently of outside pressure; the delegate attempts to represent his constituents' views; the politico is a mixture of the previous two roles.

SOURCE: From *The Role of the Congressman* by Roger H. Davidson, copyright © 1969 by the Western Publishing Company, Inc., reprinted by permission of the Bobbs-Merrill Company, Inc.

TABLE 12.8 RELATIONSHIP OF REPRESENTATIVE'S POLICY PREFERENCE AND POLICY PREFERENCE OF CONSTITUENTS   CONGRESS (1958)

	Correlation of Constituency Preference with:	
Issue area	Representative's Perception of Constituency Preference	Representative's Own Policy Preference
Social welfare	.17*	.21
Foreign involvement	.19	.06
Civil rights	.63	.39

*Correlations are Pearson r's.
SOURCE: Adapted from Warren E. Miller and Donald E. Stokes: "Constituency Influence in Congress," *American Political Science Review*, vol. 57, p. 51, March, 1963.

EXPERT OPINION

THE POWER OF COMMITTEE CHAIRMEN

This importance of the chairman flows directly from his vast array of power vis-à-vis the members of his panel. Although the precise situation will vary among the committees, most chairmen can control what their committees do. The chairman decides when the committee shall meet and presides over its sessions, exercising the parliamentary right of recognizing the members. Moreover, he sets the committee's agenda, deciding what the committee will consider, when consideration will take place, and when, and under what conditions, hearings will be held. Subcommittees have become indispensable to committee functioning, and their use is the prerogative of the full committee chairman: he creates them, establishes their jurisdictions, and appoints their members, including the subcommittee chairmen. The committee chairman, additionally, wields substantial influence during floor consideration of his committee's product; he manages the committee's bills on the floor, or appoints someone to do so in his stead; he, in fact, decides who will represent the chamber when the bill goes to a conference committee, often including himself on the delegation. Finally, the committee staff is the creature of the chairman: he determines who will be hired, how much assistance will be provided for the minority side, what the majority staff will do, and often the vigor with which it carries out its assignments. The chairman, in short, has formidable bases of power and influence, and that he can use these levers to help or hinder the goals of his committee members goes without saying.

But possession of such powers is not the same as their exercise. A chairman may be unable, or unwilling, to exploit them to their fullest extent, and the most that can be said is that the chairman has a very high potential for power. A number of limiting forces may be present. In the first place, customary ways of conducting committee business may exist; widely shared norms may require consultation with the ranking minority member, the muting of partisanship, and the observance of other proprieties. About half the committees of Congress have formal rules of procedure which a determined committee majority may invoke against a chairman who, in their view, has not met his responsibilities. An arbitrary chairman may find rules imposed upon him, as did Adam Clayton Powell (D., N.Y.) of the House Education and Labor Committee, whose colleagues chose the waning days of the Eighty-ninth Congress to pass rules limiting some of the practices in which Powell had engaged.

Moreover, personal factors are relevant; some chairmen may have no interest in exercising a tight rein on their committee colleagues. Bibby and Davidson present an interesting contrast between two chairmen of the Senate Committee on Banking and Currency, J. William Fullbright (D., Ark.) and S. Willis Robertson (D., Va.). The former's interests did not lie with the committee and he was content to exercise a "decentralized and permissive style of leadership" while he pursued his concern with foreign relations. Thus he allowed the subcommittees to work independently, under the direction of their respective chairmen, well funded and well staffed. Under his chairmanship the committee "pretty much ran itself." When Fullbright assumed the chairmanship of the Foreign Relations Committee, the leadership of Banking and Currency passed to Robertson, whose style was in sharp contrast to that of his predecessor. He held policy views at variance with others on the panel and used his powers as chairman to restrain their activities. He juggled the subcommittee structure, limited the expenditure of funds for hearings and staff studies, and generally

SOURCE: Leroy N. Rieselbach: *Congressional Politics* (New York: McGraw-Hill Book Company, 1973), pp. 67–69 and 95–100. Footnotes omitted. By permission of the McGraw-Hill Book Company.

held down the committee's activities. The chairman's leadership style and his views and interests, in sum, influence the ways in which he puts his powers as chairman to use.

Finally, the nature of the times in which he occupies his post may serve to restrain what a chairman can do with his powers. He must gauge what his majority will tolerate or insist upon; the greater the crisis or urgency, the more actions may be forced upon him against his will. The size of his majority may make a difference; a small majority may not hold together under great pressure from the chairman. He may be limited further by what the party leadership will support; he needs their backing especially if he wants his committee to act positively. Thus the chairman will seek to develop working relationships with the members of his committee, using his powers to help them whenever he can and expecting their cooperation and support in return. His ability to assist them with projects of interest, and to withhold such aid, usually dooming the project, no doubt encourages the committee members to seek such working relationships. The precise form of such chairman-member relationships would require examination of each committee, as the factors described will certainly vary among the committees.

In the last analysis, the committee chairman is a force to be reckoned with, possessing vast but not unlimited powers over the business of his panel. The use he makes of his potential for influence will depend on his own abilities, his majority, and the demands and pressures of the day. He is ultimately responsible for his actions to his committee colleagues and to the chamber as a whole. Within those limits, he will work out a *modus vivendi* which, in most cases, will guarantee him a position among the important leaders of the Senate or House.

The Power and Function of Congressional Floor Leaders. In three of the four congressional parties—both in the Senate and the minority in the House—the floor leader operates as the principal party leader. The exception, of course, is the House majority leader who shares leadership responsibility with the Speaker, and who in most cases ranks in practice as well as theory as number two in his party. Like the Speaker, the floor leaders tend to be chosen because of the widely held confidence in them; they have served for extended periods, and have earned the respect of their colleagues as trustworthy spokesmen for the party. The leaders are men who abide by the informal norms and who have avoided extreme ideological positions; they can treat all factions within the party with fairness if not impartiality.

The main function of the floor leaders is to guide the party as it seeks to create a record on which to stand at subsequent elections. This involves determining party strategy: What provisions should proposed legislation contain? What is the best method to secure passage of the desired bills? How can voting strength be mustered in support of such legislation? Once these decisions are made, the leaders have some resources at their disposal with which to implement their strategic choices, but, as with the Speaker, these provide a basis on which to negotiate arrangements rather than a means to compel compliance. Leadership remains an art, an ability to persuade those who can easily choose an independent course of action to defer to the wishes of the party, as determined by its leaders.

The majority floor leaders possess the same sorts of tools as the Speaker. They can offer tangible rewards for compliance: they are involved in the committee-assignment process; they can share the knowledge which comes to them as centers in the circulation of information as they see fit; and they can try to take advantage of the more intimate relationship with the President which they gain as leaders. Other favors are also available; the floor leaders can aid individual legislators in a number of ways. They can help congressmen with their constitutents by providing support for a pet project, support which may entail making sure a bill that has no chance to pass receives a respectable number of votes. The leaders can try to secure favorable treatment, from the perspective of the party member, of constituency-oriented proposals such as public works projects like parks, dams, and post offices. By helping in patronage matters, the leaders may assist the representative in securing his political situation in his state or district. They may also provide campaign assistance when election time rolls around. Beyond these, there are less obvious ways for the leadership to provide benefits; their involvement in the scheduling of chamber business, especially in the Senate, permits them, for instance, to try to arrange a roll-call vote at a time when a legislator will be present; they have a voice in the allocation of office space, which comes in unequal size and quality; they control desirable overseas assignments as the chamber's representative at international meetings.

The majority floor leaders are able to confer psychological, or intangible, rewards as well. By paying attention to their followers—speaking to them, communicating with them, including them in meetings and group discussion—the leaders can make them feel important cogs in the party machinery, vital to its success. Beginning with the respect which led initially to their accession to leadership and adding to this their ability to gratify the legislators' need to belong, the floor leaders can capitalize on the initial feelings of party loyalty which the rank and file often bring to congressional service. They can, through judicious dispensation of their largesse—tangible and intangible—make the party-loyalist orientation attractive to many lawmakers.

This extensive arsenal should not lead us to forget that the leaders have no way to ensure that bargains with congressmen are consummated. The techniques of one of the most successful floor leaders, Senate Majority Leader Lyndon B. Johnson, amply illustrate the essential negotiating and compromise methods which characterize the conduct of leadership. Senator Johnson, possessed with these weapons and with a mastery of parliamentary procedure, took a highly personal approach to leadership; he is reported to have talked with every Democratic senator, and many Republicans, daily. In these conversations he followed a number of strategic imperatives. First, he sought to shape situations in a way that would permit each member to stand with the party. Next, he "exploited every opportunity to get his colleagues to think, not as Northerners or Southerners, liberals or conservatives, but as Democrats." To cite one instance, Johnson managed to hold his party together in opposition to an Eisenhower appointment to the National Labor Relations Board by casting the issue not in ideological terms, which was certain to divide the party, but rather, on the basis of some inconsistent testimony by the nominee, as a question of shabby treatment of the Senate. All Democrats, he hoped, would unite to object to the "flouting of the dignity of the Senate."

The minority leaders face roughly similar leadership tasks, though their opportunities are somewhat more limited and their resources less extensive. They must, as previously noted, decide whether to offer alternatives to the majority's proposals; barter support, if the majority needs it, for concessions; or simply resist what the majority desires. To rally support for whatever choices they make, the minority leaders can employ inducements similar to those which the opposition possesses; substantial items—committee assignments, information, campaign assistance, and the like—or more ephemeral satisfactions such as the gratification which comes from proffered friendship and respect. The range of choice is more limited, however. The minority has less control over the scheduling of chamber business; it seldom has the ability to enlist the President in causes dear to the hearts of rank-and-file legislators; it has fewer opportunities to provide district-oriented patronage and projects. Moreover, situational considerations—the national mood, the desires of the President, and the personal attributes of individual leaders—constrain the minority in much the same fashion as they inhibit the majority.

The Whips. The floor leaders of each congressional party have the assistance of elaborate whip organizations. These agencies perform a variety of useful services. In the first place, they serve as the chief channels of leadership-member communication, keeping representatives "and office staff informed as to the legislative programs for the week" and informing them of the party position on the major issues. Second, the whips seek to ensure the presence on the floor, when needed, of party members, using "the telephone, telegrams, and letters . . . to determine their presence or absence for a vote." The whips seem successful in promoting attendance; Ripley found that in 1963 Democratic voting participation averaged 94 percent when the whips were active and only 84 percent when the members were not contacted.

A third function which the whips perform is to provide the leadership with intelligence about the voting intentions of the rank-and-file partisans. Polls are taken, with an error ratio of about 10 percent, which help guide the strategy of the leaders. On the basis of the sentiments which the polls uncover, targets among the undecided or uncertain lawmakers are selected. It is a waste of the leaders' time and energy to try to sway those whose minds are made up; the data which the whips produce indicate where bargaining or pressure may find needed votes or support. The whip organization can, in short, inform the members, urge their attendance, and transmit their views to the leadership. It cannot do more than transmit communications; in the words of the Republican party, "it can suggest and then it is up to the Member's party loyalty and personal responsibility" to respond as he sees fit.

The record of the whip organizations . . . is mixed. They have been successful as communications devices; they provide the leaders with a point of direct contact with party members. The information they transmit does give cues about the leadership's desires and strategy and thus may have contributed, to an uncertain extent, to party cohesion. The data which the whips collect about member sentiments and vote intentions help guide tactical decisions by locating the representatives who, with the application of suitable pressures and/or inducements, might provide needed votes. Similarly the whip apparatus has increased attendance by a factor of about 10 percent. The effectiveness of all this on the marshaling of votes for party positions is difficult to assess in the absence of information on what would have happened had the whips been inactive, but at the very least the whip network permits the leaders to undertake negotiations with reluctant members and provides the latter with a record of agreements reached. Through these activites, it appears that the whip machinery may help persuade and surely cannot hurt the efforts of the party leaders to build majorities. Where the whip organizations cooperate fully with the leadership they serve to enhance the possibility of party cohesion.

For further information:

Your library has many books about Congress; many of the political science journals and popular magazine also have useful analyses of congressional behavior. The following lists some of the best sources. Others may be found in the bibliography for Chapter 9.

Characteristics of Leaders and Their Legislative Role:
Fenno, Richard F., Jr.: "The Internal Distribution of Influence: The House," in David B. Truman, ed., *Congress and America's Future* (Englewood Cliffs, N.J.: Prentice-Hall, Inc., 1965), chap. 3.

Goodwin, George, Jr.: "The Seniority System in Congress," *American Political Science Review*, vol. 53, pp. 412–436, 1959.

Hinckley, Barbara: *The Seniority System in Congress* (Bloomington: Indiana University Press, 1971).

———: *Stability and Change in Congress* (New York: Harper & Row, Publishers, Incorporated, 1971), chap. 5 (Committees and the Distribution of Influence) and chap. 6 (Party and Party Leadership).

Huitt, Ralph K.: "The Democratic Party Leadership in the Senate," *American Political Science Review,* vol. 55, pp. 333–334, 1961.

———: "The Internal Distribution of Influence: The Senate," in David B. Truman, ed., *Congress and America's Future* (Englewood Cliffs, N.J.: Prentice-Hall, Inc., 1965), chap. 4.

Matthews, Donald R.: *U.S. Senators and Their World* (New York: Vintage Books, Inc., Alfred A. Knopf, Inc., 1960), chap. 6 (Party Leadership) and chap. 7 (The Committees).

Patterson, Samuel C.: "Legislative Leadership and Political Ideology," *Public Opinion Quarterly,* vol. 27, pp. 339–410, 1963.

Ripley, Randall B.; *Majority Party Leadership in Congress* (Boston: Little, Brown and Company, 1969), especially chap. 1 (Party Leadership and Legislative Results) and chap. 6 (Leadership in the Majority Party).

———: *Party Leadership in the House of Representatives* (Washington: The Brookings Institution, 1967), especially appendix A (Analysis of Party Leadership).

———: *Power in the Senate* (New York: St. Martin's Press, Inc. 1969).

Truman, David B.: *The Congressional Party: A Case Study* (New York: John Wiley & Sons, Inc., 1959), chap. 4 (Party Leadership Roles in the Senate) and chap. 6 (Party Leadership Roles in the House of Representatives).

Wolfinger, Raymond E., and Joan Heifetz: "Safe Seats Seniority, and Power in Congress," *American Political Science Review,* vol. 59, pp. 337–349, 1965.

Congressional Quarterly Weekly Report and *Congressional Quarterly Almanac* frequently published thumbnail sketches of congressmen, their district characteristics, and described their legislative behavior.

The Congressional Behavior and Public Opinion

Cnudde, Charles F., and Donald J. McCrone: "The Linkage between Constituency Attitude and Congressional Voting," *American Political Science Review,* vol. 60, pp. 338–348, 1966.

Cummings, Milton C., Jr.: *Congressmen and the Electorate* (New York: Free Press, 1964).

Dexter, Anthony Lewis: *The Sociology and Politics of Congress* (Chicago: Rand McNally & Company, 1969).

Erikson, Robert S.: "The Electoral Impact of Congressional Roll Call Voting," *American Political Science Review,* vol. 65, pp. 1018–1032, 1971.

Froman, Lewis A., Jr.: *Congressmen and Their Constituencies* (Chicago: Rand McNally & Company, 1963).

McPhee, William N., and William A. Glaser, eds.: *Public Opinion and Congressional Elections* (New York: Free Press, 1962).

Snowiss, Leo M.: "Congressional Recruitment and Representation," *American Political Science Review,* vol. 60, pp. 627–639, 1966.

Stokes, Donald E., and Warren E. Miller: "Party Government and the Salience of Congress," *Public Opinion Quarterly,* vol. 26, pp. 531–546, 1962.

Turner, Julius: *Party and Constituency: Pressures on Congress* (Baltimore: Johns Hopkins University Press, 1951).

Data on Characteristics of Congressional Districts

U.S. Department of Commerce, Bureau of the Census, *Congressional Data Book,* Government Printing Office, Washington. State-by-state supplements are published when congressional districts are changed. Gives census characteristics of congressional districts (e.g., percent nonwhite, education, income, etc.)

III. ANALYZING THE DATA

We have presented a considerable quantity of data on congressmen and congressional leaders. To help you interpret these data we have prepared a series of short questions and answers. As in the two previous chapters these questions will deal with the limitations of these data as well as their interpretation. The purpose of calling your attention to such limitations is to help you become aware of what assertions can and cannot be made with different types of information. Correct answers to these questions are found on p. 269.

Question 1

Tables 12.1 to 12.3 compare congressional leaders, congressmen, and the entire United States population according to a number of personal attributes. First, are leaders similar to nonleaders on most of these attributes? Second, is Congress on the whole a cross section of the American population? Finally, do these data suggest that many Americans are not represented in Congress?

Your Answer

Question 2
Do the data in Table 12.4 indicate that congressional leaders act against the interest of people residing in competitive, urban areas with large black and minority population?

Your Answer

Question 3
Do the data in Table 12.5 and 12.6 support the commonly made claim that congressional leaders are archconservatives whose power is based in their considerable seniority? To what extent do these data show that congressional leaders resist public opinion?

Your Answer

Question 4

Table 12.7 compares the legislative roles of House leaders and nonleaders. Do these data show that both leaders and nonleaders ignore popular mandates? Do these data show that nonleaders claim to be more responsive to their constituents?

Your Answer

Question 5

It is sometimes argued that despite congressmen's claims of knowing how their constituents really think, congressmen are often inaccurate in their perceptions. Do the data in Table 12.8 support this contention? What do these data say about whether or not congressmen consistently act in behest of the people they represent?

Your Answer

Question 6
Following Table 12.8 is an excerpt drawn from a study of congressional leadership. Does this expert claim that certain leaders can thwart congressional action? Does he imply that limiting leaders' power would result in a Congress more responsive to public demands?

Your Answer

Correct Answers
1. Tables 12.1 to 12.3 that compare congressional leaders with nonleaders show leaders to be unlike nonleaders in a number of ways: leaders are older, more likely to be from the South, and while there are very few black or female congressmen, no leader in either the 90th or 92nd Congress is black or female. In terms of religion (Table 12.2) the pattern is mixed—in some instances one religious group is overrepresented among leaders, but this pattern is not consistent for both sessions and in both house of Congress. The previous-occupation data shows a moderate but consistent overrepresentation of lawyers and underrepresentation of businessmen among leaders. As for the similarity of congressmen, congressional leaders, and the public, these data clearly indicate sizable differences in almost every set of comparisons. However, these personal dissimilarities tell us nothing about actual legislative behavior. Thus, if we define "representation" in terms of leaders acting for or on behalf of others (either the public or their colleagues), these data say nothing about whether leaders are representative or not. These data would be germane to the question of representation if it were defined according to similarity of personal attributes.

2. Table 12.4 shows that leaders in the House and Senate tend to come from somewhat different districts than do nonleaders (though the pattern varies by house). Here again, as was the case in our analysis of personal characteristics, we cannot automatically conclude that congressmen represent or do not represent their colleagues and constitutents. Knowing, for

example, that leaders' districts have relatively high percentages of blacks and other minorities does not tell you whether the interests of these groups is given greater weight in the legislative process. District characteristics might help explain some legislative behavior, e.g., voting for legislation to aid cities, but these data by themselves do not say whether leaders act on behest of leaders or the general public. At best, if district differences were very large and were related to legislative issues, we might *suspect* a difference in policy orientations among leaders and nonleaders. Only if we define representation in terms of similarity of characteristics would these data say something directly about representation.

3. The data in Table 12.5, which compares leaders and nonleaders' voting records, do not clearly demonstrate leaders to be overwhelmingly more conservative and obstructionist. In both Congresses, and in both Conservative Coalition scores and ADA ratings, nonleaders tend to be somewhat more liberal than leaders (though only in the Senate during the Ninetieth Congress was the difference really sizable). The pattern on presidential support is mixed—sometimes leaders are the more supportive, sometimes the opposite is true. Table 12.6 does, however, clearly show leaders to have more senority than nonleaders. What these data do not show is whether congressional voting behavior is consistent with public opinion. Merely because leaders may be more conservative than nonleaders is no evidence of ignoring public opinion. We need data on public opinion before we could make such assertions.

4. The data in Table 12.7 show that a larger proportion of nonleaders than leaders claim that their legislative role is to represent their constituents rather than act independently. Notice, however, that a clear majority of leaders and nonleaders, reject the delegate role. As for the question of ignoring popular mandates, these data are inclusive. Recall that these legislative roles are based upon congressmen's *statements,* not their behavior, It is entirely possible that these congressmen do respond to public demands, but claim otherwise.

5. Table 12.8 suggests that at least in certain policy areas a congressman's perceptions of constituency preferences and what his constituents really desire may be quite different. This is not the case, however, on the civil rights issue where the correlation is .63. Moreover, we also see that a congressman's own opinion is not highly correlated with his constituents' preferences in the social welfare and foreign involvement issue areas and only moderately correlated in the instance of civil rights. What these data do not tell us is the congressman's voting record. Without this information we can only suggest that congressmen do not translate their constituency opinion into legislative behavior. It is possible, though perhaps unlikely, that congressmen will vote their constituents' preferences without knowing what they are.

6. The expert opinion on the power of elected floor leaders and committee chairmen indicates that while their powers are considerable, it is not unlimited or prevailing in every instance. For example, floor leaders must rely on persuasion rather than raw power, and committee chairmen frequently must heed the preferences of committee members. To argue that the power of congressional leaders makes Congress inherently unresponsive to public demands is, however, to go well beyond the bounds of these data. The opinion does not suggest *what* the power will be used for. Moreover, as we have seen in much of the other data in this chapter, leaders are not always very distinct from nonleaders in many characteristics. Thus, it is plausible to believe that leaders use their power to support programs supported by many other congressmen. Whether these other congressmen follow public opinion, or even know what the public wants, is, of course, another question.

Chapter 12
Congressional Leadership

Name _____

Section _____

IV. CONCLUSION

Having reformulated the original problem and analyzed the relevant data, you can now return to the original problem. In the space below, write a short memorandum on whether Congress is an unrepresentative institution because it is controlled by unrepresentative leaders. Your essay should integrate various types of data into a coherent statement on the problem. Where outside sources are used, be sure to cite the source.

Original Problem

"Congress is not a representative institution, because not only are congressmen unrepresentative of the public, but congressional leaders, who are even more unrepresentative, dominate law making and thwart their colleagues."

Memorandum

Part Three
MORE ADVANCED ANALYSIS

Chapter 13
THE SUPREME COURT

In the previous chapter, we examined the general proposition that the President's power has become ascendant over the other two branches of government in recent years. Now we shall examine that proposition more carefully with respect to the Supreme Court alone. Comparing the two branches of government may seem like pitting David against Goliath. The Supreme Court is a tiny institution as measured by its budget or staff in comparison with the executive branch. Even if we added all the federal appeals courts and trial courts to the judiciary's measure, it would still be smaller than any single department under the President't control. Yet as the previous chapter indicated, size of budget and number of staff are not the only measures of power. Although small, the Supreme Court has immense prestige in the United States. It tries to stand aloof from partisan politics and enlists the symbolic appeal of the Law to legitimize its decisions.

In this chapter we shall examine in greater detail than possible earlier the degree of independence enjoyed by the Supreme Court. Although the Court attempts to remain remote from daily partisan strife, it decides many important issues and is the object of attempts to control its actions. For instance, one of President Nixon's most prominent election pledges in 1968 was to remold the Court from its allegedly liberal, pro-defendant bias of the Warren era into a "law and order" tribunal. However, opportunities to intervene in the Court's decisions are less plentiful than with Congress. The President has few rewards to grant Supreme Court justices and few sanctions to impose on them. It is not clear that recent Presidents have been able to assert their control over the Court to any greater degree than in the past.

Our vehicle for examining this problem is the proposition:

"Even though the President's power has grown enormously in the Twentieth Century, the Supreme Court is still a substantially independent branch of government."

I. REFORMULATING THE PROPOSITION

To simplify your analysis, you may wish to accept as a given the first part of the statement which asserts that presidential power has grown in the twentieth century. That is a generally accepted proposition; if you decided to test it here, it would lead you far astray from the main focus of this chapter on the Supreme Court.

Many special problems remain in the testing of the second portion of the statement. "Independence" is a subtle concept. It means that people do what they want to do without being forced into their actions by others. However, only gross indicators of independence exist because the concept refers to a state of mind, and we rarely have direct evidence about a state of mind. Note how each of the reformulations below treats this problem; remember too that one is limited to information that is readily available.

To complicate matters, the Supreme Court is a collective body which announces its decisions in a series of opinions. The immediate effect of a decision in a case is sometimes more important and sometimes less important than the language of the opinion accompanying the decision. That depends on how lawyers use the language of the opinion in later cases —whether they cite it as precedent or whether they ignore it. The opinion that has the greatest impact is not always the majority opinion; sometimes it is a concurring opinion and sometimes it is a minority opinion. These complications make it difficult to use Supreme Court decisions or the opinions that accompany them as absolutely valid indicators of the independence of the Supreme Court.

One must also be careful about the inferences one can make from particular bits of information. Examine each of the suggested reformulations and your own to make sure that the "because of . . ." statements really do follow both logically and empirically.

You will also want to apply the general criteria for reformulations developed in earlier chapters. If you wish to refresh your memory, you will find these rules on p. 147.

With these considerations in mind, examine the following reformulations and the comments accompanying them. Then write your own reformulation of the problem.

Partial Reformulations

1. Most Presidents appoint a majority of the Supreme Court and through their appointment power control its decisions.

2. Justices appointed by a single President usually vote together as a bloc and give the President who appointed them their support on policy issues.

3. The government wins most of the cases it brings to the Supreme Court regardless of whether the President appointed a majority of the justices.

4. Because justices have life tenure, they act independently of outside pressures.

5. Supreme Court justices come from nonpolitical backgrounds and therefore are not likely to be affected by Presidential influence.

Each of the printed reformulations are single-factor propositions. Your analysis will undoubtedly have a firmer foundation if you combine several of them. However, you must be careful to limit yourself to information that is likely to be available either in the following pages or in your library.

Some of the reformulations have more carefully defined terms than others. For instance, the second reformulation speaks of voting blocs on the Court which support or oppose the President while the fourth reformulation simply repeats the language of the original proposition without further operationalizing the term "independence."

Think about the logic of the reformulations. For instance, does life tenure always bring about independence or are some additional conditions required? When justices appointed by a President vote together as a bloc, do they always support the President who appointed them, or does their bloc sometimes oppose his position?

In the third reformulation the term "government" is used instead of "President." In this context, government means the executive branch which the President heads. But the executive branch is an enormous bureaucracy and is not always in step with the wishes of a President. Consequently, data in support of the third reformulation may not be sufficient to establish the the original statement.

Your Reformulation

II. SELECTING THE REQUIRED DATA

Examine your reformulation and list the data you think you need to test it. Write your list of required data below.

Now examine the data presented on the following pages. If you need other or more information, examine the references on p. 287.

TABLE 13.1 APPOINTMENTS TO THE SUPREME COURT BY PRESIDENT, THE APPOINTEES' PARTY AND INDEX OF PRESIDENTIAL CONTROL

President	Number of Appointments	Party* of Appointee		Index of Presidential Control†
19th Century				
Washington (F)	10	10F		100
Adams (F)	3	3F		12.0
Jefferson (D-R)	3	3D-R		12.9
Madison (D-R)	2	2D-R		14.5
Monroe (D-R)	1	1D-R		3.5
Adams (R)	1	1D-R		7.9
Jackson (D)	6	5D	1 Whig	25.9
Van Buren (D)	2	2D		11.1
Tyler (S)	1	1D		0
Polk (D)	2	2D		16.9
Fillmore (W)	1	1W		3.4
Pierce (D)	1	1D		11.1
Buchana (D)	1	1D		8.8
Lincoln (R)	5	4R	1D	29.7
Johnson	0	—		0
Grant (R)	4	4R		29.7
Hayes (R)	2	2R		8.3
Garfield (R)	1	1R		11.1
Arthur (R)	2	2R		17.2
Cleveland (D)	2	2D		5.3
Harrison (R)	4	3R	1D	15.5
Cleveland (D)	2	2D		10.8
McKinley (R)	1	1R		8.8

* The abbreviations are: F = Federalist; D-R = Democratic-Republican (the predecessor of the modern Democratic Party); W = Whig; R = Republican.

† The index is the percent of the President's term which his Supreme Court appointees served on the bench. It is calculated according to the following formula:

$$\frac{\Sigma (Am)}{Pn}$$

where: A = number of appointments by a President
m = number of months of President's term that his appointees served
P = number of months of President's term
n = total number of justices on the Court

For example, if the President appointed only one justice but the appointment came during the President's first month in office and the President served only one term and there were a total of nine justices on the court, the index would be 11.

TABLE 13.1 Continued

President	Number of Appointments	Party* of Appointee		Index of Presidential Control†
20th Century				
T. Roosevelt (R)	3	3R		22.1
Taft (R)	6	3R	3D	32.6
Wilson (R)	3	3D		22.1
Harding (R)	4	3D	1R	20.7
Coolidge (R)	1	1R		7.5
Hoover (R)	3	2R	1D	19.2
F. D. Roosevelt (D)	9	8D	1R	43.1
Truman (D)	4	3D	1R	19.9
Eisenhower (R)	5	4R	1D	32.6
Kennedy (D)	2	2D		10.8
Johnson (D)	2	2D		7.6
Nixon (R) (1st term only)	4	4R		28.4

	Summary of Index of Presidential Control		
	Mean	Median	Standard Deviation
19th century	15.8	11.1	20.0
20th century	22.2	22.1	10.7

TABLE 13.2 AGREEMENT AMONG NIXON APPOINTEES: PERCENT OF CASES ON WHICH PRESIDENT NIXON'S APPOINTEES VOTED TOGETHER DURING 1971-1972 TERM

Nixon Appointees:	Blackmun	Burger	Powell
Blackmun	—		
Burger	79.1	—	
Powell	72.4	82.9	—
Rehnquist	81.0	86.1	75.7

NOTE: These data include both unanimous decisions and decisions in which there were dissents. Twenty-two and one-half percent of all opinions were decided by unanimous vote.
SOURCE: *Harvard Law Review,* vol. 86, pp. 300–302, November, 1972.

TABLE 13.3 NIXON APPOINTEES' AGREEMENT WITH NON–NIXON APPOINTEES: PERCENT OF CASES ON WHICH JUSTICES VOTED TOGETHER DURING 1971-1972 TERM

	Stewart (Eisenhower)	White (JFK)	Brennan (Eisenhower)	Marshall (LBJ)	Douglas (FDR)
Blackmun	62.6	72.5	48.3	51.0	32.7
Burger	60.8	67.3	45.3	50.0	31.1
Powell	64.1	64.9	53.3	48.1	38.2
Rehnquist	57.0	62.5	44.9	38.8	26.9

NOTE: These data include both unanimous decisions and decisions in which there were dissents. Twenty-two and one-half percent of all opinions were decided by unanimous vote.
SOURCE: *Harvard Law Review,* vol. 86, pp. 300–302, November, 1972.

TABLE 13.4 OUTCOME OF SUPREME COURT CASES* DECIDED FOR AND AGAINST GOVERNMENT, 1960-1971

	Eisenhower Administration							
	1953	1954	1955	1956	1957	1958	1959	1960
For govt.	67%	51	51	48	49	71	67	60
Against govt.	23%	49	49	52	51	29	33	40

	Kennedy Administration		Johnson Administration						Nixon Administration		
	1961	1962	1963	1964	1965	1966	1967	1968	1969	1970	1971
For govt.	64	58	45	73	56	62	58	57	41	61	48
Against govt.	36	42	55	27	44	38	42	43	59	39	52

* The cases included in this table are civil actions from the inferior federal courts and federal criminal cases. They do not include all cases involving the federal government nor all cases of policy significance.
SOURCE: *Harvard Law Review,* November issue for years 1954–1972.

TABLE 13.5 CATEGORIES OF LAWYERS APPOINTED TO THE SUPREME COURT CLASSIFIED BY NUMBERS AND BY PERCENTAGES IN SIX HISTORICAL PERIODS

	Number of Justices						
Types	20 (100%) 1789–1828	14 (100%) 1829–1861	16 (100%) 1862–1888	18 (100%)* 1889–1919	7 (100%) 1920–1932	16 (100%) 1933–1957	Totals 1789–1957
Lawyers who were primarily politicians	17 (85%)	9 (63%)	5 (32%)	6 (33%)	2 (29%)	10 (62%)	49 (53.9%)
Lawyers who were primarily state or federal judges	3 (15%)	3 (21%)	7 (45%)	8 (45%)	2 (29%)	1 (6%)	24 (26.4%)
Corporation (primarily) lawyers	0	0	3 (19%)	4 (22%)	2 (29%)	2 (13%)	11 (12.1%)
Noncorporation (primarily) lawyers	0	2 (14%)	0	1 (6%)	0	0	3 (3.3%)
Lawyers by education who were primarily engaged in academic pursuits	0	0	0	0	1 (14%)	3 (19%)	4 (4.4%)

* Hughes was appointed a second time but is not included in the sample.

SOURCE: John Schmidhauser, "The Supreme Court: A Collective Portrait," *Midwest Journal of Political Science*, vol. 3, p. 33, 1959. Copyright, Wayne University Press. Reprinted by permission.

TABLE 13.6 HIGHEST POLITICAL POSTS HELD BY JUSTICES OF THE SUPREME COURT PRIOR TO THEIR APPOINTMENTS. CLASSIFIED BY NUMBERS AND BY PERCENTAGES IN SIX HISTORICAL PERIODS.

Occupations	Number of Justices						
	20 (100%) 1789–1828	14 (100%) 1829–1861	16 (100%) 1862–1888	18 (100%) 1889–1919	7 (100%) 1920–1932	16 (100%) 1933–1957	Totals 1789–1957
Federal political careers (totals)	8 (40%)	7 (50%)	7 (45%)	13 (74%)	6 (68%)	14 (88%)	55 (60.5%)
Federal executive	4 (20%)	4 (28%)	5 (32%)	6 (34%)	4 (57%)	8 (52%)	31 (34.1%)
Federal legislature	3 (15%)	3 (21%)	0	1 (6%)	1 (14%)	4 (26%)	12 (13.2%)
Federal judiciary*	1 (5%)	0	2 (13%)	6 (34%)	1 (14%)	2 (13%)	12 (13.2%)
State political careers	12 (60%)	6 (42%)	6 (38%)	4 (22%)	1 (14%)	2 (13%)	31 (34.1%)
State executive	4 (20%)	2 (14%)	1 (6%)	0	0	1 (6%)	8 (8.8%)
State legislature	2 (10%)	2 (14%)	1 (6%)	1 (6%)	0	0	6 (6.6%)
State judiciary*	6 (30%)	2 (14%)	4 (25%)	3 (17%)	1 (14%)	1 (6%)	17 (18.7%)
Local political careers	0	0	0	0	0	0	0
Political party management or presidential elector	0	1 (7%)	3 (19%)	0	0	0	4 (4.4%)
Those holding political positions (totals)	20 (100%)	14 (100%)	16 (100%)	17 (94%)	7 (100%)	16 (100%)	90 (99%)
Those not holding political posts	0	0	0	1 (6%)	0	0	1 (1.1%)

*It will be noted that the total of the percentages of those serving in federal or state judicial posts in this table does not, in every historical period, equal the percentages listed in Table 13.5 for lawyers who pursued primarily judicial careers. This is accounted for by the fact that some judges, such as Catron and Davis, while serving long careers as judges, were basically political managers and are considered so in this table.

SOURCE: John Schmidhauser, "The Supreme Court: A Collective Portrait," *Midwest Journal of Political Science*, vol. 3, p. 37, 1959. Copyright, Wayne University Press. Reprinted by permission.

WASHINGTON*—For a long time the U.S. Supreme Court was known as the Warren Court. Now it is often referred to as the Nixon or Burger Court. It would be closer to the mark, however, to call it the Byron White Court, for usually as he goes, so goes the court these days.

Ever since the President named four men of his leanings to the tribunal, including Chief Justice Warren Burger, many, if not most, of the significant decisions—especially in the critical areas of civil rights and civil liberties—have been settled on closely split 5 to 4 votes, with Justice White regularly casting the deciding vote, generally on the conservative or Nixon side of the issues.

In the last week or so, a whole flock of crucial censorship decisions, which will affect all of our lives in an intimate way, have turned almost exclusively on Justice White's personal viewpoint. In practice, it comes about as close as possible to one-man judicial rule, for the other eight members of the court consistently cancel out each other.

The upshot is that Byron White, temporarily at least, is one of the most powerful men in the United States. Indeed, there are days when he is even more powerful than Nixon himself, for his chance position as the "swing" man enables him to veto or, more often, affirm Presidential policies.

As many will remember, former President Eisenhower, who appointed Earl Warren and William Brennan to the court, used to groan over the liberal opinions they consistently handed down. But Eisenhower's successor, John F. Kennedy, who put White on the court, must be turning over in his grave at the satisfaction his appointee is giving Kennedy's old enemy, Richard Nixon. . . .

The high court, fulfilling a pledge of Nixon's, paved the way for a nationwide crackdown on allegedly pornographic movies, magazines, and books, by five different decisions which, in effect, invite local police and prosecutors, to say nothing of vigilantes, to have a new field day.

All the decisions were 5 to 4, with Justice White siding with Nixon's "fearsome foursome," consisting of Chief Justice Burger, plus Justices Harry Blackmun, Lewis Powell, and William Rehnquist. The dissenting justices (William Douglas, William Brennan, Thurgood Marshall, and Potter Stewart) see the decisions as an invitation to "state-ordered regimentation of our minds."

The present term of the court wound up much as it did in June of last year when, in the final weeks, there were 18 decisions that turned on 5 to 4 votes, with White siding with the conservative majority in all but two of the cases.

* By Clayton Fritchey. Copyright, Los Angeles Times. Reprinted with permission.

WASHINGTON†—There's a new Supreme Court in town, but not quite the one many people expected.

The Nixon court hasn't abolished civil rights, as some liberals darkly predicted when conservative Warren Burger was named Chief Justice in 1969. Women have gained ground in fighting sex discrimination. So have blacks, in desegregating schools.

Nor has President Nixon remade the court in his image by appointing Mr. Burger and three other conservative Justices. Since January, 1972, when the last two Nixon appointees took their seats, the high court has struck down the death penalty, which the President favored, and upheld a limited right to abortion, which he opposed. It has sharply restricted the administration's vigorous use of electronic bugging in domestic security cases. On Monday, it handed down decisions that probably killed Mr. Nixon's legislative plan for aiding church-related schools.

Thus, as the remodeled court this week completed its first full term with all four

† Excerpted from The Wall Street Journal's ledger story "The Burger Court," published June 29, 1973. © 1973 Dow Jones & Company, Inc. All Rights Reserved.

Nixon nominees participating, it's possible to look back and get some idea of the course of the court. And the trend is not any simple veer to the right. . . .

At times, Justice Powell sounds nothing like a Nixon appointee. In requiring court warrants for electronic bugging, he observed that government tends to "view with suspicion those that most fervently dispute its policies." And he warned that "unreviewed executive discretion may yield too readily to pressures to obtain incriminating evidence and overlook potential invasions of privacy and speech." That decision was issued two days after the initial Watergate arrests.

Less scholarly but more predictable among the conservatives are Justices Burger and Blackmun. Both hail from Minnesota, and they so frequently stick together in their votes that the Washington press corps once labeled them the "Minnesota Twins." They're most consistent in decisions favoring effective law enforcement over the rights of criminal suspects.

Chief Justice Burger possesses a puritanical streak that makes him predictable and rather preachy in cases involving offensive language or pornographic movies and publications. When the court upheld the distribution of a particularly graphic underground newspaper on the University of Missouri campus, Mr. Burger dissented with the admonition that universities are at least partly institutions "where individuals learn to express themselves in acceptable civil terms." More significantly, Mr. Burger wrote the recent opinion redefining obscenity in a way that will make it easier to prosecute the sale of pornographic materials.

But both the Chief Justice and Mr. Blackmun have sprung some surprises, such as voting for an absolute right to abortion during the first three months of pregnancy. Mr. Blackmun even wrote the majority opinion, which brought him the same sort of criticism frequently directed at the Warren court's civil rights opinions: that the court reached the right result, but did so by relying on concepts of human values rather than constitutional doctrine. . . .

By far the easiest Nixon appointee to anticipate is Justice Rehnquist, who rarely deserts the conservative line in cases of constitutional interpretation.

III. ANALYZING THE DATA

You now have had sufficient experience in analyzing data that you do not need specific questions and answers for every table. However, before you write your memo, there are some general considerations to keep in mind while examining the data.

You must decide whether the data are adequate indicators of the variables in your reformulation. For instance, one measure of the President's influence on the Court is the proportion of his term during which his appointees served on the Court as reported in Table 13.1. A simpler measure would be the proportion of the Court that he appointed during his term, not taking into account whether his appointees came onto the bench early or late during his term. Another measure might add the number of holdovers from previous administrations of the same party. Both indicators may be constructed from the data in Table 13.1.

You should also note carefully the reservations in the footnote to Table 13.4. That table reports the only readily available data of this sort, but its interpretation requires some care and modesty.

The same strictures may be applied to the two newspaper comments.

You need to consider the kind of biases their authors represent. Note that they are writing about the same term of the Supreme Court and were published within days of each other.

Additional information may be found as follows:

1   The official opinions of Supreme Court opinions are published by the government as *Supreme Court Reports* and are probably available in your library. These volumes also give the votes on Supreme Court cases, but all this information is in untabulated form.

2   Brief biographies of all but the most recent Supreme Court Justices may be found in Leon Friedman and Fred L. Israel, *The Justices of the Supreme Court* (4 vols.) (New York: Chelsea House Publishers, 1969).

3   Your library has many books on the Supreme Court. Among the best of the historical essays is Robert McCloskey, *The American Supreme Court* (Chicago: University of Chicago Press, 1960).

4   Statistical summaries of the Supreme Court's work are available in the U.S. Department of Commerce, *Statistical Abstract of the United States* (published annually by the Government Printing Office), in the *Annual Report of the Administrative Office of the U.S. Courts,* and in each November's issue of the *Harvard Law Review* which contains an analysis of the Supreme Court's most recent term.

Chapter 13
The Supreme Court

Name _____

Section _____

IV. CONCLUSION

Having changed the original poroposition into a more operational one, you can now return to the original problem. In the space below, write a brief memorandum on the independence of the Supreme Court. Where possible, use specific data to support your conclusions. Write a coherent essay; do not merely comment on each table of data. If you use data not found in this chapter, give your sources.

Original Problem

"Even though the President's power has grown enormously in the twentieth century, the Supreme Court is still a substantially independent branch of government."

Memorandum

Chapter 14
MINORITIES IN AMERICAN POLITICS

Equality of opportunity, before the law and by government, is one of the pillars of the American belief system. Yet people designate some persons as "minorities" and treat them in stereotyped and discriminatory ways. Such discrimination often extends to the political arena; indeed, it often hinges on governmental action or inaction. The most obvious form of such governmental discrimination was the system of segregation that pervaded the South before the 1950s. But in similar ways, the legal system discriminated against Jews by permitting many kinds of social exclusion and housing discrimination, against American Indians through the administration of the reservations, against Chicanos through farm labor policies. It is significant that those in the Women's Liberation movement consider women as a minority when numerically women are a majority in the United States; they feel that women are treated unequally as if they were a minority group.

Since the 1950s, awareness of minority groups has grown and many people feel that discrimination in the political arena has diminished and perhaps disappeared. The proposition for this chapter examines that question:

"Discrimination in the political arena against minority groups in the United States has not declined in the last 20 years."

I. REFORMULATING THE PROBLEM

Several key terms of the original proposition require careful operationalization. Without such definition, you will be unable to apply the results of empirical research to the proposition nor come to a reasonable conclusion about it.

First, you need to define "minority groups." On the one hand, you may select any group which contains less than a majority of the population. But if you follow that course, you may find that no group is a majority and that the whole country is composed of minority groups! Alternatively, you may designate as "minority" groups only those who feel as if they are in the minority, those that have developed a kind of group consciousness that makes them aware that they are set apart and treated by the outside world as different. Still a more restrictive definition would consider as "minority" groups only those groups that feel distinct and in addition feel discriminated against. However, such a definition almost settles the issue on definitional grounds because it will lead you to exclude evidence about some minority groups that may not be discriminated against.

The second term that requires careful definition is "discrimination." Although the dictionary may only speak of different treatment, the original proposition implies less than equal treatment for minority groups as compared to that received by majority groups. The term requires comparison between minorities and others. It requires some standard of judgment as to whether the treatment received by the two groups is in some way equal. That equality may in some cases be identical treatment or in others it may be proportional treatment. For instance, one might argue that the educational level of whites and blacks in the United States ought to be identical, but that the number of blacks going to college ought to be proportional to their share of the population. Note that such standards involve value judgments.

Third, "political arena" requires an operational definition. Some people would include only acts of political participation such as voting. Others would extend the definition to include office holding. Still others are more concerned with goods and services provided by government and whether they are distributed in a discriminatory fashion to minority groups.

You need, of course, to consider the usual problems of reformulating propositions. The reformulation ought to be comprehensive enough to allow you to make a judgment about the original proposition, it must be formulated so that you can find information to test it, and it must be stated in factual rather than value terms. It may be difficult to think of this problem with a cold, empirical eye because you may already have strong convictions about it. That, however, may be all the more reason to attempt a detached analysis.

Examine the following partial reformulations with these strictures in mind. Consider also the comments that follow the partial reformulations. Then construct your own reformulation from two or more of the partial ones provided here or write a reformulation of your own.

Partial Reformulations

1. Women, blacks, and Jews vote less than other groups in Presidential elections.
2. Blacks less frequently hold political office at the present time than whites, even though the number of black office holders has been increasing.
3. Minority groups have always obtained fewer benefits than majority groups from the federal government.
4. Blacks and Chicanos are oppressed by the police.
5. Women are not discriminated against because they ought to be treated differently than men.

Comments on the Reformulations

1. Note that in some of the reformulations, minority groups are specified; in others they are not. Be careful to examine the implications of the specification: does it lead to prejudgment of the issue or does it permit valid comparison?

2. Some of the reformulations are more specific than others about what is meant by the political arena. You may wish to be more specific with your own reformulation, but consider the kinds of information that may be available.

3. Consider whether the standard of comparison is explicit enough in any of the reformulations. Are some of the reformulations cast entirely in value terms?

4. In our judgment, none of the reformulations are acceptable. However, they provide sufficient guidance so that you should be able to construct your own reformulation.

Your reformulation:

II. SELECTING THE NECESSARY DATA

Examine your reformulation and then list the data you require to test it. Some of the information may be found in the following pages. You may find other information among the following sources:

The Statistical Abstract of the United States. Issued annually by the Department of Commerce, Bureau of the Census. Also available commercially as the *American Almanac.* This is a gold mine of information; the information comes from many sources but is primarily information produced by government agencies.

American Statistics Index (Washington, D.C.: Congressional Information Service). Indexes and abstracts all statistics published by the federal government. Look under such headings as Black Americans, Women, American Indians, for current information from governmental sources.

Sidney Verba and Norman I. Nie, *Participation in America* (New York: Harper & Row Publishers, Incorporated, 1972). The best social science study of political participation in the United States based on a national sample of the population.

American Jewish Yearbook. Issued annually by the Jewish Publication Society. The basic source of information about the American Jewish community.

Official Catholic Directory (New York: P. J. Kennedy & Sons). Issued annually and contains statistical information about Roman Catholics in the United States.

Harry A. Ploski and Ernest Kaiser (eds.): *The Negro Almanac* (New York: The Bellweather Co., 1971).

Editors of *Ebony, The Negro Handbook* (Chicago: Johnson Publishing Co., 1966).

List the data you believe you need in the space below. If you wish to refresh your memory about the rules governing the selection of data, refer to p. 126.

TABLE 14.1   1970 POPULATION OF "MINORITY" GROUPS

	Percent of Total Population
Blacks	11.0%
Women	51.3
Jews	2.9
Catholics	23.0
Indians	.004
Chicanos (Spanish speaking)	9.3

SOURCES: Bureau of the Census, *1970 Census;* American *Jewish Yearbook,* 1973; *Official Catholic Directory,* 1973.

TABLE 14.2 BLACK-WHITE DIFFERENCES IN CONTACTING GOVERNMENT OFFICIALS, 1967*

A. Beliefs about Contacting Government Officials	Whites	Blacks
Connections are necessary to contact government officials	21%	52%
Can easily find connection	61	50
B. Experience with Contacting Government Officials		
Have contacted government officials	33%	14%
Have not contacted government officials but:		
Feel they can contact directly	46	34
Feel they need connection	8	19
Feel they need connection and could *not* find them	13	33
	100%	100%

*NOTE: This is an abbreviated table. Each cell of this table represents a separate percentage of the entire group of whites or blacks in the sample. For example, 21 percent of the whites felt connections were necessary; 79 percent (a number not in the table) did not or were unsure. Each other cell in table should be interpreted in the same way.

SOURCE: Sidney Verba and Norman Nie, *Participation in America* (New York: Harper & Row, Publishers, Incorporated, 1972), pp. 165–166. Copyright © 1972 by Sidney Verba and Norman H. Nie. By permission of Harper & Row, Publishers, Incorporated.

TABLE 14.3 OVERREPRESENTATION AND UNDERREPRESENTATION OF SELECTED GROUPS AMONG INACTIVES AND VOTING SPECIALISTS IN A 1967 NATIONAL SAMPLE

	Political Inactives	Voting Specialists
Male	−10	−10
Female	+10	+10
White	− 3	− 1
Black	+21	+ 6
Protestant	+ 5	− 5
Catholic	−16	+16
Persons with income		
$4000 and under	+47	+17
$4000–$10,000	− 9	+ 5
$10,000 and over	−40	−31

Underrepresentation (−) means fewer people than one would expect from their proportion in population.

Overrepresentation (+) means more people than one would expect from their proportion in population.

Voting specialists are persons who vote but engage in no other political activity.

SOURCE: Verba and Nie, op. cit., p. 98. Copyright © 1972 by Sidney Verba and Norman H. Nie. By permission of Harper & Row, Publishers, Incorporated.

TABLE 14.4 NUMBER OF BLACKS IN UNITED STATES HOUSE OF REPRESENTATIVES, 80TH–93D CONGRESS

Congress	Year	Number of Blacks
80th	(1947–1949)	2
81st	(1949–1951)	2
82nd	(1951–1953)	2
83rd	(1953–1955)	2
84th	(1955–1957)	3
85th	(1957–1959)	4
86th	(1959–1961)	4
87th	(1961–1963)	4
88th	(1963–1965)	5
89th	(1965–1967)	6
90th	(1967–1969)	5
91st	(1969–1971)	9
92nd	(1971–1973)	12
93rd	(1973–1975)	15

SOURCE: *Congressional Quarterly 1972 Almanac*, p. 1036. By permission of Congressional Quarterly, Inc.

TABLE 14.5 BLACK VOTER REGISTRATION IN ELEVEN SOUTHERN STATES,* 1952-1970

Year	Percentage of Voting Age Population Registered
1952	21.3
1956	26.2
1960	28.2
1968	62.0
1970	66.3

*The states are Alabama, Arkansas, Florida, Georgia, Louisiana, Mississippi, North Carolina, South Carolina, Tennessee, Texas, and Virginia.
SOURCE: Harry A. Ploski and Ernest Kaiser, *The Negro Almanac,* (New York: The Bellweather Co., 1971), p. 281.

TABLE 14.6 NEGRO AND SPANISH-AMERICAN EMPLOYMENT IN ALL FEDERAL AGENCIES BY PAY SCHEDULE* 1962-1967 (PERCENT OF TOTAL IN EACH SET OF PAY LEVELS)

A. Negro Employment	GS 1-4	GS 5-8	GS 9-11	GS 12-18	All Levels
1962	18.1	7.7	2.6	.8	13.0
1963	18.6	8.4	2.9	1.0	13.1
1964	19.0	9.1	3.1	1.1	13.2
1965	19.3	9.6	3.4	1.3	13.5
1966	18.6	10.1	3.8	1.6	13.9
1967	20.5	11.6	4.3	1.8	14.9
B. Spanish-American Employment					
1966	2.4	1.8	1.2	.6	2.6
1967	2.6	1.9	1.2	.6	2.6

* GS 1-4 are the lowest pay levels; GS 12-18 are the highest pay levels on which information is available.
SOURCE: U.S. Civil Service Commission. Study of Minority Group Employment with Federal Government 1967, Tables 1.1 to 1.5 and Table 5.1.

TABLE 14.7 SOCIAL WELFARE EXPENDITURE UNDER PUBLIC PROGRAMS, 1950–1971 (IN MILLIONS EXCEPT PERCENTAGES)

Year	Social Insurance	Public Aid	Health & Medical	Vets Program	Education	Housing	Total Social Welfare Expenditure as Percent of		Total Govt. Expenditure
							GNP		
1950	$ 4,947	$ 2,496	$2,064	$6,866	$ 6,674	$ 15	8.9%		37.6%
1960	19,307	4,101	4,464	5,479	17,626	177	10.6		38.0
1965	28,123	6,283	6,246	6,031	29,108	318	11.8		42.4
1970	54,653	16,476	9,568	9,018	50,332	697	15.2		47.7

SOURCE: U.S. Department of Health, Education and Welfare, Social Security, Administration office, Research and Statistics, *Research and Statistics note*, no. 14, November 30, 1971.

TABLE 14.8 FAMILIES ENROLLED IN THE "AID TO FAMILIES WITH DEPENDENT CHILDREN" PROGRAM BY RACE

Year	White	Negro	American Indian	Other	Unknown	Total
1967	52.9%	44.5	1.4	.6	.6	100%
1969	48.1%	45.2	1.3	.6	4.8	100%
1971	48.3%	43.3	1.2	.7	6.5	100%

SOURCE: U.S. Department of Health, Education and Welfare, Social and Rehabilitation Service, National Center for Social Statistics, Findings of the 1967 AFDC Study, Table 2, Findings of 1969 AFDC Study, Table 2, Findings of 1971 AFDC Study, Table 2.

TABLE 14.9 UNEMPLOYMENT RATE BY SEX AND RACE, 1950-1970

Year	Male	Female	White	Black
1950	5.1%	5.7%	4.9%	9.0%
1955	4.2	4.9	3.9	8.7
1960	5.4	5.9	4.9	10.7
1965	4.0	5.5	4.1	8.1
1970	4.4	5.9	4.5	8.2

SOURCE: Department of Labor, *Handbook of Labor Statistics,* 1972, p. 129.

TABLE 14.10 MEDIAN FAMILY INCOME BY RACE, 1947-1970

Year	White	Black and Other	Black Income as Percent of White
1947	$ 3,157	$1,614	51.1
1950	3,445	1,869	54.2
1955	4,605	2,549	55.3
1960	5,835	3,233	55.4
1965	7,251	3,994	55.1
1970	10,236	6,516	63.7

SOURCE: *Statistical Abstract of the United States,* 1972, p. 322.

TABLE 14.11 MEDIAN YEARS OF
SCHOOL COMPLETED BY ALL
AMERICANS AND BY BLACKS,
1940-1970

Year	All Americans	Blacks
1940	10.3	7.0
1950	12.1	8.6
1960	12.3	10.8
1970	12.6	12.2

SOURCE: *Statistical Abstract of the United States*, p. 111.

TABLE 14.12 RACIAL COMPOSITION OF CLIENTS OF SELECTED WELFARE PROGRAMS AND FEDERAL EXPENDITURE FOR THEM, 1971

Program	Racial Composition of Clients		Expenditure (millions)	As Percent of All Welfare Expenditures
	White (Percent)	Black (Percent)		
Manpower Development and Training Program	72.4	37.6	$336	1.7
Work Incentive Program	52.0	48.0	64	.3
Job Corps	26.0	74.0	161	.8
Neighborhood Youth Corps	46.2	53.8	426	2.1

SOURCE: *Statistical Abstract of the United States,* 1972, p. 137.

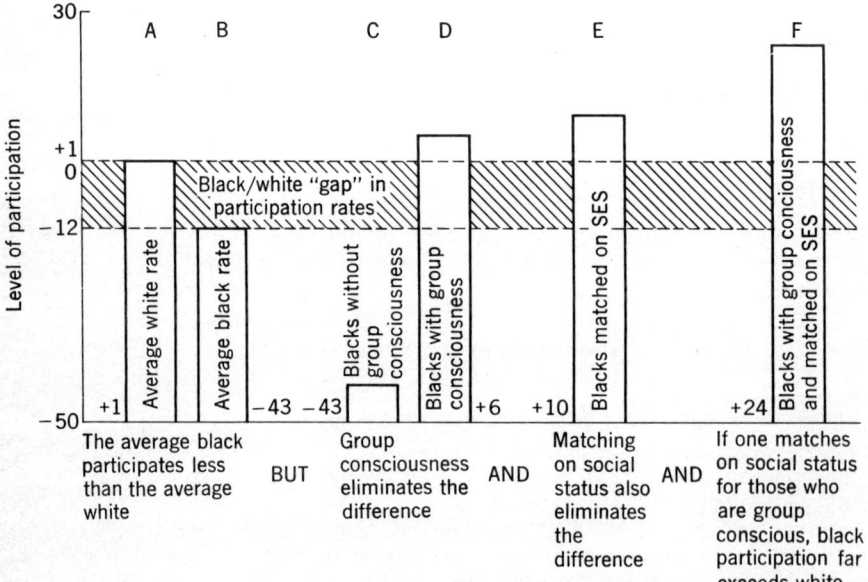

FIG. 14.1 *Effect of group consciousness and social status on black/white differences in participation. (Source: Verba and Nie,* Participation in America, *p. 161.)*

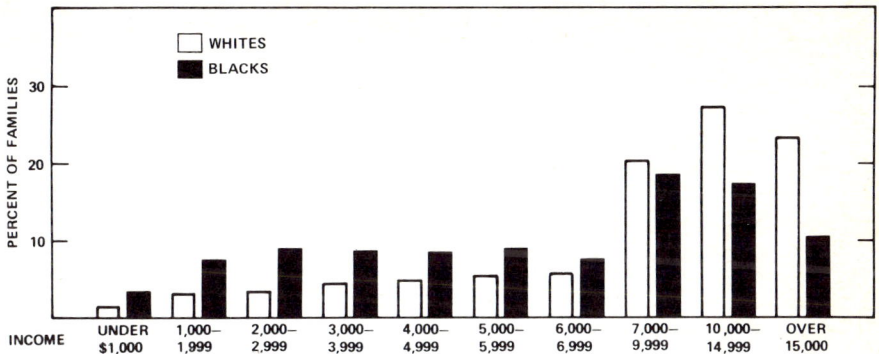

FIG. 14.2 Percent distribution of families by income and race, 1970. (Source: U.S. Department of Commerce, **Statistical Abstract of the United States,** 1972, p. 322.)

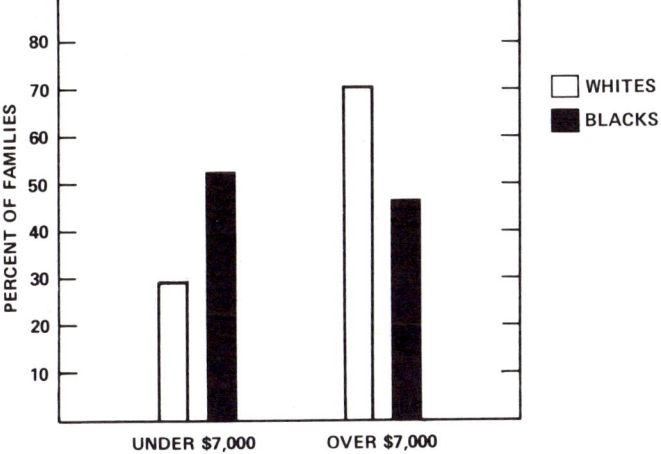

FIG. 14.3 Percent distribution of families by income and race, 1970. (Source: Ibid.)

III. ANALYZING THE DATA

Since you now have some experience in analyzing data, we will not provide you questions and answers on each of the tables. However, as you analyze the data you will use to write your memo, consider the following:

1. Compare the manner in which you operationalized key variables of your reformulation and the way in which they have been represented in the data. Are they the same or at least similar? Are the indicators which you are about to use reasonably valid reflections of the phenomena that your reformulation addresses?

2. Note some of the apparent paradoxes of the information about blacks. Some of the tables indicate that blacks participate less in the political arena than whites, but when one controls for social class, they participate as much or more than whites. However, if you look at the distribution of blacks on

income, you will find a higher proportion of blacks are poorer than whites. Consequently, if you look at *all* blacks, it appears as if blacks participate less; if one looks at the relatively few upper-class blacks, it looks as if they participate more. An issue unresolved by these data is whether the disproportionate number of poor blacks is the results of government policy. If it were, controlling for income might be inappropriate.

3. Information on some groups is much more readily available than on others. Does this in itself imply something about the "political influence" of these groups or the degree of their victimization by discrimination?

4. Can you make comparisons between several minority groups as well as between a minority group and the rest of the population? If you can, such an analysis may help you limit or broaden your generalizations about the incidence of discrimination against minority groups in the United States by letting you examine whether all minority groups are discriminated against in the same way or to the same degree.

Chapter 14
Minorities in American Politics

Name _____

Section _____

IV. CONCLUSION

Having reformulated the problem and analyzed the data, you are now ready to write a memo on the original proposition. Do not be afraid to take a strong position on the proposition, but support your conclusions with the data you have analyzed. Cite the data where relevant; cite your sources when you use data not found in this chapter.

Original Problem

"Discrimination in the political arena against minority groups in the United States has not declined in the last 20 years."

Memorandum

Chapter 15
LAW AND ORDER

Fear of the mugger, burglar, and drug addict weighs heavily on the minds of many Americans and has made law and order one of the principal political issues of American politics. No one opposes the general principle that city streets should be safe and that everyone should be able to rest at home without fear of a criminal breaking in. But there is considerable disagreement about how such objectives can be attained. Many people blame "coddling of defendants" by the courts for the rise in crime and call for harsher penalties for criminals. Others look toward increasing the competence and number of police to bring about better patrolling and more and swifter apprehension of criminals. Still others view crime as part of a widespread social pathology and would argue for improving general social conditions so that the slums which appear to breed crime could be eliminated and crime itself reduced.

This chapter puts you in the position of a government decision maker who is expected to deal with the problem of crime. The proposition you are to analyze makes assumptions that you need to analyze in the light of data presented here and available from supplemental sources. The proposition is:

"If government agencies really put their mind to it, they could reduce the amount of crime."

I. REFORMULATING THE PROBLEM

The proposition assumes that we know what causes crime and that those causes can be removed or at least addressed by appropriate remedial action. As the following partial reformulations suggest, the problem is not so simple. The causes of crime are multiple; several aspects of the problem have to be considered in order to make a fair evaluation of governmental efforts to control crime.

Note that all of the partial reformulations provide plausible explanations for the rise in crime rates. However, all of them are single-factor explanations of a phenomenon which is likely to be caused by a large number of factors. Therefore, in writing your memo, you should combine several of the reformulations into one of your own.

Some of the reformulations are much more operational than others. For instance, "moral decay" is much harder to define operationally than "density of population." When you examine the available data, you will find that other concepts mentioned in the reformulations are also not very well operationalized. Examine, for instance, the measures of severity and certainty of punishment and ponder whether they really measure what they purport to measure.

Some of the reformulations incorporate popular but ambiguous usages. Examine the reformulation linking drugs and crime. Would you include the consumption of caffeine, nicotine, and alcohol in your analysis? Each of these are powerful drugs but legal. At least one of them has been associated with crime.

All the reformulations presume that crime rates are reliable measures. There is considerable evidence that the crime rates published by the FBI reflect only a portion of the "real" incidence of crime and are unreliable as indicators of year-to-year changes or for city-by-city comparisons. But they are the best indicators of crime we possess, and therefore the policy maker must use them for making his decisions.

Note that some of the reformulations involve phenomena that a government agency might reasonably expect to affect. For instance, it is relatively easy to raise the level of expenditures for policing. Other reformulations involve phenomena that cannot be easily changed by government fiat; for instance, it is very difficult, if not impossible, for a government agency to change the density of the population or the degree of urbanization within a reasonable time span. Keep this in mind in writing your memo as the original proposition assumes that government agencies can do something about the crime problem.

Partial Reformulations

1. Crime rates reflect the amount of money spent on police. The more spent on police, the lower the crime rate.

2. Crime rates reflect the degree of punishment meted out. The more severe and the more certain the punishment, the lower the crime rate.

3. Crime rates reflect general socioeconomic conditions. The worse off people are, the higher the crime rate.

4. Crime rates reflect growing moral decay in the United States. A return to ethical and moral standards would result in a lower crime rate.

5. Crime rates reflect drug usage. The higher the drug usage, the higher the crime rate.

6. Crime rates reflect social conditions such as the degree of urbanization and the density of population. The more urban and the more dense the population, the higher the crime rate.

Keeping in mind the general rules for reformulation which you used in earlier chapters, write your own reformulation in the space below:

Your Reformulation

II. SELECTING THE NECESSARY DATA

Examine your reformulation and then list the data you require to test it. Some of the information may be found on the following pages. You may find other helpful information in the following sources:

Statistical Abstract of the United States. Issued annually by the Bureau of the Census, U.S. Department of Justice.

FBI Uniform Crime Report: Issued annually by the FBI, U.S. Department of Justice.

American Statistics Index (Washington, D.C.: Congressional Information Service). Indexes and abstracts all statistics published by the federal government. Look under such headings as crime, crime rate, police, courts or prisons for current information from governmental sources.

List the information you will look for in the space below. Then check it against the information provided on the following pages and that available from supplemental sources. If you find you have insufficient information to test your reformulation, alter it so that you can test it.

Required Data

TABLE 15.1 RELATIONSHIP* BETWEEN CRIME RATES AND CERTAINTY AND SEVERITY OF PUNISHMENT BY OFFENSE TYPES IN AMERICAN STATES

Offense Type	Certainty of Punishment†	Severity of Punishment‡
All felonies	-.45	.14
Sex offenses	-.57	.26
Assault	-.46	.18
Larceny	-.37	.14
Robbery	-.36	.05
Burglary	-.31	.14
Homicide	-.17	-.45
Auto theft	-.08	.04

*The numbers in the table are Kendall Tau rank order correlation coefficients. They may be interpreted in the same way as simple correlation coefficients.

†Certainty of punishment is measure by the ratio:

$$\frac{\text{No. of admissions to state prisons during 1959–1963}}{\text{No. of crimes known to the police in that state, 1958–1962}}$$

‡Severity of punishment is measured by the mean length of time served for felony prisoners released from state prisons in 1960.

SOURCE: Adapted from Charles R. Tittle, "Crime Rates and Legal Sanctions," *Social Problems*, vol. 16, p. 415, 1969.

TABLE 15.2 PUBLIC OPINION ON CAPITAL PUNISHMENT

	For Capital Punishment	Against Capital Punishment	No Opinion
Are you in favor of the death penalty for murder? (Gallup)*			
1936	62%	33%	5%
Are you in favor of the death penalty for persons convicted of murder? (Gallup)*			
1953	68	25	7
1960	51	36	13
1965	45	43	12
Do you believe in capital punishment or are you opposed to it? (Harris)†			Not sure
1970	47	42	11
1973	59	31	10

* *Public Opinion Quarterly*, vol. 34, p. 291, 1970.
† *Chicago Tribune*, section 1, p. 26, June 11, 1973.

TABLE 15.3 SIMPLE CORRELATIONS BETWEEN
MURDER RATE, CAR THEFT RATE, AND POLICE
EXPENDITURES IN AMERICAN CITIES BY CITY SIZE

	Relation Between	
City Size	Murder Rate and Police Expenditure	Car Theft Rate and Police Expenditure
Under 50,000	.09	.32*
50,000–99,999	.03	.51*
100,000–499,999	.10	.54*
Over 500,000	.13	.00
All cities	.03	.42*

* Statistically significant at the .001 level.
SOURCE: Based on data published in Federal Bureau of Investigation, *Uniform Crime Reports,* 1969.

TABLE 15.4 CRIME RATES, CITY SIZE AND POLICE
EXPENDITURES, IN AMERICAN CITIES, 1969

Cities	Murders/100,000 Population	Car Theft/100,000 Population	Police Expenditure/ Person
Under 50,000	7.6	355.2	$16.21
50,000–99,999	17.6	446.6	16.81
100,000–499,999	15.4	725.5	20.15
Over 500,000	24.6	1218.2	38.54
All cities	12.4	472.3	18.11

SOURCE: Herbert Jacob, *Urban Justice* (Englewood Cliffs, N.J.: Prentice-Hall, Inc., 1973), p. 24. Copyright, Herbert Jacob. By permission of Prentice-Hall, Inc.

TABLE 15.5 DEGREE OF CITIZEN SATISFACTION WITH OUTCOME OF CASE IN WHICH THEY WERE VICTIM BY TYPE OF POLICE-JUDICIAL ACTION TAKEN

	Citizen Satisfaction					
Action Taken	Very Satisfied	Somewhat Satisfied	Somewhat Dissatisfied	Very Dissatisfied	Total Percent	N
Police not notified	13%	18	28	41	100%	987
Police did not respond to call	22%	22	18	38	100%	233
Police did not consider incident a crime	24%	26	24	26	100%	190
Police considered incident a crime but made no arrest	20%	23	27	30	100%	459
Arrest made, no trial held	33%	21	22	24	100%	68
Acquittal or too lenient penalty	17%	13	26	44	100%	23
Conviction and "correct" penalty	60%	16	12	12	100%	25

SOURCE: Philip H. Ennis, *Criminal Victimization in the United States,* Field Surveys II, President's Commission on Law Enforcement and Administration of Justice, p. 15, May, 1967.

TABLE 15.6 WHY CITIZENS DON'T NOTIFY POLICE OF CRIMES BY TYPE OF CRIME

Type of Crime	Not a Concern of Police	Belief that Police Would Be Ineffective	Personal Refusal to Involve Police	Fear of Reprisal	Total Percent	N
Simple assault	50%	36	7	7	100%	54
Burglary	30%	62	6	2	100%	111
Grand larceny	24%	62	14	—	100%	68
Petty larceny	31%	57	11	1	100%	261
Malicious mischief	23%	68	7	2	100%	187
Fraud	41%	35	24	—	100%	51

SOURCE: Ibid., p. 46.

TABLE 15.7 RELATIONSHIP BETWEEN AVERAGE WEEKS OF TRAINING OF POLICE SERVING A NEIGHBORHOOD AND CITIZEN EVALUATIONS OF POLICE PERFORMANCE

Weeks of Training	Citizen Evaluations of Police Performance				
	Rate Police Service Outstanding	Rate Police Response as Very Rapid	Rate Crime as Increasing in Their Neighborhood	Rate Police-Community Relations as Outstanding	Agree or Strongly Agree Police Treat All Citizens Equally
Less than or equal to 12	34% (376)	59% (601)	24% (229)	24% (234)	79% (735)
13 to 16	27% (429)	52% (779)	29% (409)	15% (198)	84% (1069)
Over 16	22% (256)	41% (447)	39% (418)	14% (134)	82% (1790)
N for full table	(3903)	(3634)	(3414)	(3193)	(3164)
Tau	-.10	-.12	.10	-.05	-.01

SOURCE: Dennis C. Smith and Elinor Ostrom, "The Effects of Training and Education on Police Attitudes and Performance: A Preliminary Analysis," in Herbert Jacob (ed.), *The Potential for Reform of Criminal Justice* (Beverly Hills, Calif.: Sage Publications, 1974 forthcoming). By permission of publisher, Sage Publications, Inc.

TABLE 15.8 RELATIONSHIP BETWEEN TRAINING AND EDUCATION OF POLICE OFFICERS AND THEIR REPORTED PREPAREDNESS

Types of Assignment	Correlation Coefficients (Kendall's Tau)			Percent of Officers Expressing Degree of Preparedness	
	Weeks of Training	Length of Basic Training	College Credits	Percent Very Well Prepared	Percent Not Very Well Prepared
Family disturbances	.05	.01	.13	73	4
Civil disorders	.00	.05	.12	35	16
Traffic accidents	.03	-.05	.05	79	2
Narcotics cases	-.07	.01	.02	26	25
Court appearances	-.03	-.04	.08	63	6
Problem juveniles	-.03	.14	.08	37	15

SOURCE: Ibid. By permission of the publisher, Sage Publications, Inc.

Drug Use and Crime, from *Second Report of the National Commission on Marihuana and Drug Abuse,* pp 164–165, March, 1972.

The research findings concerning the associations between drug use and crime have been complicated by the interplay between the pharmacologic properties of the drugs and the psycho-social characteristics of the individuals who use them. Inferences which might have been drawn from laboratory research have suffered primarily from the difficulties attending replication of non-pharmacological variables; and while naturalistic studies are appropriate to this area of investigation, they have been plagued for the most part by deficiencies in research design and sampling procedures. Nonetheless, the following tentative conclusions appear justifiable from the data available:

> Alcohol, the most commonly used drug, is strongly associated with violent crime and with reckless and negligent operation of motor vehicles.
>
> Research findings linking barbiturate and amphetamine users with criminal behavior, especially assaultive offenses, are increasing, but no definitive association has yet been established in this country; however, a strong association has been demonstrated between amphetamine use and violence in Sweden and Japan.
>
> Research data are generally lacking regarding the actual relationship between cocaine use and criminal behavior; however, the pharmacologic effects of the drug would seem to suggest a potential for drug-induced violent behavior similar to that shown for amphetamine and barbiturate users.
>
> Marihuana use, in and of itself, is neither causative of, nor directly associated with crime, either violent or non-violent. In fact, marihuana tends to be underrepresented among assaultive offenders, especially when compared with users of alcohol, amphetamines and barbiturates.
>
> Use of opiates, especially heroin, is associated with acquisitive crimes such as burglary and shoplifting, ordinarily committed for the purpose of securing money to support dependence. Assaultive offenses are significantly less likely to be committed by these opiate users, especially in comparison with users of alcohol, amphetamines and barbiturates.
>
> Except in relatively rare instances generally related to drug-induced panic and toxic reactions, users of hallucinogens, non-barbiturate sedative-hypnotics, glue and similar volatile inhalants are not inclined toward assaultive criminal behavior. It should be noted, however, that some of the non-barbiturate sedatives, notably methaqualone, and the hydrocarbon solvents have a potential for inducing violent behavior although the incidence of such behavior is currently low.

The Effect of Drug Treatment on Crime, from *Second Report of the National Commission on Marihuana and Drug Abuse,* pp. 176–177, March, 1973.

During the past eight years, methadone maintenance has evolved from an experimental program with 22 patients into the most widely used treatment modality in the nation. Its supporters have claimed that participation in the methadone program reduces heroin-related crime, a direct function of the patient's reduced need for and use of heroin. In addition, individuals participating in methadone maintenance programs are reported to be able to function, perhaps for the first time in their adult lives, as socially responsible and economically independent and productive members of society.

> The Commission has carefully scrutinized these claims. In general, they have been based on the reported findings of a limited number of quasi-experimental studies (mostly before-after comparisons); the deficiencies in research design, sampling techniques, analysis and interpretation of the data significantly limit the reliability and validity of the conclusions and the inferences drawn therefrom. In fact, we have not found sufficiently responsible research to conclude that any of the various treatment modalities, regardless of type, actually reduce crime.

Chapter 15
Law and Order

Name _____

Section _____

III. CONCLUSION

You are now in a position to write a memo on the original proposition. Examine the conclusions you drew in the analysis of your reformulated proposition and generalize them to the original problem. Be careful not to draw unwarranted conclusions. Support your position with data; if you use data not in this chapter, cite your sources.

Original Problem

"If government agencies really put their mind to it, they could reduce the amount of crime."

Memorandum